Six Dynasties Poetry

六朝詩研究

孫康宜 著

張充和 署

Six Dynasties Poetry

Kang-i Sun Chang

PRINCETON
UNIVERSITY
PRESS

Copyright © 1986 by Princeton University Press
Published by Princeton University Press, 41 William Street,
Princeton, New Jersey 08540
In the United Kingdom: Princeton University Press,
Guildford, Surrey

All Rights Reserved

Library of Congress Cataloging in Publication Data will be found on the last printed page of this book

ISBN 0-691-06669-8

This book has been composed in Bembo by Asco Trade Typesetting Ltd., Hong Kong

Clothbound editions of Princeton University Press books are printed on acid-free paper, and binding materials are chosen for strength and durability.
Printed in the United States of America by Princeton University Press, Princeton, New Jersey

Frontispiece by Mrs. Ch'ung-ho Chang Frankel

TO MY PARENTS

Mr. and Mrs. Paul Yu-kuang Sun

Contents

	List of Illustrations	ix
	Preface	xi
	Acknowledgments	xv
	Abbreviations	xvii
I.	**T'ao Ch'ien: Defining the Lyric Voice**	3
	1. The Poet as Individual	3
	2. Poetry as Autobiography	16
	3. Sublimation through Nature	37
II.	**Hsieh Ling-yün: The Making of a New Descriptive Mode**	47
	1. Verisimilitude and Landscape Exploration	47
	2. Descriptive Language	62
	3. The Lonely Traveler	73
III.	**Pao Chao: In Search of Expression**	79
	1. From Landscape to Objects	83
	2. Description and Narration	94
	3. The Lyrical Self and Its World	102
IV.	**Hsieh T'iao: The Inward Turn of Landscape**	112
	1. The Literary Salon and Poetic Formalism	115
	2. The Structure of Feelings	125
	3. Landscape as Artistic Experience	133
	4. Aesthetics of the Miniature Form	138
V.	**Yü Hsin: The Poet's Poet**	146
	1. Literature Inside and Outside the Palace	146
	2. Conformity and Innovations	157
	3. Lyricism Regained	165
	Glossary of Chinese Characters	185
	Selected Bibliography	195
	Index	213

List of Illustrations

1. Frontispiece by Mrs. Ch'ung-ho Chang Frankel. New Haven, Yale University.   ii
2. A picture of T'ao Ch'ien by an unidentified artist, probably of the Sung and Yüan times. Collection of the National Palace Museum, Taipei, Taiwan.   4
3. "Preface to the Orchid Pavilion Collection." Calligraphy by Chao Chung of the Yüan. From his scroll, "Orchid Pavilion Gathering." Collection of National Palace Museum, Taipei, Taiwan.   8
4. From Chao Chung's scroll, "Orchid Pavilion Gathering." Each scene is accompanied by poems from the original "Orchid Pavilion" series and Chao Chung's own poems to the same rhyme schemes. Collection of the National Palace Museum, Taipei, Taiwan.   10
5. A picture of Hsieh Ling-yün. From Cheng Chen-to, *Ch'a-t'u pen Chung-kuo wen-hsüeh shih* (*History of Chinese Literature: An Illustrated Edition*). 4 vols. 1932; rpt. Hong Kong: Commercial Press, 1961, I, 183.   50
6. A painting of Hsieh An traveling with singing girls in the Eastern Mountain, by Kuo Hsü (1456–1528). Collection of the National Palace Museum, Taipei, Taiwan.   55
7. A scene of Mount Lu: "In it soaring billows leap up to touch the sky,/High waves pour onto the sun" (Pao Chao).   90
8. A picture of Emperor Wu of the Liang by an unidentified artist. Color and ink on silk. From "Portraits of Emperors and Empresses." Collection of National Palace Museum, Taipei, Taiwan.   145

Preface

The Chinese call them the Six Dynasties—Wu (222–280), Eastern Chin (317–420), Liu-Sung (420–479), Ch'i (479–502), Liang (502–557), Ch'en (557–589) —the six Nanking (then called Chien-k'ang) empires during the long political division from the end of Han to the founding of Sui. In historical terms, the Six Dynasties period marks China's first surrender to foreign invasions that resulted in its humiliating withdrawal to the valley of the Yangtze. In literary terms, it signifies the beginning of a mixture of the northern and the southern styles, and that of the old heritage and new discoveries—with an effect so powerful that it engendered a completely fresh and important poetic phenomenon that was to be recognized as characteristically Chinese. And it was this poetry which opened the way for T'ang lyricism.

The term "Six Dynasties" should not be understood literally; traditionally it serves as a convenient way of grouping together the six southern states founded at Nanking from the third through the sixth century. However, there are some who prefer to take the term to mean the six successive Chinese dynasties from the Western Chin (266–317) to the Ch'en, thus excluding the Wu kingdom from the list. And the entire period is also known generally as "the Northern and the Southern Dynasties," as an age of division.

In the chapters that follow I shall pursue the rise of a new poetry, beginning with China's southward shift in the early fourth century. For it was at this time—that is, during the last days of the Western Chin—that the Chinese fled in millions to the lower Yangtze to establish their new southern state, in open surrender to the foreign chiefs of the Tovgach (T'o-pa) tribe which was to rule North China for nearly three centuries to come. Theoretically it was the Eastern Chin founded at Nanking in 317 that marked the beginning of the "five" southern dynasties.

For the sake of convenience, the standardized term "Six Dynasties" is used throughout this book. A term such as "Southern Dynasties" may appear at first to be more appropriate, but it will in fact cause greater confusion. When the Chinese speak of the "Southern Dynasties," they often have in mind the "four" dynasties following the fall of the Eastern Chin in 420—namely Liu-Sung, Ch'i, Liang, Ch'en. The difficulty of selecting a suitable term leads me to remake an old assumption: that whatever numerical designation one chooses for this period—be it "four," "five," or "six" dynasties—it will suggest an unusually rapid movement of dynastic changes. For this was an era in which court politics was plagued by continual power struggles and turmoil.

The political unrest brings into focus what may be considered one of the

Preface

most interesting phenomena in poetry in general and Chinese poetry in particular: the intimate link between political crisis and poetic creativity. Reading this period's poetry, one is especially tempted to conclude that true literary imagination in Early China often occurs in the time of political crisis. One finds in the Six Dynasties poets a great awakening of individual sensibility which transforms the troubling political situation into poetic inspiration. Not only do these poets, through their awareness of life's tragedy and political pressure, express most forcefully their personal sense of the dilemma and perplexity of their times, but they also bring poetry into the forefront of politics.

But these poets are those who have learned, in one way or another, to transcend politics by first attempting to transform their own sense of self. A great developmental process that is particularly noticeable in the Six Dynasties poetry is the growing concern with the splendors of the physical world in general, obviously a reflection of the poet's urge to enlarge his "self" into a broader focus. Poetry may continue to be primarily an expression of internal feelings, but the poetic self is gradually externalized to see nature, often a detailed view of it, as a major part of the lyrical domain. The poet's great compulsion to orient, or reorient, himself in the external world brings about a new breadth of scope in poetic creation: at the one end of the spectrum stands an individualized "expression" of feelings, and at the other the visual "description" of natural phenomena. To a large extent, the analysis in this book has been guided by the parallel development, or the merging, of these two poles. By focusing on these two elements of poetry—the expressive and the descriptive—I do not mean to see the two in opposition. Certainly nothing is purely expressive or descriptive. But the use of such terms can still be very useful in literary analysis as long as they lead to meaningful interpretation. This methodology is particularly fruitful in studying Six Dynasties poetry, in which the relative proportion of these two poetic components often determines not only the poetic style of an individual poet but also the period style of an entire era. Moreover, the implication and application of these two terms do change with time, especially with the effect of cross-generic influences. And, later, the pairing of the expressive and the descriptive, though in a slightly modified sense, developed into a primary frame of reference for reading poetry in China. Part of my intention in adopting this approach in this book is to show that it is possible to give a systematic account of the poetic development in the Six Dynasties by tracing the complex development—including both continuities and discontinuities—of these two fundamental elements in Chinese poetry.

The five poets chosen for the present study—T'ao Ch'ien (365–427), Hsieh Ling-yün (385–433), Pao Chao (414?–466), Hsieh T'iao (464–499), Yü Hsin (513–581)—will serve as important signposts marking the long journey to-

Preface

ward a growing convergence of expression and description in Six Dynasties poetry. Chapter One explores T'ao Ch'ien's pressing search for his own selfhood in poetry which, through a genuine concern with historical consciousness and natural sublimation, crystallizes into an enlarged expression of individuality that paves the way for full-grown lyricism. Chapter Two attempts a brief survey of the Chinese poets' fascination with the rich variety of southern scenery, treating Hsieh Ling-yün as a model poet in the newly developed descriptive mode called "landscape poetry." Some of the vital elements in expression and description come to the fore in Pao Chao's poetry, and this forms the subject of Chapter Three. Chapter Four takes the reader into an innovative movement of poetic formalism current in the elite circles of the Southern Ch'i, within which Hsieh T'iao was the foremost poet. It is in this chapter that we will see how descriptive realism comes fully into its own, before retreating into an aesthetic formalism. The book ends with a final chapter in which Yü Hsin's creative synthesis of lyrical expression and self-contained description is discussed. Ultimately the southern "Palace Style" sensualism and the northern literary tendencies converge in the poetry of the old Yü Hsin in exile, and this development sets up the influence of Six Dynasties poetry on the future development of Chinese lyricism.

The interplay of tradition and individual creativity remains the central concern of this book. We will see that each poet, in developing his own individual style, seeks to relate his lyrical expression to a keen awareness of past poetic models. There is a constant dialectic between the poet's urge to express his own selfhood, on the one hand, and a sense of discipline gained from his firm grounding on a past tradition, on the other. For it is only through the consciousness of a great lyric tradition that the poet may hope to emulate or surpass his precursors. There are times when a poet needs to break with tradition in order to redefine that tradition, with a change so drastic that he may be ignored or scorned by his own contemporaries. Yet the ultimate reward for such a poet lies in his firm belief that his work will have won him a kind of immortality, in the sense that sometime in future generations there will be one who "appreciates his tone" (*chih-yin*). This notion of later understanding was to become one of the most significant determinants of literary revivals in China.

Living with the burden of this cultural heritage, each of the poets whose works form the core of this book strives to find a new lyrical voice of his own, in the hope that his poetry will ultimately contribute to the larger vision of immortality through literary creativity.

Acknowledgments

It is a pleasure to acknowledge and thank those who read one draft or another of my manuscript and offered valuable criticism: Hans H. Frankel, C. T. Hsia, Karl Kao, Yu-Kung Kao, Shuen-fu Lin, Earl Miner, F. W. Mote, Stephen Owen, Andrew H. Plaks, Hugh M. Stimson, and Anthony C. Yu. All of them were generous with their time in the midst of their own busy schedules. I am further indebted to Hans H. Frankel, who gave an exhaustive critical reading of the first draft of my translations.

My thanks are also due to many friends who helped out in a variety of ways. Richard Barnhart is my most reliable guide to Chinese art, and the choice of the illustrations in this book has in many ways benefited from his advice. Ch'ung-ho Chang Frankel, an expert in Chinese poetry, calligraphy, and other arts, has written the initial calligraphy which graces this volume. Parker Huang's advice on my study of T'ao Ch'ien has been fruitful and constructive. Edwin McClellan has been a congenial and encouraging colleague; he took a strong interest in my subject from the start and kept me from delays in completing this book. Judith Rabinovitch informed me of the important text of *Kakyō hyōshiki* (dated 772), and discussed with me the many crucial issues in it. William Kelly invited me to give a talk to the East Asian Discussion Group at Yale, and the questions raised by the audience were helpful. Jonathan Spence's intellectual curiosity has been most inspiring, and the last sentence in this book is a direct response to a question that he raised casually one day: "How do you explain the relationship between literary creativity and political disunity?" Stanley Weinstein has tried to keep me up-to-date regarding Japanese reference sources, a guidance most needed for my research. Ying-shih Yü has enlightened me on many issues pertaining to literature and history, and given me the privilege of reading his draft article on the Neo-Taoist movement in Wei-Chin China. Others who offered similar help are: Ta-tuan Ch'en, Hsiao-ch'iang Ch'en, Susan Cherniack, Dore J. Levy, Mary G. Neill, Kate Simpson, Hai-t'ao T'ang, James Trilling, and King-lui Wu. To all of them, I give my thanks.

The names of authors to whom I owe an intellectual debt are too many to list here. I have tried to acknowledge their help in my footnotes and bibliography. However, I would like to express my special thanks to those scholars whose critical works or translations have been most frequently consulted: J. D. Frodsham on Hsieh Ling-Yün; William T. Graham on Yü Hsin; James R. Hightower on T'ao Ch'ien; Donald Holzman on Juan Chi; David R. Knechtges on *Fu* poetry and on *Wen Hsüan*; Lin Wen-yüeh on landscape poetry;

Acknowledgments

James J. Y. Liu on theories of Chinese literature; Richard B. Mather on Hsieh Ling-yün and on *Shih-shuo hsin-yü*; Vincent Yu-chung Shih on *Wen-hsin Tiao-lung*.

I am also grateful to Anthony Marr, Associate Curator of the East Asian Collection at Yale, for his excellent service in research matters. To Diane Perushek, Curator of the Gest Oriental Library at Princeton, I owe a debt of gratitude for all she has done for me—in both professional and personal ways. My thanks are also due to T. P. Liu of the National Palace Museum in Taipei, who made available prints of some of the Museum's oldest holdings, and to Geri Mancini of Yale University, who provided photographic services for me. One of my delights in the process of research was my several visits to the Harvard-Yenching Library, and I am especially grateful to Eugene Wu, the curator, and Sidney Tai, the rare book librarian. I wish to thank the Whitney Humanities Center at Yale for a Griswold Research Award that made it possible for me to take these important trips.

A special note of thanks goes to R. Miriam Brokaw, Associate Director and Editor of Princeton University Press, without whose encouragement and professional assistance this book could not have been completed so much sooner than expected; and to Marjorie Sherwood for her enthusiastic response to my work, which I very much enjoyed and appreciated. To the readers of my manuscript for Princeton University Press I am most grateful for their useful comments and suggestions.

Finally, I wish to thank Chézy Chang, to whom I owe the greatest debt for both intellectual stimulation and personal support.

K.S.C.
Yale University
December, 1984

Grateful acknowledgment is made to the following for
permission to reprint copyrighted material:

Cambridge University Press: Excerpts from William T. Graham, Jr., trans., *The Lament for the South*, 1980.

Columbia University Press: Excerpts from Burton Watson, trans., *Chinese Rhyme Prose*, © 1971 by Columbia University Press.

David Hawkes: Excerpts from his *Ch'u Tz'u: The Songs of the South* (Oxford University Press, 1959).

National Palace Museum, Taipei, Taiwan: Five photographs from the National Palace Museum Collection.

Oxford University Press: James Robert Hightower, trans., *The Poetry of T'ao Ch'ien*, 1970.

Abbreviations

Works most frequently cited have been abbreviated according to the list below

CHSK   Ting Fu-pao 丁福保, ed. *Ch'üan Han San-kuo Chin Nan-pei-ch'ao shih* 全漢三國晉南北朝詩. Shanghai, 1961. Rpt. in 3 vols. Taipei: Shih-chieh shu-chü, 1969.

CKLT   Kuo Shao-yü 郭紹虞, ed. *Chung-kuo li-tai wen-lun hsüan* 中國歷代文論選. Rev. ed., 4 vols. Shanghai: Ku-chi ch'u-pan-she, 1979–1980.

CKWH   Lo Lien-t'ien 羅聯添, ed. *Chung-kuo wen-hsüeh shih lun-wen hsüan-chi* 中國文學史論文選集. Vol. II. Taipei: Student Book Co., 1978.

CYK   Ch'en Yin-k'o 陳寅恪. *Ch'en Yin-k'o hsien-sheng wen-shih lun-chi* 陳寅恪先生文史論集. Vols. I and II. Hong Kong: Wen Wen Publications, 1973.

ESP   Lin, Shuen-fu and Stephen Owen, eds. *The Evolution of Shih Poetry from the Han through the T'ang*. Princeton: Princeton Univ. Press. Forthcoming.

HHCC   Hsieh T'iao 謝朓. *Hsieh Hsüan-ch'eng chi [chiao-chu]* 謝宣城集 [校注]. Ed. Hung Shun-lung 洪順隆. Taipei: Chung-hua shu-chü, 1969.

HHCS   Hsieh T'iao 謝朓. *Hsieh Hsüan-ch'eng shih [chu]* 謝宣城詩 [注]. Ed. Lee Chik-fong 李直方. Hong Kong: Universal Book Co., 1968.

HLYS   Hsieh Ling-yün 謝靈運. *Hsieh Ling-yün shih-hsüan* 謝靈運詩選. Ed. Yeh Hsiao-hsüeh 葉笑雪. Shanghai: Ku-tien wen-hsüeh ch'u-pan-she, 1957.

PTCC   Pao Chao 鮑照. *Pao Ts'an-chün chi [chu]* 鮑參軍集 [注]. Ed. Ch'ien Chung-lien 錢仲聯. Shanghai: Ku-tien wen-hsüeh ch'u-pan-she, 1980.

SPC   Chung Jung 鍾嶸. *Shih-p'in [chu]* 詩品 [注]. Commentary by Ch'en Yen-chieh 陳延傑. Hong Kong: Commercial Press, 1959.

SS   Shen Yüeh 沈約. *Sung shu* 宋書. 8 vols. Ed. Editorial Board of Chung-hua shu-chü. Peking: Chung-hua shu-chü, 1974.

TYMC   T'ao Ch'ien 陶潛. *T'ao Yüan-ming chi* 陶淵明集. Ed. Lu Ch'in-li 逯欽立. Peking: Chung-hua shu-chü, 1979.

WH   Hsiao T'ung 蕭統, ed. *[Chao-ming] Wen-hsüan* [昭明] 文選. Commentary by Li Shan 李善. 2 vols. Rpt. Taipei: Ho-lo t'u-shu ch'u-pan-she, 1975.

Abbreviations

WHTL	Liu Hsieh 劉勰. *Wen-hsin tiao-lung* [*chu*] 文心雕龍 [注]. Commentary by Fan Wen-lan 范文瀾, 1947; rpt. in 2 vols. Peking: Jen-min wen-hsüeh ch'u-pan-she, 1978.
YFSC	Kuo Mao-ch'ien 郭茂倩, ed. *Yüeh-fu shih-chi* 樂府詩集. Ed. Editorial Board of Chung-hua shu-chü. 4 vols. Peking: Chung-hua shu-chü, 1979.
YTSC	Yü Hsin 庾信. *Yü Tzu-shan chi* [*chu*] 庾子山集 [注]. Commentary by Ni Fan 倪璠. Peking: Chung-hua shu-chü, 1980.

Six Dynasties Poetry

In the chaos of the Yung-chia period,
When the Central Plain lost its ruler,
The people lay down against ruined walls;
Jackals and tigers prowled the roads.
Then, when five horses fled to the South,
And three stars joined in the East,
A man crossed the Yangtze to found a new state,
Thus uprooting my ancestors.

Yü Hsin, "Lament for the South,"
TRANSLATED BY WILLIAM T. GRAHAM

I

T'ao Ch'ien

Defining The Lyric Voice

I. The Poet as Individual

T'ao Ch'ien (365–427) has been celebrated for centuries as one of the few greatest poets in China—perhaps only Tu Fu (712–770) can rank with him—who combined superb literary innovation with a powerful and enduring lyrical tradition that is distinctly Chinese. Such a powerful creativity and synthesis in one poet needs a strong age to support it, but one gets the curious feeling that T'ao Ch'ien was born either too early or too late. The period that he lived in, the Eastern Chin (317–420), was relatively unexciting in terms of poetic vitality, one which the Liang critic Liu Hsieh (ca. 465 to ca. 522) criticizes thus:

> During the period of the Eastern Chin [317–420], literary writings were mired in Neo-Taoistic discussions ... (*WHTL*, I, 67)
> 江左篇製，溺乎玄風 ...

And Chung Jung (459–518) in his *Shih-p'in (Poetry Ratings)* eloquently gives a similar description of the age:

> During the Yung-chia period [307–312] Taoism was highly valued, and people took pleasure in abstract philosophizing. The writings of the time were characterized more by intellectual reasoning than by literary aesthetics; their lack of flavor makes them quite dull. This tendency was thus passed on to the Eastern Chin. Poems by Sun Ch'o [320–377], Hsü Hsün [?–365], Huan Wen [312–373], and Yü Liang [289–340] were all simple, unadorned dicta like Lao Tzu's *Tao-te ching* (*SPC*, 1–2).
> 永嘉時，貴黃老，稍尚虛談，于時篇什，理過其辭，淡乎寡味。

陶淵明晉名也在宋易名潛字元亮
世號靖節先生著五柳傳親老家
貧湉人曰聊欲絃歌以為三逕之
資可乎起為彭澤令解官賦歸去
來辭有酒輙醉嘗九日採菊盈
把適太守王弘遣白衣送酒至因
醉而歸恥事二姓宋召之不起故
朱子書鑑曰晉傲士云

2. A picture of T'ao Ch'ien by an unidentified artist, probably of the Sung and Yüan times.

T'ao Ch'ien
DEFINING THE LYRIC VOICE

爰及江表，微波尚傳。孫綽、許詢、桓庾諸公詩，皆平典似道德論。

The fact is that T'ao Ch'ien's poetry differs vitally not only from the contemporary poetry, but also from that immediately following the Eastern Chin. His poetry as literary art was unappreciated by his age and misunderstood by critics and poets alike for hundreds of years to come. But posterity would not let him disappear into oblivion, and in time it gave him the popular approval that he so well deserved but had been denied. To be sure, as students of literature, we cannot help but be fascinated by this particular case of misunderstanding and literary revisionism. Can we simply assume that great poets must always meet with a certain degree of resistance or indifference, if not as dramatic as in T'ao Ch'ien's case? Yet history informs us that no rational arguments can support such an assumption; there are overwhelming examples—as in a great majority of the poets under study in this book—in which contemporary approval stands the test of future generations. Who, then, is responsible for the judgment of literary taste? What makes posterity revive a certain poet but not others? These questions cannot really be answered, but they are particularly relevant in our study of T'ao Ch'ien. And my attempt to reread T'ao Ch'ien's poetry reflects most appropriately a modern reader's sympathy with the process of literary revisionism.

Let us now go back to the contemporary literary scene in which the poet T'ao Ch'ien found himself. In literature the entire period of the Eastern Chin has been known as an age of *hsüan-yen* poetry (Neo-Taoistic poetry). This poetry, characterized by philosophical propositions, was itself a reflection of an increasingly important intellectual movement called "pure conversation" (*ch'ing-t'an*) in vogue since the third century.[1] By definition, the *hsüan-yen* poetry is primarily discursive, a deliberate mimesis of "pure conversation." The most famous author in this genre, Sun Ch'o (320–377), for instance, uses various shades of the *ch'ing-t'an* language in his poem to Hsü Hsün, another *hsüan-yen* poet:

> Looking up, I view the vastness of creation,
> Looking down, I survey the existence of living things.
> Contingencies come and go, disasters arise,
> The good and the bad displace one another.   4
> Man's wisdom is clouded by greed,
> His understanding cramped by feelings.
> In the wilds, he suffers from withering cold,
> At court, he meets with sultry heat.   8

---

[1] Ying-shih Yü, "Individualism and the Neo-Taoist Movement in Wei-Chin China" (draft, 1982), p. 19.

T'ao Ch'ien
DEFINING THE LYRIC VOICE

    Failure would strike him with sudden terror,
    Success would make him unable to contain himself for joy.
       (CHSK, I, 434)

仰觀大造
俯覽時物
機過患生
吉凶相拂
智以利昏
識由情屈
野有寒枯
朝有炎鬱
失則震驚
得必充詘

Clearly the basic attitude in this poem is not emotional but philosophical, as it is essentially about the reasoning of a philosophy which preaches the necessary alternation of *yin* and *yang*, and of fortune and misfortune.

    A similar tone of rationalism also characterizes Wang Hsi-chih's (303–379) poem "Orchid Pavilion" (*Lan-t'ing*):[2]

    Looking up, I view the outer limit of the blue sky,
    Looking down, I survey the cerulean water's edge.
    So vast and tranquil, the scene is boundless,
    In whatever strikes my eyes, the principle is evident.   4
    Great indeed are the workings of creation,
    Ten thousand different phenomena: none of them are unequal.
    Natural stirrings of various kinds, however diverse,
    Are all in rapport with me.   8
       (CHSK, I, 431)

仰視碧天際
俯瞰淥水濱
寥闐無涯觀
寓目理自陳
大矣造化工
萬殊莫不均
羣籟雖參差
適我無非親

The philosophy that the speaker attempts to illustrate is that of the universal equality (lines 5–6) central to Neo-Taoist thinking. This poem appears to be

---

[2] For Wang Hsi-chih's dates, see Chiang Liang-fu, *Li-tai jen-wu nien-li pei-chuan tsung-piao* (rpt. Taipei: Hua-shih ch'u-pan-she, 1976), p. 51.

more personal than the one by Sun Ch'o, as the dominant acceptance of a philosophical principle comes from the observation of a particular phenomenon, that of a riverbank (line 2). But it still reads like a proposition based on a well-established doctrine, exhibiting little emotion. Indeed it is the lack of emotional overtones in the *hsüan-yen* poetry that makes it philosophical rather than lyrical.

When one compares Wang Hsi-chih's poem with the preface, the "Lan-t'ing chi hsü," one is struck by the difference: whereas the poem proper is marked by discursive reason, the preface is distinguished by lyrical directness. In fact, Wang's well-known "Preface to the *Orchid Pavilion Collection*" is one of the most lyrical items of prose literature ever produced in the Chinese tradition. The preface is about a late spring purification ritual held at the beautiful Orchid Pavilion in the year 353. As a leader of a powerful aristocratic family, Wang Hsi-chih gathered for this occasion some forty influential members of Eastern Chin society—among them the brothers Hsieh An and Hsieh Wan from the powerful Hsieh clan, and the *hsüan-yen* poets Sun Ch'o and Hsü Hsün. Wang Hsi-chih and his guests sat, arranged according to age, along the riverbank, where they drank wine and wrote poetry. Wang's "Preface" was then written for the thirty-seven poems composed at this gathering, each entitled "The Orchid Pavilion" (*CHSK*, I, 431–443). The lyrical immediacy of the "Preface" arises from a sad feeling of life's transience on the part of the author, who has just turned fifty *sui*:

> Every time I examine the reasons why the emotions of people of former times were aroused, it is as though they all fit the same mode,[3] and I bend over their writings with grief and sighs, unable to understand it in my breast. I certainly know that to equate death and life is an empty lie, and to even up a P'eng with one who has died early is a false construct. The future views the present in the same way that the present views the former times. Is it not sad![4]
> 每覽昔人興感之由，若合一契，未嘗不臨文嗟悼，不能喻之於懷。固知一死生爲虛誕，齊彭殤爲妄作。後之視今，亦猶今之視昔，悲夫。

Wang's "Preface" concludes with a desire to overcome his sorrow by making the "Orchid Pavilion" poem-series a permanent record of the occasion. Yet, ironically, it is the "Preface" itself, rather than the poems, that is celebrated by

---

[3] This line may also be taken to mean: "it is as though I have a bond with them."

[4] I am indebted to Hugh M. Stimson for the privilege of using his translation here. (See Stimson, "Preface to the *Orchid* Pavilion Collection," unpublished trans., 1983.) For another translation, see H. C. Chang, *Chinese Literature, Vol. 2: Nature Poetry* (New York: Columbia Univ. Press, 1977), pp. 8–9. The original passage can be found in Fang Hsüan-ling, et al. *Chin shu*, *chüan* 80 (Peking: Chung-hua shu-chü, 1974) VII, 2,099.

3. "Preface to the Orchid Pavilion Collection." Calligraphy by Chao Chung of the Yüan. From his scroll, "Orchid Pavilion Gathering."

T'ao Ch'ien
DEFINING THE LYRIC VOICE

posterity. This suggests that to the traditional critics the expression of feeling is a literary requisite of Chinese poetry. When the purpose of a poem is philosophical discourse, as in Wang's "Orchid Pavilion" poem, poetry tends to lose its aesthetic appeal. Usually when one speaks of *hsüan-yen* poetry at all, one tacitly assumes its non-lyrical character. It is only natural that literary critics such as Chung Jung and Liu Hsieh would regard the period of Eastern Chin, a period dominated by the *hsüan-yen* poetics, as a rather lifeless age in poetry.

T'ao Ch'ien's poetic style represents a sharp break from that of Wang Hsi-chih and Sun Ch'o, though traditionally his poetry is placed with theirs in the same category of "Eastern Chin poetry." It seems curious that the Liang critic Liu Hsieh, who attempts to systematize Chinese literature in an all-inclusive manner, does not mention T'ao Ch'ien's name even once in his *Wen-hsin tiao-lung*.[5] In my opinion, the conventional way of designating period style is partially responsible for the general neglect of T'ao Ch'ien's literary innovation. We must consider T'ao Ch'ien's "An Outing to Hsieh Brook," a poem written under the influence of Wang Hsi-chih, to see the essential difference between T'ao Ch'ien's poetics and the general poetic style of the Eastern Chin:

> On this new year's day all at once I'm fifty,
> My life is about to return to its rest.
> Pondering over this, my heart stirs within:
> Let me enjoy an outing on this seasonable day.   4
> The weather is fair, the sky cloudless,
> When we sit together by the far-running stream.
> Colorful mullet dart through the weak currents,
> Crying gulls take wing from the quiet valley.   8
> Letting our vision wander over the distant marshes,
> We gaze afar at the Layered Wall Mountain:
> Though not majestic like the Ninefold Peak,
> Its grandeur is unmatched by anything else in sight.   12
> I carry a jar, serving wine to my companions,
> Filling each cup to the brim, as we drink to each other's health.
> Who knows whether after today
> There will be another time like this.   16
> In our cups we let our unbounded thoughts go,
> Troubled no more by those thousand-year cares.

---

[5] A Late Ming edition of *Wen-hsin tiao-lung* added a paragraph of about 400 characters to the chapter entitled "*Yin hsiu,*" in which T'ao Ch'ien's name is mentioned. But most scholars since the time of Chi Yün have considered this addition a Ming forgery. Recently Chan Ying argued that the Ming edition was based on a genuine Sung edition. (See Chan Ying, *Wen-hsin tiao-lung te feng-ke hsüeh* [Peking: Jen-min wen-hsüeh ch'u-pan-she, 1982], pp. 78–94.)

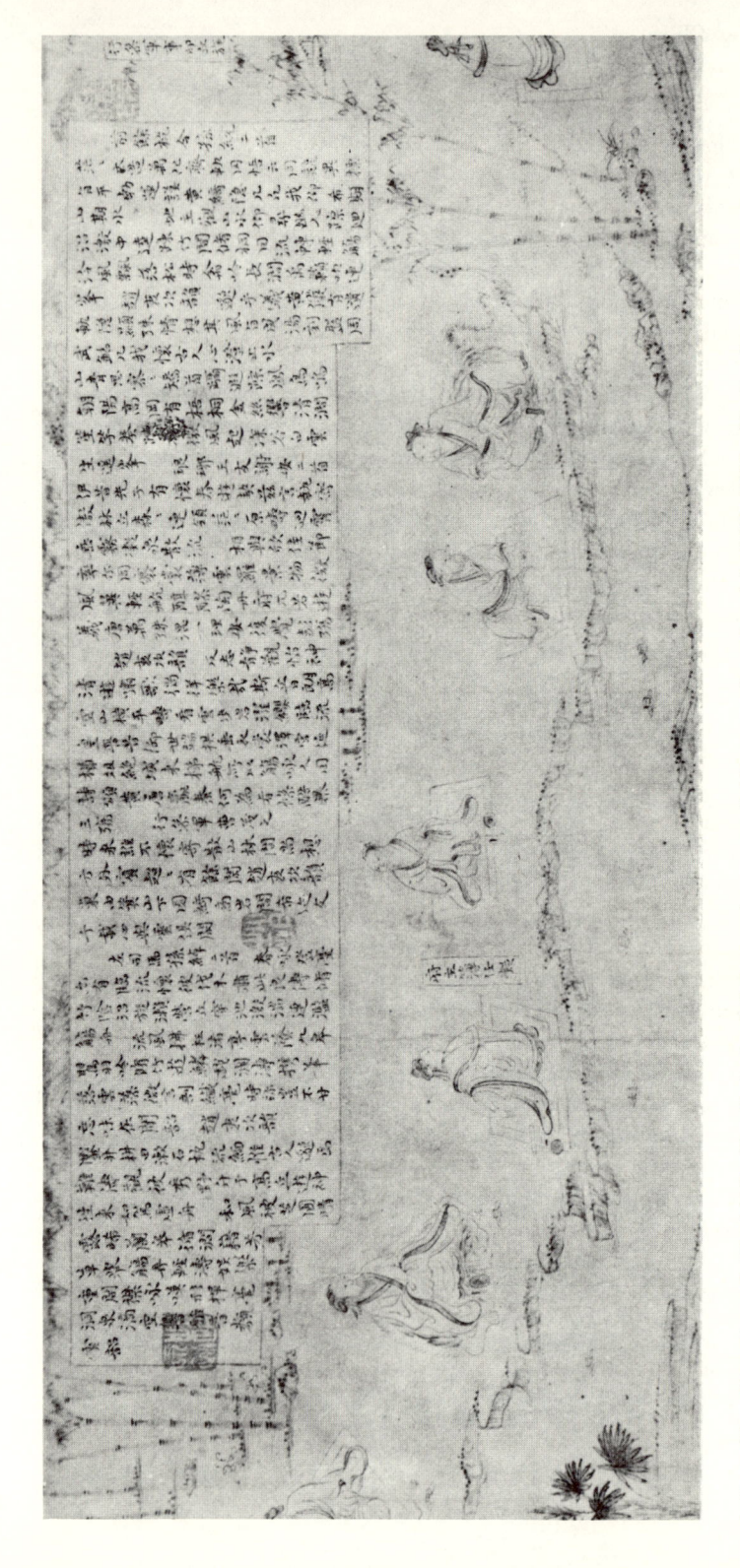

4. From Chao Chung's scroll, "Orchid Pavilion Gathering." Each scene is accompanied by poems from the original "Orchid Pavilion" series and Chao Chung's own poems to the same rhyme schemes.

T'ao Ch'ien
DEFINING THE LYRIC VOICE

> Let us make the most of today's happiness,
> For tomorrow is not worth pursuing. 20
> (*TYMC*, 44)

開歲倏五十
吾生行歸休
念之動中懷
及辰爲茲遊
氣和天惟澄
班坐依遠流
弱湍馳文魴
閑谷矯鳴鷗
迥澤散游目
緬然睇曾丘
雖微九重秀
顧瞻無匹儔
提壺接賓侶
引滿更獻酬
未知從今去
當復如此不
中觴縱遙情
忘彼千載憂
且極今朝樂
明日非所求

The poem opens with an expression of personal feeling reminiscent of Wang Hsi-chih's "Preface"—again, it is about the same lament for mortality: that life is slipping away and that "this" moment should be treasured. The possibility of T'ao Ch'ien's composing this poem at fifty *sui* makes his work an allusion to Wang Hsi-chih's spring purification ritual.[6] The description of sitting by a stream (line 6) and of drinking wine together (lines 13–18) recalls the occasion of the Orchid Pavilion.

[6] There is no general agreement about the date of this poem. Hightower sums it up correctly: "This one is plagued with variant readings." (See Hightower, *The Poetry of T'ao Ch'ien*, p. 57.) The problem of dating in this case arises from the ambiguous nature of the term *hsin-yu* in T'ao Ch'ien's Preface. Most scholars take *hsin-yu* to mean the year designation for A.D. 421. But recently Lu Ch'in-li held that *hsin-yu* refers to a day rather than a year—i.e., the New Year's day of A.D. 414. According to Ch'en Yüan's *Erh-shih shih shuo-jun piao*, this date was indeed the day *hsin-yu*. Suppose that we accept this time designation, then it would be very convenient for us to see T'ao Ch'ien's piece as following the tradition of Wang Hsi-chih's spring purification ritual at 50 *sui*. (See Lu Ch'in-li, "T'ao Yüan-ming shih-chi shih-wen hsi-nien," in *TYMC*, 281.) This interpretation would then make the first line of the poem very convincing. In any case, T'ao Ch'ien's attention to age is quite notable, as may be seen in his Preface to this poem, which includes the line: "Each of us wrote down his age and birthplace to commemorate the occasion (James R. Hightower, *The Poetry of T'ao Ch'ien* [Oxford: Calrendon Press, 1970], p. 56).

T'ao Ch'ien
DEFINING THE LYRIC VOICE

Our interest in T'ao's poem arises from a larger concern with the idea of artistic expression. Whereas Wang Hsi-chih reserves the expression of feelings primarily for his prose "Preface," T'ao Ch'ien makes his poem a lyrical articulation of feelings. "My heart stirs within ...," so T'ao Ch'ien says directly in the opening section of his poem. The implication of this statement is of great importance to our study of this period's literary history. For the subject of poetry here is the poet's own feeling, and we immediately recognize this individual accent as the distinctive voice that marks classical Chinese lyricism. As stated in the "Great Preface" to *Shih ching*,

> Poetry is that which expresses the heart's intent (*chih*). When it is within the heart it is called *chih*. When expressed in words, it is poetry.[7]
> 詩者志之所之也，在心爲志，發言爲詩。

It is the personal voice of T'ao Ch'ien that restores the ancient lyricism and announces his departure from the discursive mode of poetry that dominated the literary scene for over a century. Whereas *hsüan-yen* poetry is devoid of emotional tone, it is precisely this lyrical quality that characterizes T'ao Ch'ien's poetry.[8]

As soon as T'ao Ch'ien's expressive lyricism is recognized, one can see his individual style in a better light. For what he brings to the poetic tradition is more than a restoration of classical lyricism. His poetry is the expression of the total person. This individuality permits him to treat subjects in ways different from his contemporaries. A case in point is the series of three poems on his own imagined death, opening with the following statement:

> If there is life, there must be death.
> He who dies young has not hastened to his doom....
>   (*TYMC*, 141)
> 有生必有死
> 早終非命促....

Upon first reading this opening couplet the reader would expect the series of poems to be a *hsüan-yen* piece. For this does sound like an introduction to philosophical discourse. Yet very soon the reader is struck by its forceful lyricism—the dramatic "self" proceeds to tell us how his dead body first fills

---

[7] See *Mao shih chu-shu* (rpt. Hong Kong: Chung-hua shu-chü, 1964), 1.3a. See also James J. Y. Liu, "The Individualist View: Poetry as Self-Expression," *The Art of Chinese Poetry* (Chicago: Univ. of Chicago Press, 1962), pp. 70–76.

[8] This is not to deny the fact that a few of T'ao Ch'ien's poems were still under the influence of *hsüan-yen* poetry. (For a discussion of this point, see Wang Yao, *Chung-ku wen-hsüeh feng-mao*, 1951 [Shanghai; rpt. Hong Kong: Chung-liu ch'u-pan-she, 1973], p. 58.) Yet the general style of T'ao's poetry is lyrical rather than discursive.

T'ao Ch'ien
DEFINING THE LYRIC VOICE

the coffin (poem 1), how his relatives and friends weep by his side (poem 2), and how he is finally buried underground (poem 3). All this is expressed through a lyrical voice that intends to reveal the innermost feelings which lie close to the poet's heart. It is a grasp of life which is intensely personal:

> In the old days I used to dwell in the highest halls,
> Now I make my home among the desolate wilds.
> Once I go beyond the gate,
> My return will never come to pass.
>   (Poem 2, lines 9–12)
> 昔在高堂寢
> 今宿荒草鄉
> 一朝出門去
> 歸來良未央

It should be mentioned that T'ao Ch'ien was not an exact contemporary of Wang Hsi-chih and the other prominent *hsüan-yen* poets such as Sun Ch'o and Hsü Hsün. These poets had died before T'ao Ch'ien turned twenty, and gradually an entirely different literary style from that of *hsüan-yen* poetry was beginning to develop. What finally emerged was a new aesthetic taste characterized by literary embellishment, an obvious reaction to the rather dry and plain style of the typical Eastern Chin poetry. This new stylistic tendency, through various forms of expression, was to dominate the literary scene in China for the next one hundred and fifty years.

However, T'ao Ch'ien stood apart from both the *hsüan-yen* style and the newly emerging aesthetic movement. He was all alone, for he lived in a period of transition, and was judged by a set of poetic criteria directly opposed to his own literary taste. Critics of the next several decades more or less agreed that T'ao Ch'ien's style was impaired by its unadorned diction. For example, Yang Hsiu-chih (509–582) says: "T'ao Ch'ien's literary style is deficient in verbal ornament." [9] 陶潛之文，辭采未優. Chung Jung appears to be more sympathetic to T'ao Ch'ien's individual style, but he is nonetheless reluctant to place him in the "first rank" (*shang-p'in*). He regards T'ao Ch'ien as a poet of the "middle rank" (*chung-p'in*) despite his admiration for the poet's general accomplishment. And his reason is clear enough—that "the world at large" laments T'ao's "plain and straightforward" style (*chih-chih*). Chung Jung attempts to justify T'ao Ch'ien's literary position by arguing that T'ao Ch'ien's poetry is not always devoid of "the elegant and the flowery" (*feng-hua ch'ing*-

---

[9] See his Preface to *Ching-chieh hsien-sheng chi*, in *Ssu-pu pei-yao*, (Shanghai: Chung-hua shu-chü, 1936), 2a. See also David R. Knechtges' Introduction to his translation of *Wen xuan, or Selections of Refined Literature, Vol. 1: Rhapsodies on Metropolises and Capitals*, by Xiao Tong (Princeton: Princeton Univ. Press, 1982), p. 41.

T'ao Ch'ien
DEFINING THE LYRIC VOICE

mi), and it thus should not be regarded as "rustic language" (*t'ien-chia yü*).[10] Yet the fact that Chung Jung finds it necessary to defend T'ao Ch'ien's lack of verbal ornament reveals precisely the enormous influence of a new aesthetic standard.

Yen Yen-chih (384–456), the author of "Eulogy on T'ao Ch'ien" (*WH*, II, 1237–1241), was a major poet in the new stylistic movement emerging in the late years of the Eastern Chin. A close friend of T'ao Ch'ien, Yen had a genuine respect for T'ao Ch'ien's lofty disposition.[11] He was only nineteen years younger than T'ao Ch'ien, but, unlike the older poet, who was regarded as an Eastern Chin poet, he belonged essentially to the following dynasty, the Liu-Sung (420–479). Known to be one of the "Three Literary Giants in the Yüan-chia Reign" (425–453), along with Hsieh Ling-yün (385–433) and Pao Chao (414–466), Yen was particularly skillful in producing poems that are full of colorful images and meticulous embellishment. That he was conscious of T'ao Ch'ien's "faulty" poetic style may be proved by the fact that his "Eulogy" focuses merely on the noble character of the poet without once mentioning T'ao Ch'ien's literary merits.

It must be noted that this preference for ornate style on the part of Yen Yen-chih and his contemporaries is not at all unknown to Chinese literature. Many earlier leading poets in the Western Chin (265–316), such as P'an Yüeh (247–300) and Lu Chi (261–303), already reveal in their poetry an unmistakable preference for flowery diction.[12] Indeed, Chung Jung singles out Lu Chi as Yen Yen-chih's precursor:

> His poetic style originates in that of Lu Chi.... It is refined and dense. (*SPC*, 43)
> 其源出於陸機。…體裁綺密。

This proves that the new stylistic movement which Yen Yen-chih identified himself with began first as a revival of a predominant literary phenomenon of the Western Chin, the period immediately preceding the Eastern Chin. And T'ao Ch'ien must have been familiar with the general tendency in Western Chin poetry, but, unlike his younger contemporaries, he chose not to emulate

---

[10] See *SPC*, 41. For a discussion of Chung Jung's view of T'ao Ch'ien's poetry, see Chia-ying Yeh and Jan W. Walls, "Theory, Standards, and Practice of Criticizing Poetry in Chung Hung's *Shih-p'in*," in *Studies in Chinese Poetry and Poetics*, vol. 1, ed. Ronald C. Miao (San Francisco: Chinese Materials Center, 1978), p. 44; and Knechtges, *Wen xuan*, pp. 40–41.

[11] Yen Yen-chih served in T'ao Ch'ien's home town Hsün-yang in 415–416. Yen was believed to be one of T'ao Ch'ien's two friends who gave him a constant supply of wine. See *SS, chüan* 93; VIII, 2,288; and Hightower, *The Poetry of T'ao Ch'ien*, p. 5.

[12] See Chung Jung, *SPC*, 24–26. Both of these poets are judged to be "first-ranking" poets by Chung Jung.

it. Indeed, we see a deliberate attempt on his part to create the impression of an easygoing style that is dramatically opposed to that of verbal refinement. In his poetry expressions of daily conversation often merge smoothly into the narrative context:

(1) Although I have five sons,
　　None of them is fond of brush and paper.
　　　　(*TYMC*, 106)
　　雖有五男兒
　　總不好紙筆

(2) If I do not amuse myself now,
　　Who knows if there will be another year?
　　　　(*TYMC*, 59)
　　今我不爲樂
　　知有來歲不

(3) If by any chance I do not get along with them,
　　The whole world would forever laugh at me.
　　　　(*TYMC*, 112)
　　萬一不合意
　　永爲世笑之

Unusual, too, in T'ao Ch'ien's poetry is his frequent use of questions followed by answers. It is a device that gives his poetry a quality of living presentness through directly imitating daily discourse:

(1) "May I ask you how this is possible for you?"
　　When the mind is remote, so is the place.
　　　　(*TYMC*, 89)
　　問君何能爾
　　心遠地自偏

(2) Who made me take this trip?
　　It seems I was driven by hunger.
　　　　(*TYMC*, 93)
　　此行誰使然
　　似爲饑所驅

(3) "May I ask you the purpose of your journey today?"
　　It is not for business, nor for war.
　　　　(*TYMC*, 110)
　　問君今何行
　　非商復非戎

T'ao Ch'ien
DEFINING THE LYRIC VOICE

On the whole we see in T'ao Ch'ien a general preference for a more elastic structure in poetry, a freer play in its syntactic variety. And this stylistic originality is an expression of his individuality. For T'ao is an individual working against the tides of his time, and his ordinariness is itself a sign of self-expression.

II. Poetry as Autobiography

T'ao Ch'ien's aspiration for self-expression leads him to create an autobiographical mode in poetry, making himself the prime subject of his work. His poetic autobiography is not autobiographical in the literal sense, but rather one of "self-biography" that addresses the problems of self-definition figuratively. T'ao Ch'ien uses a number of literary forms for his autobiography. Sometimes it takes the form of the factual account, with documentation of place and time.[13] At other times the self of the poet may be revealed through primarily fictive modes. Despite the wide range of forms employed, most of T'ao Ch'ien's poetic autobiography express a consistent desire to define his ultimate self-realization in life.

Yet the effect of T'ao Ch'ien's autobiography will be not only to reveal the self but to touch the heart of the reader with the power of universality. This the poet often accomplishes through a fictional voice: by focusing his attention on the immediate experiences of the protagonist, the poet succeeds in bringing the poem to a level of universality with which the reader can identify. Poised between the poles of factuality and fiction, T'ao Ch'ien turns Chinese literature into something more complex and multifaceted. And the power of T'ao Ch'ien's poetry lies precisely in this dual function.

The perfect union of T'ao Ch'ien's autobiographical and fictional impulses can be found in his famous description of an ideal land, "The Peach Blossom Spring." The poem is preceded by a prose account (*chi*) of the story that opens like a typical fantastic tale (*chih-kuai*) in which the protagonist, a fisherman, rowing along a stream, continues on aimlessly until he suddenly finds himself

---

[13] Many of the titles of his poems indicate clearly the time and the situation of composition, revealing the poet's deliberate attempt to provide factual data on his life. (See especially *chüan* 3 in *TYMC*, 71, 72, 74, 76, 78, 79, 81, 83, 84, 85.) His prefaces to his poems often serve a similar referential function. (See *TYMC*, 11, 13, 15, 18, 22, 35, 39, 44, 51, 64, 106, 145, 159.) In general, his poetry takes his daily life as its main subject. Details about his neighbors, his thatched hut, his family, his love of drinking, the misery of famines, and the joy of harvests—all give us a vivid picture of his life. His poetry even informs us that his house in Hsün-yang was destroyed by fire in A.D. 408, and that he moved to the "Southern Village" soon after that incident. It is through referential details such as this that we find it easy to construct a biography of T'ao Ch'ien in the literal sense of biography.

T'ao Ch'ien
DEFINING THE LYRIC VOICE

passing through a narrow entrance to a wonderland:[14]

> During the T'ai-yüan period of the Chin dynasty a fisherman of Wu-ling once rowed upstream, unmindful of the distance he had gone, when he suddenly came to a grove of peach trees in bloom. For several hundred paces on both banks of the stream there was no other kind of tree. The fragrant flowers [*fang-ts'ao*] growing under them were fresh and lovely, and fallen petals covered the ground—it made a great impression on the fisherman. He went on for a way with the idea of finding out how far the grove extended. It came to an end at the foot of a mountain whence issued the spring that supplied the stream. There was a small opening in the mountain and it seemed as though light was coming through it. The fisherman left his boat and entered the cave, which at first was extremely narrow, barely admitting his body; after a few dozen steps it suddenly opened out onto a broad and level plain where well-built houses were surrounded by rich fields and pretty ponds. Mulberry, bamboo and other trees and plants grew there....[15]
> 晉太元中，武陵人捕魚為業。緣溪行，忘路之遠近。忽逢桃花林，夾岸數百步，中無雜樹。芳草鮮美，落英繽紛，漁人甚異之。復前行，欲窮其林。林盡水源，便得一山。山有小口，髣髴若有光，便捨船，從口入。初極狹，纔通人，復行數十步，豁然開朗。土地平曠，屋舍儼然，有良田美池，桑竹之屬。...

Yet, unlike a tale of pure fantasy, the narrative proceeds to dwell on the description of a simple farm community which appears to be rather down-to-earth. It is an ideal land in which all men and women enjoy working in the fields, live in peace with their neighbors, and are secure against the vicissitudes of dynastic changes. The prose account is then followed by the poem proper, which compresses the details of the anecdote into verse:

> When Ying overturned the heavenly principle,[16]
> Virtuous men retired from the world.

---

[14] See also the collection of *chih-kuai* tales in *Sou-shen hou-chi*, (*Ku chin shuo-pu ts'ung-shu*, *chi* 2), 1a–1b. Modern scholars, such as Ch'en Yin-k'o, have confirmed T'ao's authorship of *Sou-shen hou-chi*, and this view has had a long impact on the field since the 1930's. (See Ch'en Yin-k'o, "T'ao-hua yüan chi p'ang-cheng," posthumously reprinted in his *CYK*, I, 188–189.) The story called "The Peach Blossom Spring" in *Sou-shen hou-chi* (#5) deserves our special attention, as it seems to have a direct relationship with T'ao Ch'ien's "Peach Blossom Spring" and its Preface.

[15] The translation is Hightower's (see *The Poetry of T'ao Ch'ien*, p. 254), except that "wild flowers" is changed to "fragrant flowers" here to give a more literal rendering of *fang-ts'ao*.

[16] This alludes to Ying Cheng, the first Emperor of Ch'in. During his rule many worthy men fled into hiding, chief among them Hsia Huang Kung and Ch'i Li-chi. (See line 3 of the poem.)

T'ao Ch'ien
DEFINING THE LYRIC VOICE

When Huang and Ch'i left for Mount Shang,
The ancestors of these people also went into hiding.[17]   4
Slowly their tracks were buried,
Their trodden paths gave way to weeds.
They encouraged one another to be diligent in farming,
At sunset each returned to his home to rest.   8
Mulberry and bamboo gave ample shade,
Beans and millet were planted in season.
From spring silkworms long silk threads were gathered,
On the autumn harvest no official tax was levied.   12
Overgrown roads were bare of traffic,
Cocks and dogs crowed and barked at one another.
Their ritual vessels still followed the old designs,
Their clothes were not in the new fashions.   16
Children sang their songs with abandonment,
Gray-haired men wandered about in high spirits.
When grass was lush and green, they realized the season was mild,
When trees withered, they knew the winds were chilly and harsh.   20
Although they had no calendar to mark the time,
The four seasons naturally made a year.
Joyfully they lived in ample happiness,
Why should they tire themselves with knowledge?   24
Their extraordinary existence had lain hidden for five hundred years,
Then one day this heavenly land was discovered.
Since the pure and the low-minded are different in nature,
Shortly after, their world vanished from sight again.   28
Let me ask you who wanders within the conventional world,
Can you imagine those who live outside the earthly dust and noise?[18]

[17] This line corresponds to a passage in T'ao Ch'ien's own prose account of the Peach Blossom Spring story which reads: "They told him that their ancestors had fled the disorders of Ch'in times and, having taken refuge here with wives and children and neighbors, had never ventured out again...." (See translation by Hightower, in his *The Poetry of T'ao Ch'ien*, p. 255.)

[18] According to traditional critics, these two lines are an allusion to Chapter Six of *Chuang Tzu* ("*Ta tsung shih*"), where Confucius distinguishes himself from the Taoists: "Such men as they ... wander beyond the realm; men like me wander within it." (For translation, see Burton Watson, trans., *The Complete Works of Chuang Tzu* [New York: Columbia Univ. Press, 1968], p. 86.) For a discussion of T'ao Ch'ien's use of the allusion, see Hightower, *The Poetry of T'ao Ch'ien*, pp. 257–258.

T'ao Ch'ien
DEFINING THE LYRIC VOICE

I wish to move astride the clear breeze,
And fly high to find my understanding friends. 32
 (*CHSK*, I, 485)

嬴氏亂天紀
賢者避其世
黃綺之商山
伊人亦云逝
往迹浸復湮
來逕遂蕪廢
相命肆農耕
日入從所憩
桑竹垂餘蔭
菽稷隨時藝
春蠶收長絲
秋熟靡王稅
荒路曖交通
雞犬互鳴吠
俎豆猶古法
衣裳無新製
童孺縱行歌
班白歡游詣
草榮識節和
木衰知風厲
雖無紀歷誌
四時自成歲
怡然有餘樂
于何勞智慧
奇蹤隱五百
一朝敞神界
淳薄既異源
旋復還幽蔽
借問游方士
焉測塵囂外
願言躡輕風
高舉尋吾契

The world of "The Peach Blossom Spring," however plausible, is sharply different from actual Eastern Chin society. T'ao Ch'ien's time was one of the most chaotic in Chinese history, and farmers in particular confronted the problem of survival. From the beginning of the Eastern Chin, the government, whose existence was so dependent on the powers of the large families, was unable to set limits on the size of private lands. As a result, numerous local

T'ao Ch'ien
DEFINING THE LYRIC VOICE

farmers and immigrants from the north quickly became the suffering dependents of the powerful landowners. The situation culminated in a series of uprisings that began in the last years of the fourth century, of which the Rebellion of Sun En from 399 to 402 was the most menacing. Several army leaders, chief among them Huan Hsüan and Liu Yü, rose to fight against these insurrections and took advantage of the situation to gain power which would otherwise have been denied them in a society mainly controlled by an aristocracy. It so happened that T'ao Ch'ien grew up in Kiangsi, one of the main bases of these continuous struggles and campaigns.[19]

It was at about this time that T'ao Ch'ien began to seek government employment. In 393, at age twenty-eight, he obtained the post of Libationer (*chou chi-chiu*) in the local province Chiang-chou, but resigned from the post only a few months afterward. His reason for resignation was clear enough: he refused to yield to the authority of Wang Ning-chih, the Provincial Governor of Chiang-chou (*TYMC*, 265). Wang Ning-chih, a son of the famous aristocrat Wang Hsi-chih, perhaps appeared to be somewhat disdainful of those who were not members of the great families. And T'ao Ch'ien found this aristocratic snobbishness, pervasive throughout elite society, especially difficult to bear. T'ao Ch'ien's great-grandfather T'ao K'an was a distinguished general in the early years of the Eastern Chin who made important contributions to the nation. But T'ao's family, which had since become poor, lacked the nobility that characterized the so-called *shih-tsu* (gentry families)—such as the families Wang, Hsieh, Yüan, Hsiao from the north; and the Chu, Chang, Ku, Lu, which originated in the south. The Wangs and the Hsiehs were the most influential among these noble families, and their very existence seemed to threaten the power of the central government.

Thus, T'ao Ch'ien resigned from his post and spent six years in his home town Hsün-yang, tilling the small piece of land owned by his family. He did not come back to serve in the government until after Wang Ning-chih's death in 399. This time T'ao Ch'ien worked for Huan Hsüan, the new Provincial Governor of Chiang-chou, who first distinguished himself by victorious campaigns against the troublesome rebels. But two years later T'ao Ch'ien asked for leave of absence to work as a self-supporting farmer again. Soon afterward Huan Hsüan usurped the throne at Chien-k'ang, and in 403 named his unlawful dynasty Ch'u. The treacherous Huan Hsüan had Emperor An of the Chin (Chin An-ti) imprisoned in Hsün-yang, the home town of T'ao Ch'ien. It was at this time of national crisis that T'ao Ch'ien served under Liu Yü as an inspector of troops (*chen-chün ts'an-chün*), in a collective effort to save the Emperor. Huan Hsüan's forces were crushed by Liu Yü in 404, and Emperor

---

[19] Jacques Gernet, *A History of Chinese Civilization*, trans. J. R. Foster (Cambridge: Cambridge Univ. Press, 1982), p. 182.

T'ao Ch'ien
DEFINING THE LYRIC VOICE

An regained his throne the following year. The Eastern Chin government breathed a sigh of relief.

In 405 T'ao Ch'ien was appointed the Prefect of P'eng-tse, but he resigned after some eighty days of service. Whatever his reasons, this resignation marked the most uncompromising and irreversible decision that he ever made. For never again in his lifetime would T'ao Ch'ien come back to service. In a tone of self-reliance, the poet sings his final farewell to the political world:

> Let me go back home!
> My fields and garden will soon turn into wastelands—Why not
>   go back now?
> For it was I who made my mind the slave of my body,
> Why should I be disheartened and feel sad myself now?
> I am aware the past is beyond remedy,
> Yet I know the future can be pursued.
> After all I have not strayed far on the wrong path,
> And I understand today's move is right, yesterday's wrong....
>   (*TYMC*, 160)

歸去來兮
田園將蕪胡不歸
既自以心爲形役
奚惆悵而獨悲
悟已往之不諫
知來者之可追
實迷途其未遠
覺今是而昨非....

He explains the reason for his radical choice:

> When a closely knit net is cast, the fish are frightened,
> When a big trap is set, the birds are terrified.
> Wise men are quick to understand this,
> So they flee from official service to return to farming.
>   (*TYMC*, 147)

密網裁而魚駭
宏羅制而鳥驚
彼達人之善覺
及逃祿而歸耕

Indeed politics in T'ao Ch'ien's time was as dangerous as the fish net and the bird's snare, and he was wise enough to see through it early. Of course, the statement above may reflect only the poet's general disillusionment with the government and the governing elite of his time. But there is a strong possi-

T'ao Ch'ien
DEFINING THE LYRIC VOICE

bility that he wished to make his resignation a specific political protest. For history informs us that the same Liu Yü who rescued Emperor An at Hsün-yang was also the one who murdered the Emperor fourteen years later, and eventually usurped power at Chien-k'ang in 420. And for more than a decade Liu Yü controlled the political and military powers at court, provoking great resistance from the great families. T'ao Ch'ien might not have predicted that the fall of the Chin dynasty would take place so soon, but he must have seen in the army chief Liu Yü the same kind of dissident ambition exhibited by Huan Hsüan. It seems that these faithless generals, who rose from humble origin, were even worse than the proud members of the noble families. T'ao Ch'ien's disappointment with politics was most understandable.

Thus, T'ao Ch'ien creates an ideal world in literature in his "The Peach Blossom Spring." Any reader can delight in the beauty of its fictional world, knowing that the world outside is undesirable and that the free society is possible only in the realm of imagination. But what is striking is that this Utopia reminds us of the brighter side of T'ao Ch'ien's own life in retirement. As has been cited, "The Peach Blossom Spring" describes an agricultural society where

> They encouraged one another to be diligent in farming,
> At sunset each returned to his home to rest.   8
> Mulberry and bamboo gave ample shade,
> Beans and millet were planted in season.
> From spring silkworms long silk threads were gathered,
> On the autumn harvest no official tax was levied.   12
> Overgrown roads were bare of traffic,
> Cocks and dogs crowed and barked at one another ...
> 相命肆農耕
> 日入從所憩
> 桑竹垂餘蔭
> 菽稷隨時藝
> 春蠶收長絲
> 秋熟靡王稅
> 荒路曖交通
> 雞犬互鳴吠 ....

This is very similar to the real world which the poet describes in his "Returning to My Farm to Dwell":

> Elms and willows give shade to the back eaves,
> Peach and plum grow in front of the house.
> Hazy, hazy—the distant village,
> Gently, gently, the chimney smoke rises from the hamlet.   4

> Dogs bark in the hidden lane,
> Cocks crow atop the mulberry tree....
> When we meet we talk not of irrelevant things,
> But about how hemp and mulberry have grown.
> Day after day the hemp and mulberry thrive,
> Everyday my tilled lands are wider....
>   (*TYMC*, 40–41)
>
> 8
>
> 榆柳蔭後簷
> 桃李羅堂前
> 曖曖遠人村
> 依依墟里烟
> 狗吠深巷中
> 鷄鳴桑樹巔....
> 相見無雜言
> 但道桑麻長
> 桑麻日己長
> 我土日己廣....

It seems that the Utopian society has only one significant advantage over T'ao Ch'ien's village community—exemption from taxes.

It is said that "The Peach Blossom Spring" might have been inspired by a contemporary report of some secluded settlements actually in existence.[20] But, in any case, since the Utopia is modeled after T'ao Ch'ien's ideal vision of his own farm life, it is the poet's desire for self-definition that underlies the main theme of his Utopia. What makes "The Peach Blossom Spring" autobiographical, in other words, is not the reference to any specific time and place, but rather the poet's goal to establish an imaginative world for self-realization. It is worth noting that the poem ends with the statement of a personal wish:

> I wish to move astride the clear breeze,
> And fly high to find my understanding friends.
>   (*TYMC*, 168, lines 31–32)
> 願言躡清風
> 高舉尋吾契

This conclusion clearly spells out the main message that the poet hopes to convey: that his "Peach Blossom Spring" is nothing more than the ideal realization of his lifelong search for persons of his own kind. The conformists might reject people in his Utopia. Yet these unconventional men, living in the anarchic society of the ideal land, are precisely those with whom T'ao Ch'ien would like to identify himself. It is at this point that the distinction between

[20] See Ch'en Yin-k'o, "T'ao-hua yüan chi p'ang-cheng," in his *CYK*, I, 185–191.

T'ao Ch'ien
DEFINING THE LYRIC VOICE

fiction and autobiography, between imaginative self-realization and autobiographical reflection, begins to blur.

In very much the same way, T'ao Ch'ien narrates his dramatic meeting with an uncommon man in Poem 5 of "Imitations of the Ancient Style":

> In the east there lives a gentleman,
> His clothes are always in tatters.
> In a month he eats only nine meals,
> For ten years he has worn the same old hat.   4
> No one bears more hardships than he,
> But he always has a cheerful face.
> I desired to see this man,
> At dawn I set out, crossing rivers and passes.   8
> Green pines grew on both sides of the road,
> White clouds leaned on the edge of the eaves.
> He knew the purpose of my coming,
> And took his zither to play for me.   12
> At first he played the thrilling tune of the Departing Crane,
> Then he played the second tune, the Lonely Phoenix.[21]
> "I want to stay and live with you,
> From now until the cold season."   16
>   (*TYMC*, 112)
> 東方有一士
> 被服常不完
> 三旬九遇食
> 十年著一冠
> 辛苦無此比
> 常有好容顏
> 我欲觀其人
> 晨去越河關
> 青松夾路生
> 白雲宿簷端
> 知我故來意
> 取琴為我彈
> 上絃驚別鶴
> 下絃操孤鸞
> 願留就君住
> 從今至歲寒

[21] "The Departing Crane" was attributed to Ling Mu-tzu of the Shang, and "the Lonely Phoenix" was invented in the Han. These tunes were often sung to celebrate the moral integrity of a recluse, who withdraws from office and is alone in the world.

24

T'ao Ch'ien
DEFINING THE LYRIC VOICE

The gentleman in the poem reveals traits typical of T'ao Ch'ien himself, especially in his ability to maintain a cheerful disposition in the face of poverty (lines 1–6). That this fictional character may be an allegorical equivalent of the poet's self is of great importance.[22] T'ao Ch'ien seems to see no necessary conflict between fiction and autobiography. His is a technique that primarily seeks to create an objective perspective, to recreate a more public view of himself in poetry. When a poem centers on the narration of a human encounter, this effect of objectivity can be substantially enhanced. As in the poem above, the "I" serves as the explicit narrator who tells his motives of making the journey (lines 7–8), reports on the spontaneous friendship he has with the respectable gentleman (lines 11–14), and even records "verbatim" his request to stay with this understanding friend (lines 15–16). Clearly what T'ao Ch'ien does is to invent a dramatic rhetoric, set against the limitations of traditional lyric poetry. His new lyricism is characterized by both expressive impulse and narrative distance. We find that the narrator says scarcely a word without some kind of explicit clarification of his thoughts and impressions. And yet throughout the poem the gentleman remains silent. Confident that his music will be appreciated by "the one who knows the tone" (*chih-yin*), he relies for his self-expression solely on the playing of the tunes. Though this final message is only subtly conveyed in the poem, we learn from it the precise quality of this gentleman's (T'ao Ch'ien's) heart.

A similar image of the self can be found in T'ao Ch'ien's famous prose piece, "The Biography of Mr. Five Willow Trees." The poet takes the stance of a historian, writing in a highly stylized form reminiscent of Ssu-ma Ch'ien's (ca. 145 B.C. to ca. 86 B.C.) *Records of the Grand Historian* (*Shih-chi*):[23]

> We do not know what sort of man he was, nor are we sure of his name. There were five willow trees beside his house, and thus he was so called.
> (*TYMC*, 175)
> 先生不知何許人也，亦不詳其姓字。宅邊有五柳樹，因以爲號焉。

The reader is soon to discover that again T'ao Ch'ien's device of anonymity has a familiar symbolic function. The core personality, the real T'ao Ch'ien, is expressed in a veiled autobiography in the guise of biography (*chuan*). Following the example of the historian Ssu-ma Ch'ien, the poet judges objectively

---

[22] See Su Shih's remark on this poem in *T'ao Yüan-ming shih-wen hui-p'ing* (Peking: Chung-hua shu-chü, 1961), p. 233. See also Hightower, *The Poetry of T'ao Ch'ien*, p. 177.

[23] For a partial but extensive translation of *Shih-chi*, see Burton Watson, trans., *Records of the Grand Historian of China*, 2 vols. (New York: Columbia Univ. Press, 1961).

and seems to assume that his evaluation of Mr. Five Willow Trees will have permanent historical value:

> The judgment: "never feel distressed in poverty; never eager for material wealth," so Ch'ien-lou's wife has said. Perhaps these words can best describe the kind of people like him [Mr. Five Willow Trees]? He delights his heart by drinking and writing poems....
> (*TYMC*, 175)
> 贊曰：黔婁之妻有言，不戚戚於貧賤，不汲汲於富貴。其言茲若人之儔乎？酣觴賦詩，以樂其志...。

Aware of this being a veiled confession of the author, T'ao Ch'ien's contemporary readers simply regarded this fictional biography as the poet's own autobiography.[24]

T'ao Ch'ien's allegorical tendencies in biography are closely related to his metaphorical conception of nature. If a parallel can be drawn between Mr. Five Willow Trees and himself, the same may be drawn between nature and himself. What follows is a poem that demonstrates T'ao Ch'ien's typical projection of himself into nature:

> There is a green pine in the eastern garden,
> Its beauty obscured by the profusion of plants.
> But after frigid frost kills the other vegetation,
> Its lofty branches stand out majestically.   4
> In the midst of other trees it goes unnoticed,
> All by itself, it now seems extraordinary.
> I bring along my jug to hang on a cold branch,
> And gaze at it from time to time at a distance.   8
> Our life is in the midst of a dream,
> Why should we be burdened with earthly concerns?
>   (*CHSK*, I, 472)
> 青松在東園
> 衆草沒其姿
> 凝霜殄異類
> 卓然見高枝
> 連林人不覺
> 獨樹衆乃奇
> 提壺挂寒柯
> 遠望時復爲
> 吾生夢幻間
> 何事紲塵羈

---

[24] See Hsiao T'ung's "Biography of T'ao Yüan-ming," in *T'ao Yüan-ming chi chiao-chien*, ed. Yang Yung (Hong Kong: Wu-hsing chi shu-chü, 1971), p. 385.

T'ao Ch'ien
DEFINING THE LYRIC VOICE

The green pine, a recurrent symbol of enduring fortitude in T'ao Ch'ien's poetry, stands out most clearly like an individual person in this poem.[25] Looking admiringly at this tree, the poet imagines that he has found in it a true friend. He then roams contentedly in this ecstatic world of mutual understanding, hangs his beloved wine cup on its branch, and finally arrives at a conscious confirmation of his own life-philosophy. The green pine forces the reader to view it as the allegorical reflection of the poet's true self. The tree, through its silent existence, suggests a convivial and benevolent nature like T'ao Ch'ien's. It is endowed with an identity, in a manner that is characterized by the poet's own vision of himself.

At this point we may refer again to the important idea of *chih-yin* (the one who knows the tone) that has not yet been fully elaborated upon. By now it should be clear to readers that T'ao Ch'ien's persistent search for deeply understanding friends adds a special depth to his self-definition. Yet it is in the realm of history that T'ao Ch'ien explores the idea of *chih-yin* to the utmost.

A man who creates *chih-yin* in his fictional world will also look for enduring "friends" in history. T'ao Ch'ien is precisely such a poet. A brief survey of the titles of his poems will demonstrate this point: "Ode to the Two Shus" (*TYMC*, 128–129), "Ode to the Three Good Men" (*TYMC*, 130–131), "Ode to Ching K'o" (*TYMC*, 131), "Odes to the Impoverished Gentlemen, Seven Poems" (*TYMC*, 123–128). And several of his poems from the "Imitations of the Ancient Style" series are in fact celebrations of virtuous men in times past.

T'ao Ch'ien's historical odes are an effective means of providing an enlarged perspective for his lyrical voice. If the traditional Chinese critics seldom talked about T'ao Ch'ien's substantial contribution to this particular mode in poetry, it was only because they took it for granted. "Historical odes" (*yung-shih shih*) as a sub-genre of *shih* poetry were first made popular by Tso Ssu (ca. 250 to ca. 305), but T'ao Ch'ien carries this poetry's expressive function much further—indeed, far beyond the limits of Juan Chi's (210–263) *yung-huai* poetry (poems on feelings).[26] In T'ao Ch'ien the *yung-shih* poetry has acquired a new meaning and perspective—that of the dynamic overcoming of loneliness. The passive complaint so typical of Tso Ssu's *yung-shih* poetry is now gone (*CHSK*, 385–386). We feel that the individual, though intensely lonely in his heart, is now freer to realize his ideals. In my opinion, the rise of the individual

---

[25] For similar symbolic devices with regard to the image of the green pine, see "Poems on Drinking Wine" #4, *TYMC*, 89; "Imitations of the Ancient Style" #6, *TYMC*, 112.

[26] There are eighty-one poems in Juan Chi's *Yung-huai* series, and traditional commentators have attempted to make an allegorical interpretation of these poems. For Juan Chi's poetry, see Donald Holzman, *Poetry and Politics: The Life and Works of Juan Chi, A.D. 210–263* (Cambridge: Cambridge Univ. Press, 1976); J. D. Frodsham and Ch'eng Hsi, trans., *An Anthology of Chinese Verse: Han Wei Chin and the Northern and Southern Dynasties* (Oxford: Clarendon Press, 1967), pp. 53–67.

T'ao Ch'ien
DEFINING THE LYRIC VOICE

to this self-fulfilling vision in T'ao Ch'ien's poetry comes largely from his basic confidence in finding "the one who knows the tone" in history. But how does T'ao Ch'ien produce this new perspective in poetry? Does he always achieve this sublime state of mind in his poems?

In one of his "Miscellaneous Poems" T'ao Ch'ien expresses his melancholy mood:

> As the weather changes I realize the turn of the season,
> Sleepless, I feel the night is forever.
> I want to talk, but no one is there to respond,
> I raise my cup, offering a drink to my lonely shadow.
> Days and months cast me away,
> My innermost ambition cannot be fulfilled.
> Thinking of this, I feel grief and sorrow,
> Until dawn, I cannot still my heart.
> (*TYMC*, 115)
> 氣變悟時易
> 不眠知夕永
> 欲言無予和
> 揮杯勸孤影
> 日月擲人去
> 有志不獲騁
> 念此懷悲悽
> 終曉不能靜

The intensely pensive tone, coupled with the frustration of sleeplessness, immediately recalls Juan Chi's famous *Yung-huai* poem #1 (*CHSK*, I, 215). Yet, whereas Juan Chi leaves his inner thoughts and purpose partly unexpressed, T'ao Ch'ien brings all his reflections to the foreground. The reason for his low spirits is explicitly stated—that his innermost ambition (*chih*) has not yet been attained, and that he is running out of time. T'ao Ch'ien's lyrical directness is a form specifically adapted to his conception of the self, and his self-consciousness has given a new force to Chinese poetry. More importantly, he lets us know what his innermost ambition (*chih*) is:

> My fierce ambition (*meng-chih*) reaches the four seas,
> Soaring on my wings I wish to go afar.
> (*TYMC*, 117)
> 猛志逸四海
> 騫翮思遠翥

The "vigorous ambition" (*meng-chih*) of traveling afar is a metaphor of youthful aspirations for the heroic. We are told in poem #8 of his "Imitations of the Ancient Style" that his ambitious, though imaginary, "journey" extends as far

T'ao Ch'ien
DEFINING THE LYRIC VOICE

as the border:

> When I was young, I was strong and brave,
> With sword in hand I roamed alone.
> Who says my journey was short,
> From Chang-i to Yu-chou? ...²⁷
>   (*TYMC*, 113)
> 少年壯且厲
> 撫劍獨行遊
> 誰言行遊近
> 張掖至幽州....

Indeed, the trip is no ordinary venture; it is a quest for heroic deeds—either one of unyielding loyalism in the manner of Po-i and Shu-ch'i, or one of chivalrous defiance like that of the assassin Ching K'o:

> When hungry I ate the ferns on Mount Shou-yang,
> When thirsty I drank the water of the Yi River.²⁸
> 飢食首陽薇
> 渴飲易水流

But we are informed that this "journey" is halfway abandoned, because

> I saw no understanding friend,
> I saw only the mounds of ancient times.
> By the side of the road stood two lofty graves—
> One belonged to Po-ya, the other to Chuang Chou.
> Such men are hard to find these days,
> What better things could I expect of my quest?
> 不見相知人
> 惟見古時丘
> 路邊兩高墳
> 伯牙與莊周
> 此士難再得
> 吾行欲何求

---

²⁷ Chang-i was in Kan-su Province—i.e., on the northwestern frontier of China. Yu-chou was a town on the northeastern frontier, situated in modern Hopei. These two places were separated by several thousand *li*. There is no doubt that the itinerary as described in the poem is imaginary, for it was impossible for any subject of South China to travel so far into the northern territory during the period of division.

²⁸ Po-i and Shu-ch'i were two loyalists of the Shang Dynasty, who refused to serve the new dynasty Chou, and fled to Mt. Shou-yang. They ate the ferns on Mt. Shou-yang, and finally starved to death. The Yi refers to the river from which the heroic Ching-k'o left for his assassination trip to Ch'in.

T'ao Ch'ien
DEFINING THE LYRIC VOICE

The allusions to Po Ya and Chuang Tzu reveal the lonely self of the poet that lies hidden behind his contented outlook. His *chih* is frustrated because there is no understanding friend to appreciate his innate quality. He wishes that he had ideal friends like Po Ya and Chuang Tzu: Po Ya stopped playing music after the death of his *chih-yin* Chung Tzu-ch'i; Chuang Tzu felt that he had no one to talk to after his friend Hui Shih met his death.

To T'ao Ch'ien this ethos of friendship is the basis of everything noble in man, for it imparts courage, sincerity, and the ability to recognize the essential quality in another person. That it is the search for *chih-yin* which lies at the very core of T'ao Ch'ien's innermost ambition is unmistakable. His great admiration for men who practice this "code" of morals is most clearly expressed in his "Ode to Ching K'o." The courageous Ching K'o is asked by Prince Tan of Yen (Yen T'ai-tzu Tan) to undertake an assassination attempt on the life of the King of Ch'in (later Emperor of Ch'in, reigned 221 B.C. to 210 B.C.).[29] Ching K'o agrees to perform the dangerous mission, all for the sake of Prince Tan, a friend who recognizes and appreciates his innate worth. T'ao Ch'ien talks in the voice of the hero:

> A gentleman dies for his understanding friend (*chih-chi*),
> So with my sword in hand, I set out from the Capital of Yen.
> My white horse moans on the road;
> With fervent feelings, my friends see me off.
>   (*TYMC*, 131, lines 5–8)
> 君子死知己
> 提劍出燕京
> 素驥鳴廣陌
> 慷慨送我行

This willingness to die for the understanding friend is rooted in the concept of immortality, a critical concept in the traditional Chinese ethos. According to the ancient commentary *Tso-chuan*, one attains immortality through three means: moral perfection (*te*), meritorious service (*kung*), important words (*yen*). Ching K'o's ethos of friendship is a recasting of this traditional notion, as he believes that his willingness for martyrdom for the sake of Prince Tan is an act of immortality itself:

> He knows in his heart once he departs he will never return,
> But he will have a name in posterity [*hou-shih ming*].
> Getting on to his cart, he never again looks back,
> Chariot canopy flying, he makes way into the Ch'in court.

---

[29] For an English summary of Ssu-ma Ch'ien's biography of Ching K'o, See Hightower, *The Poetry of T'ao Ch'ien*, pp. 225–227. See also James J. Y. Liu, *The Chinese Knight-Errant* (London: Routledge and Kegan Paul, 1967), pp. 78–79, for a discussion of T'ao Ch'ien's poem.

T'ao Ch'ien
DEFINING THE LYRIC VOICE

心知去不歸
且有後世名
登車何時顧
飛蓋入秦庭

The hero's hope for "a name in posterity" (*hou-shih ming*) should not be scorned as a vain wish on his part. The view he wishes to express is simply this: the ethical force of his devotion and heroic action must be registered as a larger historical fact that goes beyond him as an individual.

The tone is definitely T'ao Ch'ien's. For who can deny that this is one of the most energetic poems that he has written in defense of his own ethics of *chih-yin*? Clearly triumph over time and death remains a permanent value in his thoughts. One cannot fail to see that the concluding couplet in the "Ode to Ching K'o" expresses this wish:[30]

> Although the man perished long ago,
> After a thousand years some of his feelings still remain.
> 其人雖已沒
> 千載有餘情

In very much the same way, he expresses the desire to emulate the great Han patriot and recluse T'ien Ch'ou, who leaves a name that is forever remembered:

> In his lifetime he was known to all,
> After his death his name was celebrated without cease.
> I will not copy those who madly pursue earthly matters,
> And live only for this short life-span.
>   (*TYMC*, 110)
> 生有高世名
> 既沒傳無窮
> 不學狂馳子
> 直在百年中

In fact, T'ao Ch'ien followed the exact footsteps of T'ien Ch'ou in dealing with a real event. In 404, in the middle of the civil war in Hsün-yang, the usurper Huan Hsüan suddenly abducted Emperor An and fled to Chiang-ling (in modern Hupei). This incident recalls an important episode in Han history: in 190 a rebel named Tung Cho held Emperor Hsien of the Eastern Han (Han Hsien-ti) as hostage and escaped to Ch'ang-an. T'ien Ch'ou, a well-trusted scholar-official serving the Governor of Yu-chou, immediately made a trip to Ch'ang-an to deliver a secret document from the Governor to the Emperor

---

[30] Note that Tso Ssu's "Historical Ode" (*Yung-shih*) on Ching K'o (*CHSK*, I, 386) does not emphasize the hero's enduring name in history.

T'ao Ch'ien
DEFINING THE LYRIC VOICE

under duress. Confronted with a similar national crisis, T'ao Ch'ien compared himself to T'ien Ch'ou, for he too would risk his life for the love of his Emperor. Thus in 404 T'ao Ch'ien worked as Inspector of Troops and traveled between Hsün-yang and the capital Chien-k'ang to transmit information to Liu Yü about Emperor An's situation. The poet wrote the following lines, it is believed, in celebration of his important mission:[31]

> At dawn I bade farewell to my family and got ready to go,
> My mind was set for my destination, Wu-chung.
> "May I ask you the purpose of your journey today?"
> It is not for business, nor for war.   4
> I have heard there was a T'ien Tzu-t'ai[T'ien Ch'ou],
> A man of moral fortitude, and a hero among men.
> He has been dead for a long time,
> But those in his hometown still follow his teaching....   8
>   (*TYMC*, 110)

辭家夙嚴駕
當往志無終
問君今何行
非商復非戎
聞有田子泰
節義爲士雄
斯人久已死
鄉里習其風....

Like T'ien Ch'ou, who retired into the mountains after the fall of the Eastern Han, T'ao Ch'ien chose to become a recluse when Liu Yü came to power. Indeed it is said that T'ao Ch'ien, formerly named Yüan-ming, did not adopt the name "Ch'ien" (meaning "in hiding") until sometime in 420, for that was the year that Liu Yü founded his new dynasty, Liu-Sung. T'ao Ch'ien's refusal to acknowledge the legitimacy of the Liu-Sung government may be further proved by the fact that he never once used the reign title of the new dynasty in any of his works. It is the ancient loyalists such as T'ien Ch'ou with whom T'ao Ch'ien wished to identify himself.

For T'ao Ch'ien, writing poetry is his means of achieving immortality, or rather of finding understanding readers in future generations. He writes in the preface to one of his poems:

> As this year is drawing to its close, my heart is bursting with cares. If I do not put my feeling in writing now, how will posterity know?
>   (*TYMC*, 106)

歲云夕矣，慨然永懷。今我不述，後生何聞哉？

---

[31] See Lu Ch'in-li's discussion of this poem in *TYMC*, 232–233.

T'ao Ch'ien
DEFINING THE LYRIC VOICE

This reads almost like a prophecy. Six centuries later T'ao Ch'ien was to find a most unusual *chih-yin* in the Sung poet Su Shih (1037–1101). For the first time in Chinese literary history we see such a powerful affinity and bond between two poets separated by well over 600 years.[32] For almost every poem by T'ao Ch'ien, Su Shih composes a verse to match it. In addition, Su Shih speaks of himself as a reincarnation of the former poet:

> Alert in my dream, wide-awake in drunkenness,
> It is only because Yüan-ming [T'ao Ch'ien]
> Was my previous incarnation.[33]
> 夢中了了醉中醒
> 只淵明
> 是前生

And he announces, with magnificent conviction, that if dead men could all come back to life, he would choose to be a follower of T'ao Ch'ien:

> I wish the dead could be revived,
> And I would follow Yüan-ming alone.[34]
> 我欲作九原
> 獨與淵明歸

This mythical identification on the part of Su Shih is probably more than what T'ao Ch'ien could expect. At the very least it proves that T'ao Ch'ien's idea of *chih-yin* has helped form a strong heritage of conscious poetic emulation or influence in Chinese poetry. If reading is the art of knowing one's ideal friends in the past, then writing poetry is surely the best means by which one could hope to touch the heart of future readers. Indeed it is this notion of immortality that helps T'ao Ch'ien overcome the harsh reality of life. He notices that those who have left behind them an everlasting name were often deprived one way or another during their lifetime:

> Though they have left behind eminent names,
> Throughout their lifetime, they suffered many privations.
>   (*TYMC*, 93)

---

[32] Of course, many other Sung poets referred to T'ao Ch'ien as their poetic model. See Jonathan Chaves, *Mei Yao-ch'en and the Development of Early Sung Poetry* (New York: Columbia Univ. Press, 1976), pp. 104–105.

[33] Translation taken from my *The Evolution of Chinese Tz'u Poetry* (Princeton: Princeton Univ. Press, 1980), p. 163.

[34] See "Harmonizing with T'ao Ch'ien's 'Odes to the Impoverished Gentlemen'," in *Su Shih shih-chi, chüan* 39 (Peking: Chung-hua shu-chü 1982), VII, 2,137. For a discussion of these two lines, see Sung Ch'iu-lung, *Su Tung-p'o ho T'ao Yüan-ming shih chih pi-chiao yen-chiu* (Taipei: Commercial Press, 1980), p. 94.

T'ao Ch'ien
DEFINING THE LYRIC VOICE

雖留身後名
一生亦枯槁

This historical fact provides our poet with exactly the kind of stoical courage that he needs in face of an impoverished life. Toward the end of his life, T'ao Ch'ien became increasingly poor, so poor that he frequently suffered from hunger and cold. He admits in his "Complaint in the Ch'u Mode, a Poem to Show to Secretary P'ang and Scribe Teng":

> During summer days I suffer from continued hunger,
> Through wintry nights I sleep without bedcovers.
> When evening comes, I long impatiently for the cockcrow,
> At dawn I wish the sun would hurry off to the west.[35]
>   (*TYMC*, 49–50)

夏日抱長飢
寒夜無被眠
造夕思雞鳴
及晨願烏遷

Another poem, entitled "Begging for Food," describes the misery of hunger most poignantly:

> Hunger came, it forced me to go out,
> I did not know where I was heading for.
> I wandered and wandered, till I reached this village,
> I knocked at a door, and muttered a few words,   4
> The man of the house understood my intent;
> He gave me what I desired—so my trip was not in vain.
> We talked happily from morning to night,
> And emptied our cups as we drank to each other.   8
> Delighted by the joy of this new friendship,
> We chanted verse and composed poetry.
> "I appreciate your generosity; you are as kind as
>   the washerwoman,
> But I feel shame at not having Han Hsin's talents.[36]   12

[35] The original line reads literally: "At dawn I wish the crow would pass quickly." The crow stands for the sun here for, according to ancient mythology, there is a three-footed crow residing in the sun.

[36] Han Hsin was a famous general who helped Liu Pang found the Han Dynasty. When he was young, he was extremely poor and underprivileged. Once a washerwoman sympathized with his misfortune and gave him food. Later, when Han Hsin was enfeoffed as Lord of Ch'u, he repaid the washerwoman with several thousand pieces of gold. For a biography of Han Hsin, see Burton Watson, trans., *Records of the Grand Historian of China*, by Ssu-ma Ch'ien (New York: Columbia Univ. Press, 1961), I, 208–232.

T'ao Ch'ien
DEFINING THE LYRIC VOICE

My gratitude to you—how can I express it?
I can only repay you from the underworld after my death."
    (*TYMC*, 48)

飢來驅我去
不知竟何之
行行至斯里
叩門拙言辭
主人解余意
遺贈豈虛來
談諧終日夕
觴至輒傾杯
情欣新知勸
言詠遂賦詩
感子漂母惠
愧我非韓才
銜戢知何謝
冥報以相貽

It was during T'ao Ch'ien's later years, when he began to live in much reduced circumstances, that the poet Yen Yen-chih, then the provincial Governor of Chiang-chou, came to know him. In his "Eulogy on T'ao Ch'ien" Yen Yen-chih expresses his admiration for T'ao Ch'ien's ability to maintain unbending integrity in the face of poverty:

> He lived an industrious and frugal life. He suffered from both poverty and illness. Other people would find it hard to bear such adversity, but he accepted it as a decree of fate.... Middle-aged, he was often afflicted with fever and malaria. But he looked upon death as going home, and took misfortune for fortune.... (*WH*, II, 1240)
> 居備勤儉，躬兼貧病，人否其憂，子然其命。...年在中身，疢維痁疾，視死如歸，臨凶若吉。...

T'ao Ch'ien explains in his poetry the source of his comfort:

> How can I find comfort for my soul?
> Only with the help of all those ancient worthies.
>   (*TYMC*, 123)
> 何以慰吾懷
> 賴古多此賢

Indeed many of T'ao Ch'ien's poems attempt to bring to light this self-realization—that his deliberate choice of farming and poverty, rather than a life of moral compromise, is not to be regretted. One has the impression that, despite all the real hardship, there is a genuine joy in T'ao Ch'ien that comes

T'ao Ch'ien
DEFINING THE LYRIC VOICE

from the realization of the self. What T'ao Ch'ien values most is the fulfillment of his individuality. And this he defends with confidence and wit in his "Poems on Drinking Wine" #9:

> I heard a knock at my door early in the morning,
> Tripping on my gown, I go to open the door,
> I asked who the caller was;
> A good-hearted farmer   4
> Came with a jug of wine to call upon me from afar.
> He suspected I was in disagreement with the times:
> "Dressed in rags, living under a thatched roof—
> This is not good enough for a lofty recluse.   8
> All the world likes to live a similar life,
> I wish you would go along with the muddy crowd."
> "I am deeply grateful to you for your advice, old man.
> But my intrinsic nature puts me at odds with the times.   12
> Of course, one can learn to twist the reins,
> But isn't it wrong to go against one's nature?
> Now let's have a happy drink together—
> My carriage can never turn back!"   16
> 　　(*TYMC*, 91–92)

清晨聞叩門
倒裳往自開
問子為誰歟
田父有好懷
壺漿遠見候
疑我與時乖
繿縷茅簷下
未足為高栖
一世皆尚同
願君汩其泥
深感父老言
稟氣寡所諧
紆轡誠可學
違己詎非迷
且共歡此飲
吾駕不可回

The dialogue between the persona of the poet and the farmer recalls a poem in the *Ch'u-tz'u* entitled "Fisherman," where a fisherman advises the unhappy yet upright poet Ch'ü Yüan (ca. 340 B.C. to 278 B.C.) to be more flexible in his attitude to the world in general:

> If all the world is muddy, why not help them to
> 	stir up the mud and beat up the waves?
> And if all men are drunk, why not sup their dregs
> 	and swill their lees?[37]
> 舉世皆濁
> 　何不淈其泥而揚其波
> 衆人皆醉
> 　何不餔其糟而歠其醨

T'ao Ch'ien's farmer seems to give him the same advice that the fisherman gave the ancient poet. But T'ao Ch'ien's poem reveals a radical shift not only in the perspective of its vision but also in its style. Now the persona of the poet no longer has Ch'ü Yüan's sneering contempt for the world at large. Gone are the anger, cynicism, and suicidal despair that prevail in the Ch'ü Yüan tradition. Instead we hear a crushingly rhetorical question addressed with equal pertinence to each human individual: "Isn't it wrong to go against one's nature?" (line 14). This simple question has the power of awakening the reader to a true sense of individuality. Most important of all, the poet does not claim that "all men are drunk and I alone am sober" as did Ch'ü Yüan. Instead he invites the farmer to get drunk with him (line 15), to accept the fact that his deliberate choice of life-style has a positive value in itself.

There is no doubt that the expression of this positive attitude to life in general is one of T'ao Ch'ien's greatest contributions to poetry. As the protagonist of his "autobiographical" poetry, T'ao Ch'ien tells us not only all his joys and sorrows but also the moral value of his feelings. For the first time since classical antiquity Chinese poetry has gained a large measure of confidence.[38]

III. Sublimation through Nature

The source of T'ao Ch'ien's confidence comes essentially from his trust in nature—the ageless nature that constantly recreates itself. According to his view of nature, everything moves in a cyclical order, and life and death are only the necessary phases of nature's creation. If life is spontaneous and inevitable, so is death. For nature is not static; it is time and movement. Perceiving nature as such, T'ao Ch'ien often tells of his feeling of repose in the face of

---

[37] Translation taken from David Hawkes, trans., *Ch'u Tz'u: The Songs of the South, An Ancient Chinese Anthology* (London: Oxford Univ. Press, 1959), p. 90.

[38] This is not to deny the importance of earlier literature, such as poetry of the Chien-an period (196–220), which is noted for its intense individuality. T'ao Ch'ien's positive attitude should be seen as a further development of that tradition.

T'ao Ch'ien
DEFINING THE LYRIC VOICE

life's transience. To demonstrate the power of this philosophy in T'ao Ch'ien's poetry, I shall cite a poem from his "Dirge" series which I have briefly mentioned earlier:

> How boundless are the barren grasslands,
> The white poplars moan in the wind.
> Bitter frost penetrates the ninth month,
> When they accompany me to the distant rural area.   4
> All around no one dwells,
> The lofty grave mounds alone loom high.
> Horses lift up their heads to neigh,
> The wind wails by itself.   8
> Once the dark tomb is closed,
> I shall never see the sunlight again for a thousand years.
> Not being able to see the sunlight again for a thousand years,
> Even sages and worthies can do nothing about it.   12
> Those who have come to escort me
> Will each return to his home.
> My relatives may still grieve over my death,
> The others have already begun singing.   16
> Dead and gone, what is there to say?
> Let me entrust my body to the hillside.
>   (*TYMC*, 142)

荒草何茫茫
白楊亦蕭蕭
嚴霜九月中
送我出遠郊
四面無人居
高墳正嶕嶢
馬爲仰天鳴
風爲自蕭條
幽室一已閉
千年不復朝
千年不復朝
賢達無奈何
向來相送人
各自還其家
親戚或餘悲
他人亦已歌
死去何所道
託體同山阿

T'ao Ch'ien
DEFINING THE LYRIC VOICE

What is particularly remarkable about this poem is the delicate balance the poet strikes between his feelings of solitude and unqualified trust in nature. Being human, he laments his own death—that he will be forever left alone in the graveyard, like the white poplars which stand all by themselves in the desolate wilderness. And yet, understanding the natural imperfection inherent in individual existence, the poet finally learns to entrust his own smallness and misery to nature's perpetual greatness and joy: "Dead and gone, what is there to say?/Let me entrust my body to the hillside."

We see in T'ao Ch'ien a heightened consciousness and a positive attitude toward death unknown to earlier poets.[39] This signifies a critical turning point in poetry, for the anguish of death had been a predominant theme in Chinese poetry after the Han dynasty, as may be seen in the "Nineteen Old Poems," where men are portrayed consistently as victims of the transient life.[40] Yet T'ao Ch'ien's originality lies in his expression of triumph over death—the feeling that life's insufficiency is itself a necessary phenomenon of the larger nature that continuously reaches beyond us. This faith in nature gives T'ao Ch'ien's work the impression of an unusually objective perspective rarely encountered in Chinese poetry. As in the poem above, the persona (the dead person) seems to have more of a sense of detachment than the living people who participate in the funeral procession. The possibility that the poem was written by T'ao Ch'ien shortly before his own death in 427, but surely in contemplation of impending death, makes its view of objectivity seem particularly noteworthy. It is an objectivity born of a reconciled confidence, not of cold reasoning.

T'ao Ch'ien's stoical acceptance of death in fact originates in the idea of "transformation" (*hua*) in Chuang Tzu's Taoism. To Chuang Tzu both life and death are the forces of natural transformation, and therefore man should welcome death as he would life, so as not to "disturb the process of change."[41] As a true believer in Chuang Tzu's philosophy, T'ao Ch'ien seems to be able to put life outside himself and achieve the sense of completion in the process of *hua*. The fine passage from his "Elegy for Myself" expresses this firm conviction:

> Content with the ways of Heaven and accepting my fate, I have lived out my mortal span.... Knowing the inevitability of my des-

---

[39] Of course, one might argue that the dirge as a genre was not invented by T'ao Ch'ien and that poets such as Lu Chi (261–303) had already written similar poems about impressions of the "dead" persona (*WH*, II, 399–400). But the tone of total reconciliation with nature in T'ao Ch'ien's poem is in sharp contrast to the despairing note characterizing the earlier models.

[40] See Sui Shu-sen, *Ku-shih shih-chiu shou chi-shih* (Hong Kong: Chung-hua shu-chü, 1958).

[41] Burton Watson, trans., *The Complete Works of Chuang Tzu* (New York: Columbia Univ. Press, 1968), p. 85.

tined end, how can I not cherish my life? But my present transformation [*hua*] is no cause for regret.... (*TYMC*, 197)

樂天委分，以至百年。...識運知命，疇能罔眷，余今斯化，可以無恨。...

His famous poem series on the three aspects of man, "Form, Shadow, and Spirit," also concludes with the same acceptance of nature's changing rhythm:

> Let yourself go, following the waves of the Great Transformation,
> Neither happy nor frightened.
>   (*TYMC*, 37)

縱浪大化中
不喜亦不懼

This spiritual liberation from fears leads him to view death as a final return to the "original home" (*pen-chai*, or *chiu-chai*),[42] a permanent dwelling place.

T'ao Ch'ien's return to nature, to the Great Transformation of things, may be regarded as the culmination of an increasingly widespread belief in what Ying-shih Yü calls the "Neo-Taoist Naturalism" characterizing Wei-Chin thought.[43] But T'ao Ch'ien's greatest achievement lies in his creation of a lyrical world in poetry by drawing inspiration from the Neo-Taoist attitude toward nature which he practices faithfully in life. The nature portrayed in his poetry is often synonymous with the simple Tao:

> The clouds make their movement without consciousness from mountain peaks,
> The birds, growing tired of flying, know it is time to return.
>   (*TYMC*, 161)

雲無心以出岫
鳥倦飛而知還

> Joyfully the trees are flourishing,
> Trickling, the streams begin to flow.
>   (*TYMC*, 161)

木欣欣以向榮
泉涓涓而始流

Just like clouds, birds, trees, and streams which delight in the spontaneous movement of nature, man should freely participate in the infinite vitality of cyclical changes, in other words, the Tao of things. It is this return to nature

---

[42] See "Elegy for My Self" (*TYMC*, 197), and "Miscellaneous Poems" #7 (*TYMC*, 119).

[43] Ying-shih Yü, "Individualism and the Neo-Taoist Movement in Wei-Chin China." See also Ch'en Yin-k'o, "T'ao Yüan-ming chih ssu-hsiang yü ch'ing-t'an chih kuan-hsi," in his *CYK*, II, 399.

which sets T'ao Ch'ien apart from the fantasy world in the "poetry of Wandering Immortals" (*yu-hsien* poetry) prevalent since the third century. Most important, T'ao Ch'ien frequently reminds his readers that he wishes to be dissociated from the then current vogue of the elixir of immortality and alchemy:

> I do not have the magic of immortality,
> It must be so; there should be no more doubt.
> (*TYMC*, 36)
> 我無騰化術
> 必爾不復疑

> If there ever existed in this world the immortals Sung and Ch'iao,
> Where do they have their place today?
> (*TYMC*, 55)
> 世間有松喬
> 於今定何間

> If my understanding of life is already superior,
> Why do I need to climb [the immortals' mountains] Hua and Sung?
> (*TYMC*, 53)
> 即事如已高
> 何必升華嵩

We must not forget that for a long time T'ao Ch'ien had been viewed primarily as a recluse who went into retreat. The famous Prince of Chao-ming, Hsiao T'ung (501–531), calls him "one of the three recluses from Hsün-yang."[44] The critic Chung Jung (fl. 502–519) honors him with the title: "the model recluse-poet at all times" (*SPC*, 41). And the T'ang poet Tu Fu (712–770) criticizes him for being "one who evades the common crowd."[45] These traditional views, either as expressions of admiration or criticism, have the effect of producing a distorted image of T'ao Ch'ien that does not do full justice to the true quality of the poet. Of course, T'ao Ch'ien did share with the traditional recluses a refusal to take office. But he was never cut off from the normal way of life, as some "Taoists" or Buddhist recluses might have been.[46] In T'ao Ch'ien's poetic world of *tzu-jan* (nature), which James R. Hightower perceptively translates as "freedom," there are farmers, children,

---

[44] See Hsiao T'ung's "Biography of T'ao Yüan-ming," in *T'ao Yüan-ming chi chiao-chien*, p. 385.
[45] See Tu Fu, *Tu shih hsiang-chu*, chüan 7 (Peking: Chung-hua shu-chü, 1979), II, 563.
[46] F. W. Mote's term "Confucian eremitism" may be most suitable for describing T'ao Ch'ien's way of life—i.e., withdrawal from public service, but not from "the everyday world of man." See Mote's article, "Confucian Eremitism in the Yüan Period," in *The Confucian Persuasion*, ed. Arthur F. Wright (Stanford: Stanford Univ. Press, 1960), pp. 202–240.

T'ao Ch'ien
DEFINING THE LYRIC VOICE

drinking friends, and poets.[47] One has the impression that whenever the poet is on his way to an outing, he would call to the children or neighbors to join the occasion.[48]

In contrast, T'ao Ch'ien's Buddhist friend Liu I-min, also known as "one of the three recluses from Hsün-yang," was a hermit in the true sense of the word. Liu, formerly named Ch'eng-chih, had been the Prefect of Ch'ai-sang in Hsün-yang until the winter of 403, at which time Huan Hsüan usurped the throne and stirred up a large-scale civil war. Liu resigned from his post and changed his name to "I-min" (meaning "surviving adherent of the former dynasty"). He then abandoned his wife and children to join Hui Yüan's White Lotus Society in Mount Lu, situated not far from T'ao Ch'ien's village.[49] It is said that sometime in 409 Liu I-min invited T'ao Ch'ien to join him in his mountain retreat, but T'ao Ch'ien declined with the following reply:

> "Mountains and lakes" have long invited me to join them,
> For what reason did I hesitate to make a move?
> It is only because of my relatives and old friends
> That I have not the heart to think of living apart....
>   (*TYMC*, 57)
> 山澤久見招
> 胡事乃躊躇
> 直爲親舊故
> 未忍言索居....

Clearly there is no need for T'ao Ch'ien to escape to the remote "mountains and lakes." His thatched hut is situated in a noisy human world, and yet with a detached heart he is able to maintain an inner serenity (*TYMC*, 89). The sense of "being-with-oneself" makes the poet confident enough to move beyond his own subjectivity.

But the important thing is that T'ao Ch'ien does not go outside himself to appreciate the beauty of nature, for he is no longer an external spectator. As part of nature, the poet's self views every aspect of the world from a mingled perspective. Reading T'ao Ch'ien's poetry one is often astonished by the extraordinary way in which the poet mingles his feelings and the external world. For his poetry is no longer confined to subjective expression, but is rather extended to embrace the movement of nature. This explains why critics after the T'ang often used the term "the fusion of feeling and scene" (*ch'ing-ching chiao-jung*) to describe the special quality of T'ao Ch'ien's poetry.

It cannot be denied that T'ao Ch'ien has given a new meaning to the lyrical

---

[47] For Hightower's translation of *tzu-jan*, see his *The Poetry of T'ao Ch'ien*, p. 50.

[48] See, for example, "On Moving House" and "To Liu, Prefect of Ch'ai-sang," in Hightower, trans., *The Poetry of T'ao Ch'ien*, pp. 74, 78.

[49] For a biography of Liu I-min, see citations in *TYMC*, 272.

T'ao Ch'ien
DEFINING THE LYRIC VOICE

voice, and he is the first to awaken in poetry the full potentiality of the Chinese attitude toward nature. The increasing emphasis on man's response to nature, the so-called *kan-wu*, was already a significant literary phenomenon that started long before T'ao Ch'ien's time. A case in point is the *"Wen-fu"* (*"Fu* on Literature") by Lu Chi (261–303), which introduces a new responsive attitude towards the movement of nature:

> Moving along with the four seasons, he sighs at the passing of time;
> Gazing at the myriad objects, he thinks of the complexity of the world.
> He sorrows over the falling leaves in sinewy autumn;
> He takes joy in the delicate bud of fragrant spring.[50]
> 遵四時以歎逝
> 瞻萬物而思紛
> 悲落葉於勁秋
> 喜柔條於芳春

Yet nature in T'ao Ch'ien does not merely stir man's heart as Lu Chi so perceives; it actually cools and sublimates feelings. And T'ao Ch'ien's "*Fu* on Calming the Passions" (*"Hsien-ch'ing fu"*) centers on this important theme. We find from the outset of this *fu* the voice of a man in love; his object of passion is a graceful beauty who passes the day playing the zither and lamenting the transience of human life.[51] So moved by her beauty and music the "I" in the poem confesses:

> I am moved as she quickens the clear notes' tempo
> And wish to speak with her, knee to knee.[52]
> 激清音以感余
> 願接膝以交言

Afraid to transgress against propriety, he is swallowed up in his emotional turmoil and cannot free himself from it. His heart is like a room that does not have enough space. He goes out to nature:

> Overcome with sadness, and no one to confide in,
> I idly walk to the southern wood.
> I rest where the dew still hangs on the magnolia
> And take shelter under the lingering shadows of the green pines.[53]

---

[50] Achilles Fang, trans., "Rhyme Prose on Literature," in *Studies in Chinese Literature*, ed. John L. Bishop (Cambridge: Harvard Univ. Press), p. 12. I have changed "virile autumn" to "sinewy autumn" (line 4) here in order better to convey the literal meaning of *chin-ch'iu*.

[51] The image of a beautiful woman playing music and lamenting the transience of life can also be found in "Imitations of the Ancient Style" #7 (*TYMC*, 113).

[52] Translation taken from Hightower, trans., *The Poetry of T'ao Ch'ien*, p. 264.

[53] Hightower, trans., *The Poetry of T'ao Ch'ien*, p. 266.

T'ao Ch'ien
DEFINING THE LYRIC VOICE

擁勞情而罔訴
步容與於南林
栖木蘭之遺露
翳青松之餘陰

At this juncture his helpless preoccupation with passion leads him to believe that nature will come to his aid, will help him attain his beloved. But he soon becomes conscious of the fact that he is seeking an illusion, and this disappointment brings more disunity within himself:

> To the end all is desolate, no one appears;
> Left alone with restless thoughts, vainly seeking....
> Hoping to follow her in my nighttime dream,
> My soul is agitated and finds no rest:
> Like a boatman who has lost his oar,
> Like a cliff-scaler who finds no handhold.[54]

竟寂寞而無見
獨悁想以空尋....
思宵夢以從之
神飄颻而不安
若憑舟之失棹
譬緣崖而無攀

His hope is once again aroused by the sad note of the flute coming from afar. Thinking that it is the lady who is playing the flute, he entrusts the passing cloud to communicate his love to her. But the cloud pays no attention to his wish. So suddenly comes the moment of the great unfolding when he looks outward to nature again:

> But the passing cloud departs without a word,
> It is swift in its passing by.[55]

行雲逝而無語
時奄冉而就過

The passing cloud that he formerly regarded as a messenger of love has now become the message of nature itself: like everything else in nature the cloud passes freely without saying a word. Should he not learn from the silent cloud to transform disquieting passion into exalted pleasure? Should he not try to be wholly contained in the open space of nature? In this very moment, the persona for the first time is able to hold his head above water:

[54] Hightower, trans., *The Poetry of T'ao Ch'ien*, pp. 266–267.
[55] Hightower, trans., *The Poetry of T'ao Ch'ien*, p. 267.

T'ao Ch'ien
DEFINING THE LYRIC VOICE

> I welcome the fresh wind that blows my ties away
> And consign my weakness of will to the receding waves....
> I level all cares and cling to integrity,
> Lodge my aspirations at the world's end.[56]
> 迎清風以祛累
> 寄弱志於歸波....
> 坦萬慮以存誠
> 憩遙情於八遐

The final transformation experienced by the speaker of the poem is one of great importance. It is a realization coming from a period of inner struggle. Because it is won with difficulty, it also tends to be enduring and true. What the persona achieves is a conscious self-realization, a sublimated feeling of getting hold of himself. He is no longer a victim of his passion, for his "exhausting passion" (*lao-ch'ing*) has now turned into "distant feeling" (*yao-ch'ing*).[57] Besides, it is through nature that his instinct is finally transformed into the state of harmony between feeling (*ch'ing*) and propriety (*li*).[58] The *fu* concludes with a rather vigorous and explicit statement:

> I disapprove the lovers' meeting in the "*Man-ts'ao*" poem,
> But celebrate the old song from "Shao-nan." ...[59]
>   (*TYMC*, 156)
> 尤蔓草之爲會
> 誦邵南之餘歌....

T'ao Ch'ien's "*Fu* on Calming the Passions" is dramatically opposed to such earlier *fu* as Sung Yü's (3rd century B.C.) "*Kao-t'ang fu*" and Ts'ao Chih's "*Lo-shen fu*" in one significant aspect: whereas nature provides convenient settings for erotic love in these earlier *fu*,[60] it serves a completely different function in T'ao Ch'ien's *fu*. Certainly T'ao Ch'ien's piece, as is expressed clearly in his "Preface," is written in perfect awareness of the convention in *fu*

---

[56] Hightower, trans., *The Poetry of T'ao Ch'ien*, p. 267.

[57] See *TYMC*, 155, 156.

[58] For a discussion of the conflict between *ch'ing* and *li* typical of the Wei-Chin intellectuals, see Yü Ying-shih, *Chung-kuo chih-shih chieh-ts'eng shih-lun, ku-tai p'ien* (Taipei: Linking Publishing Co., 1980), pp. 350–372.

[59] "*Man-ts'ao*" refers to Song #94 of the *Shih-ching*. "Shao-nan" (literally "Shao and the South") is Section II of the *Shih-ching*, and the reference may be to Song #14, where conjugal affection, rather than illicit love, is celebrated.

[60] See Andrew H. Plaks, "The Chinese Literary Garden," in his *Archetype and Allegory in the Dream of Red Chamber* (Princeton: Princeton Univ. Press, 1976), p. 151. It should be noted that the attribution of "*Kao-t'ang fu*" to Sung Yu is still doubtful.

T'ao Ch'ien
DEFINING THE LYRIC VOICE

to write about quieting the passions.[61] But his remarkable description of nature's power to transcend excessive feeling is an original contribution to the *fu* tradition.[62] The belief that nature, in the sense of *tzu-jan*, is the key to self-realization is uniquely at the heart of T'ao Ch'ien's poetics, one which I would call "lyrical sublimation."

Yet by and large T'ao's contemporaries were unprepared for his new lyrical voice, and could not see the implications of his individuality. We will have to await three hundred years to see a sympathetic revisionist movement with regard to T'ao Ch'ien's poetic ideal.[63] Yet, before the appearance of that large-scale revival, T'ao Ch'ien continues to serve as an important source of inspiration for the strong minds who sincerely try to grapple with their individual voices. His poetry represents to a great extent the hidden power of that lyrical impulse.

[61] For T'ao Ch'ien's possible precursors in this case, see a thorough study by James R. Hightower: "The *Fu* of T'ao Ch'ien," *Studies in Chinese Literature*, ed. John L. Bishop (Cambridge: Harvard Univ. Press, 1966), pp. 45–72.

[62] Hsiao T'ung was obviously missing the point when he said that, compared to the other writings by T'ao Ch'ien, this *fu* is like "a minor flaw in a piece of white jade." The true value of this work would not be recognized until the Sung Dynasty, when Su Shih praised this *fu* for its theme of "sensuality without lust." See *T'ao Yüan-ming shih-wen hui-p'ing*, p. 322.

[63] Stephen Owen, *The Great Age of Chinese Poetry: The High T'ang* (New Haven: Yale Univ. Press, 1981), p. 6.

II

Hsieh Ling-yün

The Making of a New Descriptive Mode

I. Verisimilitude and Landscape Exploration

We have observed briefly in the preceding chapter that T'ao Ch'ien's lyrical directness is dynamically opposed to the general taste of the Eastern Chin and that of the new aesthetic movement emerging in the Liu-Sung period. Yet the reasons underlying the development of this new poetic tendency in early fifth-century China have not yet been explored. The critic Liu Hsieh gives us the best explanation of the nature of this new literary movement:

> In recent years, literature has been prized for verisimilitude [*hsing-ssu*]. Poets perceive [*k'uei-ch'ing*] the true form of landscape, and pierce through [*tsuan-mao*] the appearance of grass and plants.... Thus, this technique of skilled expression and precise description may be compared to the use of ink for imprinting seals, for the copy so made reproduces the seal in its finest detail without the need for further cutting and shaping. (*WHTL*, II, 694)
> 自近代以來，文貴形似，窺情風景之上，鑽貌草木之中。...故巧言切狀，如印之印泥，不加雕削，而曲寫毫芥。

The above passage identifies a particular way of viewing nature that is crucial to this new poetics. The prevailing trend dictates that good poetry must be lavish in descriptive details, details that capture the various perspectives of scenery. If description was regarded as mere background for the lyrical expression in the traditional *shih*, it has now become the primary element that defines the subject of poetry. No longer decorative or accessory, the descriptive mode has for the first time acquired a legitimate status in *shih* poetry.

Hsieh Ling-yün
A NEW DESCRIPTIVE MODE

Even critics a hundred years later voiced their overwhelming consensus on these values in poetics. Liu Hsieh, as in the passage cited above, calls this new orientation one of *"hsing-ssu,"* meaning "verisimilitude."[1] Chung Jung in his *Shih-p'in* also uses this term, or sometimes *ch'iao-ssu* ("artistic similitude"), to describe individual styles that are particularly successful in sensory descriptions.[2] Hsieh Ling-yün (385–433) was the most famous poet in this new mode of description. And Yen Yen-chih, the author of "Eulogy on T'ao Ch'ien," was also praised by Chung Jung for his stylistic quality of verisimilitude.

The spirit of this new descriptive mode lies in the sheer joy of observing the landscape. As Liu Hsieh points out, these poets "perceive the true form of landscape" and "pierce through the appearance of grass and plants." Thus, the increasingly elaborate descriptions of nature in poetry are only the reflection of a new way of "seeing" landscape that is typical of the age. Liu Hsieh places this literary phenomenon in its historical context:

> In the early part of the Liu Sung, there were changes and developments in the literary style: the philosophy of Chuang Tzu and Lao Tzu receded into the background, while literature of mountains and waters began to thrive.... Feelings in poetry must always accord with the forms of the things described; in the choice of words every effort should be made to be original and fresh. These are the things that modern writers strive to achieve. (*WHTL*, I, 67)
> 宋初文詠，體有因革，莊老告退，而山水方滋。…情必極貌以寫物，辭必窮力而追新，此近世之所競也。

The Chinese remember the fifth century as a period of "mountains and waters" poetry (*shan-shui shih*), and they feel a particular nostalgia when looking back to it. For that era marks the culmination of a particular kind of cultivated taste characteristic of the aristocratic families. When the northern aristocrats first fled south along with the Eastern Chin government in the early fourth century, they were struck by the unusually mild climate and the beautiful landscape in the south. Although they were grieving over the loss of northern territory to the "barbarians," they began to spend much of their

---

[1] Although the literary term "verisimilitude" carries many different connotations in the context of English criticism, it is used here in its particular sense of "presenting details" so as to give "the semblance" of reality. (See C. Hugh Holman, *A Handbook to Literature*, 4th ed. [Indianapolis: Bobbs-Merrill, 1980], p. 459.) This idea of description may be similar to the concept of "verism" in art history.

[2] See Chung Jung's comments on Chang Hsieh, Hsieh Ling-yün, Yen Yen-chih, and Pao Chao in *SPC*, 27, 29, 43, 47. For a more detailed discussion of the subject, see my "Description of Landscape in Early Six Dynasties Poetry," in *ESP*. See also Liao Wei-ch'ing. "Ts'ung wen-hsüeh hsien-hsiang yü wen-hsüeh ssu-hsiang te kuan-hsi t'an Liu-ch'ao ch'iao-kou hsing-ssu chih yen te shih," in *Chung-kuo ku-tien wen hsüeh lun-ts'ung* (Taipei: Ch'un-wen-hsüeh yüeh-k'an-she, 1976), pp. 126–128.

Hsieh Ling-yün
A NEW DESCRIPTIVE MODE

leisure time in pleasure tours around the scenic country. For traveling had gradually become the supreme rite for the upper class, as is witnessed by Wang Hsi-chih's "Orchid Pavilion" outing. However, still burdened with patriotic sentiment and a keen nostalgia for the north, these people could not quite fully enjoy the gaiety of travel. Liu I-ch'ing (403–444), the author of *Shih-shuo hsin-yü* (*A New Account of Tales of the World*), records an event that is particularly telling in this aspect:

> On their free days those gentlemen who had crossed the Yangtze River would always invite each other to go for an outing to Hsin-t'ing [near Chien-k'ang], where they drank and feasted on the grass. Once Chou I, seated among the company, sighed and said: "The scenery is just as good as in the North, but these are the wrong mountains and rivers." They all looked at each other and shed tears....[3]
> 過江諸人，每至暇日，輒相要出新亭，藉卉飲宴。周侯中坐而嘆曰："風景不殊，舉目有山河之異。"皆相視流淚。...

The champion poet of "mountains and waters" poetry, Hsieh Ling-yün, was born at a time when such nostalgic feelings for the northern lands were long gone. At last the aristocrats seemed to feel well settled in the scenic south. As a member of one of the most powerful aristocratic families, Hsieh Ling-yün had the good fortune to be born rich, and to live at the center of cultural and literary movements. Besides being a famed poet, he was a talented calligrapher and painter.[4] For him leisure tours, like all daily luxuries, were a way of life. Endowed with an unusual love of landscape and travel, Hsieh was also the originator of "travel literature" in China, the so-called *yu-chi*. His *Travels to Famous Mountains* (*Yu ming-shan chih*), with detailed geographical information about scenic mountain sights, was extremely popular among his contemporaries, although only portions of it are extant today (*HLYS*, 219–220). But, most important, he was the first and most distinguished *shan-shui* poet in China. Hsieh's distinctive achievement in poetry became that of the entire age, for his contemporary readers seemed to see literature through his eyes:

> Whenever a poem by him [Hsieh Ling-yün] got to the city, the high and the low alike all vied with one another in copying it.

---

[3] Liu I-ch'ing, *Shih-shuo hsin-yü* [*chiao-chien*], ed. Yang Yung (Hong Kong: Ta-chung shu-chü, 1969), Section 2, Item 31, p. 71. For an English translation of the book, see Richard Mather, trans., *Shih-shuo hsin-yü, A New Account of the World* (Minneapolis: Univ. of Minnesota Press, 1976).

[4] Note that Hsieh's mother, Madame Liu, was a grand-niece of Wang Hsi-chih. Hsieh had obviously learned calligraphy from the Wang family, for whom calligraphy was almost like a hereditary trademark. For his accomplishments as a calligrapher and painter, see Yeh Hsiao-hsüeh, "Hsieh Ling-yün chuan," in *HLYS*, 185–186.

5. A picture of Hsieh Ling-yün.

Hsieh Ling-yün
A NEW DESCRIPTIVE MODE

Overnight the poem would be circulated everywhere, among both officials and commoners. People from afar and nearby all looked up to him, and his name created a sensation in the capital. (*Sung shu*, chüan 67, VI, 1754)
每有一詩至都邑，貴賤莫不競寫，宿昔之間，士庶皆徧，遠近欽慕，名動京師。

True enough, the critic Chung Jung rates Hsieh Ling-yün among the few first-ranking poets since classical antiquity, and lauds him especially for his "artistic similitude" (*ch'iao-ssu*) in poetry. What Hsieh has done is to turn life into art, to make travel experiences the very substance of poetic structure. If Wang Hsi-chih's aristocratic gathering in Orchid Pavilion represents a casual pursuit of joy in life, then Hsieh Ling-yün's *shan-shui* poetry is the very expression of artistic creation. The older generation enjoys nature as one who regards an outing as good; the younger generation believes that beauty in nature is the ultimate good. The former contents itself with the mere viewing of landscape; the latter challenges itself to the artistic representation of landscape in poetry, in what is called *hsing-ssu* (verisimilitude). In other words, Hsieh's approach is aesthetic, and his poetry a product of artistic consciousness.

Here I would like to quote a typical poem by Hsieh that gives an excellent illustration of his descriptive skills:

ON MY WAY FROM SOUTH MOUNTAIN TO NORTH MOUNTAIN, I GLANCE AT THE SCENERY FROM THE LAKE

At dawn I set out from the sunlit cliffs,
At sunset I take my rest by the shaded peaks.
Leaving my boat, I turn my eyes upon the distant sandbars,
Resting my staff, I lean against the lush pine.   4
The small mountain paths are far and deep,
The ring-like islets are beautiful and pleasing.
I view the twigs of tall trees above,
I listen to the torrents in the deep valley below.   8
The rocks lie flat, and the river divides its flow.
The forest is dense, tracks are buried and lost.
What is the effect of Nature's "deliverance" and "becoming"?
All things growing are lush and thriving.   12
Young bamboos are wrapped in green sheaths,
Fresh rushes embrace their purple flowers.
Seagulls play by the springtime banks,
Wild pheasants sport in the gentle breeze.   16

Hsieh Ling-yün
A NEW DESCRIPTIVE MODE

A heart that embraces natural transformations is never bored,
Yet the more I contemplate nature, the more my concerns deepen.
I do not lament that the departed is remote,
I only regret that I have no friend as companion.   20
Traveling alone is not what makes me sigh,
But to whom can I convey the reasons of my appreciation and dissatisfaction?
(*HLYS*, 90)

於南山往北山，經湖中瞻眺

朝旦發陽崖
景落憩陰峯
舍舟眺迥渚
停策倚茂松
側逕既窈窕
環洲亦玲瓏
俛視喬木杪
仰聆大壑灇
石橫水分流
林密蹊絕蹤
解作竟何感
升長皆豐容
初篁苞綠籜
新蒲含紫茸
海鷗戲春岸
天鷄弄和風
撫化心無厭
覽物眷彌重
不惜去人遠
但恨莫與同
孤遊非情歎
賞廢理誰通

The title of the poem is significant; what is being conveyed here is a new way of description intended to outline the itinerary of an actual excursion. North Mountain and South Mountain are real place-names, both belonging to Hsieh's extensive estate at Shih-ning. The title informs us that the poet is both a traveler and a viewer of scenery.

Reading the poem from the beginning to the end, we can see that the poet has a particular system of scanning the landscape. His descriptive procedure

Hsieh Ling-yün
A NEW DESCRIPTIVE MODE

follows a distinct method of alternation, one which moves between mountain scenes and water scenes:

line 3: water scene
line 4: mountain scene
line 5: mountain scene
line 6: water scene
line 7: mountain scene
line 8: water scene
line 9: water scene
line 10: mountain scene

Even the plants and birds are distributed according to the mountain/water spectrum:

line 13: mountain plant (bamboos)
line 14: water plant (rushes)
line 15: water bird (seagulls)
line 16: mountain bird (pheasants)

As a whole, the poem progresses from larger scenes in nature (lines 3–10) to smaller objects (lines 13–16). The impression is that of a perceptive traveler constantly exploring complex scenes around him and yet simultaneously ordering them into meaningful units. There are comprehensive views and close-up views, depending upon the visual perspective of the viewer at a particular moment. What we call "verisimilitude" in *shan-shui* poetry refers to this description of multiple views. The T'ang poet Po Chü-i (772–846) sums up most eloquently Hsieh's descriptive comprehensiveness:

His large images always encompass the sky and the sea;
His small images never leave out the grass and the trees.[5]
大必籠天海
細不遺草樹

Hsieh's particular descriptive method reflects the variety of his own travel and visual experiences. It is the continuous unfolding of scenes that gives rise to the detailed description in his *shan-shui* poetry. In passing, we must mention that the Hsieh family had already produced many noted travelers in the past, chief among them Hsieh Ling-yün's great grand-uncle Hsieh An (320–385). During his late years Hsieh An had retired to his family estate "The Eastern

---

[5] See Po Chü-i's poem on Hsieh Ling-yün, in *Po Chü-i chi*, ed. Ku Hsüeh-chieh (Peking: Chung-hua shu-chü, 1979), I, 131.

Hsieh Ling-yün
A NEW DESCRIPTIVE MODE

Mountain" in Shih-ning, where he enjoyed his pleasure tours in the mountains, in the constant company of singing girls.[6] He was a good friend of Wang Hsi-chih, and a distinguished guest at the "Orchid Pavilion" occasion in 353. However, like all the other travelers in his generation, Hsieh An produced very little poetry, if at all, on his actual touring experiences. His two contributions to the "Orchid Pavilion" series (*CHSK*, I, 439) are among the very few pieces in Eastern Chin poetry that can be called descriptive. For that period's literature was predominantly *hsüan-yen* and philosophical.

Thus, like T'ao Ch'ien, Hsieh Ling-yün also reacted against the discursive reasoning of the *hsüan-yen* poetry, though not totally free from its influence. What T'ao Ch'ien brought to the poetic tradition was a new dynamic sense of expression, but it was Hsieh Ling-yün who first stimulated a profound awareness of description in *shih* poetry. Hsieh happened to live in an age that supported his artistic tendencies, and as a result Chinese poetry became visually more descriptive and stylistically more sensory. Yet for all his literary originality he too lived in the domain of tradition, like all creative poets. Before we can fairly attest to his true accomplishments, we must ask: What literary precursors did Hsieh Ling-yün have? In what way did he surpass his masters?

Among the earlier poets, Chang Hsieh (?–307) of the Western Chin comes nearest to Hsieh in terms of poetic style. Chung Jung considers Chang Hsieh a first-ranking poet who excels in the art of "verisimilitude" (*hsing-ssu*), and believes that there is a profound affinity between Hsieh Ling-yün and Chang in terms of poetic style:

> [Hsieh Ling-yün's style] somewhat resembles Chang Hsieh's, and so he also favors the device of artful structure and verisimilitude....
> 〔謝靈運〕…雜有景陽〔張協〕之體，故尚巧似。…

We need only read one of Chang's "Miscellaneous Poems" (*tsa-shih*) to see the validity of Chung Jung's judgment:

> Rosy morning clouds greet the white sun,
> Cinnabar vapor penetrates the Sunny Valley.
> Hazily, hazily, the multitude of clouds gather,
> Densely, densely, a scattering rain pours down.   4
> A gentle wind blows on the sinewy grasses,
> The frigid frost bristles on the lofty trees.
> Dense leaves wither away by day and night,
> Crowded trees become like a bundle of twigs.   8

---

[6] For a biography of Hsieh An, see Fang Hsüan-ling, et al., *Chin shu*, chüan 79, VII, 2,072–2,091.

6. A painting of Hsieh An traveling with singing girls in the Eastern Mountain, by Kuo Hsü (1456–1528).

Hsieh Ling-yün
A NEW DESCRIPTIVE MODE

> In the past I would sigh because time passed too slowly,
> Now in old age I lament that the years are hurrying by.
> At year's end, my heart is filled with a hundred worries,
> I shall follow Chi-chu to become a fortuneteller.[7]   12
> (CHSK, I, 393–394)

朝霞迎白日
丹氣臨暘谷
翳翳結繁雲
森森散雨足
輕風摧勁草
凝霜竦高木
密葉日夜疎
叢林森如束
疇昔歎時遲
晚節悲年促
歲暮懷百憂
將從季主卜

The stylistic resemblance of this poem to Hsieh Ling-yün's *shan-shui* poetry is very striking. In both, descriptive detail dominates the movement of poetry. The persona here, like Hsieh's perceptive viewer, surveys a sequence of scenes in a meticulous fashion—from the bright sun to the clouds, from the mists to the rains, from the full-grown grass to the tall trees (lines 1—8). This realistic attitude toward nature suggests a fundamental difference from the "poetry of wandering immortals" (*yu-hsien* poetry). And it is in this sense that Chang Hsieh's poetry represents a new movement of "realism" and a gradual departure from the magical world of immortals. His subject is not the awesome fantasy of an imaginary world but the actual scenery in his daily surroundings. Living in the mountains, he views nature through the lens of a self-contained recluse. Nothing moves him more deeply than the changing phenomena of seasons and landscapes. Nature is recognized by him as an overwhelming power that is capable of stirring man's heart, as he often says in his "Miscellaneous Poems":

> Moved by natural objects [*kan-wu*], my heart is filled with feelings.
> (Poem #1)

感物多所懷

---

[7] Ssu-ma Chi-chu was a famous fortuneteller in Ch'ang-an during the Han. When asked why he chose to be a poverty-stricken fortuneteller, he replied: "The virtuous men refuse to engage in the same pursuit as the wicked. Thus, I would rather remain poor, to avoid the attention of the World." (See Ssu-ma Ch'ien, *Shih-chi*, *chüan* 127.) What Chang Hsieh means here is that he would like to withdraw from officialdom and become a recluse.

Hsieh Ling-yün
A NEW DESCRIPTIVE MODE

> Moved by natural objects [kan-wu], my thoughts are many.
> (Poem #6)
> 感物多思情

This emotional response to physical nature, called *kan-wu*, represents not only Chang Hsieh's own individual attitude to natural scenery but also the general tendencies of Western Chin poetry. The *shih* poetry of that period witnesses a gradual concern with the world outside. Instead of saying merely "I feel," the poet describes the changing phases of nature and his confrontation with them. We have already mentioned in the previous chapter that the Eastern Chin poet T'ao Ch'ien also exhibits an intimate feeling for nature typical of *kan-wu*. Yet there is a significant difference between Chang's descriptive technique and T'ao Ch'ien's. Whereas Chang's poetry is full of descriptive details of landscape, T'ao Ch'ien's images of nature are generally brief and less concrete. While Chang Hsieh searches for the particularity of scenes and colors, T'ao Ch'ien's descriptions are often marked by symbolism—that of the pine tree, homing birds, and floating clouds. Undoubtedly Chang Hsieh's and T'ao Ch'ien's poetry each represents a distinct type of description, though both reveal a natural realism in sharp contrast to the magical world of wandering immortals.

Like his friend Yen Yen-chih, Hsieh Ling-yün draws many of his stylistic devices from Western Chin poetry. His descriptive techniques in particular show traces of Chang Hsieh's influence. Yet Hsieh Ling-yün turns Chang's mountain-oriented landscape into a balanced world of *shan-shui*, and the effects are powerful and dynamic. For Chang Hsieh lived at a time and a place where the southern river scenes were not readily accessible to him. As a result, descriptions of landscape in his poetry are generally limited to those of the mountains. With Hsieh Ling-yün the landscape looks more picturesque and diverse, for the south has always been noted for its variety of mountain and water scenes. As has been mentioned, sightseeing had become a cultural phenomenon for the fashionable aristocrats from the early years of the Eastern Chin. Hsieh's dazzling landscape based on the traveler's perspective is thus very different from the rather static world in Chang Hsieh.

Hsieh Ling-yün's disposition to explore undiscovered regions and perilous paths may be largely responsible for the unusually dramatic effect in his scenic descriptions. The speaker in his poetry travels through remote places where hidden scenes are revealed bit by bit as he proceeds. Seen from afar, the mountains are layered and trees crowded—indeed, one cannot discern everything at one glance:

> The never-ending ranges of mountains are piled high and overlap,
> Their greens and blues are deep and impenetrable.
> (*HLYS*, 32)

Hsieh Ling-yün
A NEW DESCRIPTIVE MODE

連障疊巘崿
青翠杳深沈

It is the closer views that gradually unfold the details of the winding mountain roads and intricate twists of currents:

> I keep to the winding path that curves around the mountain side,
> I labor up treacherous slopes and hills....
> The riverbank keeps on twisting and turning,
> Merrily I go round and round, following the meandering stream.
>   (*HLYS*, 92–93)

逶迤傍隈隩
迢遞陟陘岘....
川渚屢逕復
乘流翫迴轉

Such varied landscape offers the explorer delight. The poet insists on seeking secluded and obscured areas hidden from ordinary view:

> So craggy are the mountains, the roads seem to be blocked,
> The thick bamboos obscure the tracks.
> Those who come cannot remember the new route,
> Those who leave forget the old path they took.
>   (*HLYS*, 87)

連岩覺路塞
密竹使逕迷
來人忘新術
去子惑故蹊

To be sure, it is the constant search for variety that produces such wide-ranging adventurous exploration. Thus, in Hsieh Ling-yün one often sees a hurried traveler incessantly looking for new sights:

> I spend my nights on the water, and stay there from dawn till dusk,
> Dark clouds rise and withdraw intermittently.
> I have toured all over this place, and am tired of the sea-coast,
> So I set sail for the distant ocean.[8]
>   (*HLYS*, 51–52)

---

[8] The "distant ocean" (literally "the bald and barren north") is an allusion to Chapter One of the *Chuang Tzu*: "In the bald and barren north, there is a dark sea, the Lake of Heaven. In it is a fish which is several thousand *li* across...." (Burton Watson, trans., *The Complete Works of Chuang Tzu*, p. 31.)

Hsieh Ling-yün
A NEW DESCRIPTIVE MODE

水宿淹晨暮
陰霞屢興沒
周覽倦瀛壖
況乃陵窮髮

I become weary of seeing the country in the south of the river,
It has been long since I explored the north of the river.
I yearn for new sights, but the roads are long and winding,
I go after rare scenery, but time is short.
    (*HLYS*, 54)

江南倦歷覽
江北曠周旋
懷新道轉迥
尋異景不延

The pressing need to move on to new undiscovered regions is reflected in the language above: the recurrent word *chüan* reinforces the image of a traveler easily weary of the familiar old scenes.[9] The desire to proceed is so overwhelming that traveling by boat is ultimately more exciting than a leisurely walk. Many of Hsieh's *shan-shui* poems describe the flashing speed of river crossing, with the persona viewing the progressive scenery from a fast-moving boat:

    The islets quickly go around and close in on us,
    While craggy shores repeatedly crush the swift flow.
        (*HLYS*, 114)

洲島驟迴合
圻岸屢崩奔

These lines produce the illusion that it is the islands and riverbanks, not the boat, that are moving. For, to the traveler, nature is resolved into a series of pictures which are progressive and continuously changing.

    The fact that traveling is full of risks and beset with uncertainty makes the sightseeing more exciting. To Hsieh landscape exploration is itself a challenge, and he takes delight in describing the perilous aspect of his adventure:

    Going upstream, we meet the terrifying currents head-on,
    Sailing along the craggy shore, we are obstructed by a mess of
        rocks.

---

[9] See also Hans Frankel's discussion of the typical traveler in Hsieh's poetry: *The Flowering Plum and the Palace Lady: Interpretations of Chinese Poetry* (New Haven: Yale Univ. Press, 1976), p. 14.

Hsieh Ling-yün
A NEW DESCRIPTIVE MODE

> I certainly lack the gallant spirit of Po-hun,[10]
> But the perils of this journey exceed those of Lü-liang Gorge.[11]
>   (*HLYS*, 28)
> 溯流觸驚急
> 臨圻阻參錯
> 亮乏伯昏分
> 險過呂梁壑

"Terrifying" (*ching*), "perilous" (*hsien*)—such are the words that Hsieh employs to depict the dynamic movement of his journey. If normal life is restricted by the narrowness of its scope, then it is the journey that brings about the breadths and depths of life. This is why Hsieh Ling-yün considers his "heroic" voyaging as his greatest pride in life, as he reveals in his longest poem "Return to the Old Garden," an autobiographical piece which sums up the chief glories of his ancestors and himself:[12]

> I boated down gorges ten thousand feet deep,
> I galloped across peaks a hundred thousand feet high.
> The perils of the "surging currents" seem small to me,
> And who says the "Forest of Stones" is steep....[13]
>   (*HLYS*, 75)
> 浮舟千仞壑
> 總轡萬尋巔
> 流沫不足險
> 石林豈爲艱....

It is this dramatic exploration that makes Hsieh Ling-yün's journey so fundamentally different from Wang Hsi-chih's casual tour-like "Orchid Pavilion" outing. Whereas Wang and his friends enjoy looking at the mountain scenery from a distance, Hsieh often aims at conquering nature, building his grand resort at the mountaintop. Hsieh Ling-yün's expedition to the highest peak of the Stone Gate in Chekiang can best demonstrate this adventurous attitude:

> I climb the steep mountain to build a secluded lodge,
> I smooth away the clouds and rest at Stone Gate.

---

[10] Po-hun Wu-jen was known as an extremely brave adventurer who would walk near the brink of an abyss without any hesitation. (See A. C. Graham, *The Book of Lieh-tzu* [London: J. Murray], p. 38.)

[11] Confucius once observed that even fish dared not swim in the hazardous waterfall at Lü-liang Gorge. (See Graham, *The Book of Lieh-tzu*, p. 44.)

[12] The only poem in Hsieh's collection which details his life in a manner reminiscent of historical writings. See Yeh Hsiao-hsüeh's comment in *HLYS*, 80.

[13] The "surging currents" refer to the rapid flows in Lü-liang gorge. The "Forest of Stones" is the name of a rocky mountain in modern Honan.

Hsieh Ling-yün
A NEW DESCRIPTIVE MODE

>Who can walk on these slippery mosses?
>The kudzu vines are too brittle to hold on to.
>(*HLYS*, 69)
>躋險築幽居
>披雲臥石門
>苔滑誰能步
>葛弱豈可捫

Clearly this *shan-shui* poetry mirrors a very vigorous conception of man, based on constant striving and experiencing. This basic philosophy gives Hsieh's style an extremely vital flavor. Nature to Hsieh is something not only to commune with, but to touch and feel.

Yet, ironically, the joy of exploring physical nature in Hsieh Ling-yün's poetry is the product of a disconsolate heart. For Hsieh's *shan-shui* poetry came to be written only after he suffered the severe blow of a political setback. His dynamic sense of struggle in poetry reflects his unhappiness in life. It is only natural that the poet lacked the casual cheerfulness typical of the "Orchid Pavilion" literati some decades before.

From the beginning of his political career, Hsieh Ling-yün was doomed to fail. When he was old enough to seek office around 405, Liu Yü had already come to power. As has been mentioned in the previous chapter, this was also the time when T'ao Ch'ien retired from public service for good. In his quick rise to power, Liu Yü had become the common enemy of the great families. In an attempt to protect the imperial authority, Hsieh Ling-yün's uncle Hsieh Hun and his friend Liu I eventually launched an attack upon Liu Yü that resulted in their tragic deaths in 412.[14] This event led to Liu Yü's continuous distrust of the members of noble families.

In consideration of the practical situation, Hsieh Ling-yün was determined to compromise. He remained socially involved with Liu Yü and continued to serve in the government well into Liu's new Liu-Sung dynasty. Gradually the poet's literary talents won him the affection of Prince Lu-ling (Liu I-chen), the second son of Liu Yü (Emperor Wu). Their friendship grew rapidly, and in no time a small literary group was formed, with Prince Lu-ling at its center. The poet Yen Yen-chih also became an active member of the circle.

Hsieh's happy association with Liu I-chen soon brought about an unexpected mishap. Their literary group had incited the suspicion of a powerful official, Hsü Hsien-chih, who brought a slander action against Prince Lu-ling, and charged Hsieh Ling-yün and his friends with forming a political clique. Prince Lu-ling defended the innocence of their friendship:

---

[14] For a biography of Hsieh Hun, see Li Yen-shou, *Nan shih*, *chüan* 20 (Peking: Chung-hua shu-chü, 1975), II, 550–551.

Hsieh Ling-yün
A NEW DESCRIPTIVE MODE

> Ling-yün is shallow and uninhibited; Yen-chih is prejudiced and selfish. They are no different from those whom Emperor Wen of the Wei described as "being unable to establish themselves through honor and integrity." However, because of my natural disposition I am unable to detach myself from the worldly bond with my friends. That's why I still keep company with them. (*Sung shu, chüan* 61, VI, 1636)
> 靈運空疎，延之隘薄，魏文帝云，鮮能以名節自立者。但性情所得，未能忘言於悟賞，故與之遊耳。

But in due time this literary group was to encounter a greater blow. Soon after Liu Yü's death, the new Emperor, Sung Shao-ti, had Prince Lu-ling degraded to commoner status and had the prince's friends sent into exile, so as to dissipate this "dangerous" group. Thus, in 423 Hsieh Ling-yün was forced to leave the capital for a small seaport, Yung-chia, to assume the position of Commandery Administrator.

One can well imagine how disheartened the poet must have felt. Filled with shame and anger, Hsieh Ling-yün deliberately neglected his official duties in Yung-chia. And, as if he was destined to devote his life to the development of *shan-shui* poetry, Yung-chia happened to be a place of spectacular scenic sights. It was in Yung-chia that Hsieh Ling-yün came to learn the joy of travel, and began to develop a poetry that attempted to describe his experience of seeing from detail to detail.[15] For only landscape could inspire him to a world of tranquility.

II. Descriptive Language

Although Hsieh Ling-yün participates actively in the temporal progression of traveling from place to place, it is important for him to stop to contemplate the landscape during the "timeless" moments of ecstasy. Indeed, beauty is in the instant of mental stillness when the past and future no longer exist. There are moments when the traveler, facing a beautiful scene, would find in himself an imaginary space where time seems to be transformed and lost. What he sees in front of him is a picture, an artistic formulation of his perceptions. To a despairing poet, nothing is more valuable than such an aesthetic experience,

---

[15] Yung-chia is modern Wen-chou in southern Chekiang. A brief survey of the titles of his poems written in Yung-chia in 423 will reveal that he visited practically all the famous scenic sites in that area—Ling-men Mountain, Eastern Mountain, Shih-ku Mountain, Shih-shih Mountain, Red Stone, Ku-yu Mountain, White Stone Rock, Green Crag Mountain, P'an-yü Mountain (*HLYS*, 36, 39, 41, 89, 51, 54, 55, 34, 58). Hsieh Ling-yün's service in Yung-chia lasted only a year, and in 424 he made a decision to retire to his family villa in Shih-ning, where he continued to tour extensively in nearby places.

Hsieh Ling-yün
A NEW DESCRIPTIVE MODE

and Hsieh Ling-yün repeatedly tells himself to hold fast to this moment of rapture:

> Let me express my desire to walk my own path,
> While there is moonlight, let me play with the murmuring stream.
> I shall always make the most of this transient moment;
> Why worry about the then-and-now?
> (HLYS, 118)
> 且申獨往意
> 乘月弄潺湲
> 恆充俄頃用
> 豈爲古今然

The visual experience is what makes this moment permanent. It is also the greatest of our consolations, for viewing the landscape will enlarge ourselves. Unlike T'ao Ch'ien, who often looks to the ancient sages (i.e., his *chih-yin*) for inspiration, Hsieh almost always regards the "visual experience" (what he calls *kuan*) as the ultimate relief from his troubles:

> The voyaging is hard—how do I get comfort?
> By looking at [*kuan*] the sea in the morning wind.
> (HLYS, 58)
> 羈苦孰云慰
> 觀海藉朝風

> Looking at [*kuan*] this scenery I can cast off the burdens of things,
> Once enlightened, I let everything go its own way.
> (HLYS, 93)
> 觀此遺物慮
> 一悟得所遣

Thus there is almost a formula in Hsieh's poetry to begin with the narrative account of a journey and then to move on to the descriptive scenes of mountains and waters. And readers are led to expect in the middle of his poems a change of tone—from the action-oriented narration to the object-oriented description.

Hsieh's impulse to describe is clearly revealed in his attempt to capture his momentary impressions in a high descriptive fashion. As has been said, the power of scanning detailed scenes in nature is strongly felt in Hsieh's *shan-shui* poetry. Yet, rather than giving us one random detail after another, Hsieh's persona carefully selects and organizes his impressions. We have already mentioned his method of alternation between mountain and water scenes, but have not yet touched upon the nucleus of his descriptive procedure, namely, the art of parallelism.

Hsieh Ling-yün
A NEW DESCRIPTIVE MODE

The Chinese fascination for seeing things parallel and complementary with each other is most successfully conveyed by Hsieh's scenic delineation, what may be called "synchronic description." In sharp contrast to the temporal movement in an actual progressive journey, the visual images of landscape in Hsieh's poetry are synchronically balanced. For his is a device of parallelism where things are viewed and juxtaposed as necessary correlations. In this orderly scanning, however diverse the chosen images are for each parallel couplet, the impression is inevitably one of simultaneous occurence:

Example 1:
The forest and the valley are wrapped in dusky colors,
Rosy clouds merge into evening mist.
Caltrop and waterlily brighten each other,
Reeds and rushes grow side by side.
    (*HLYS*, 72)
林壑斂暝色
雲霞收夕霏
芰荷迭映蔚
蒲稗相因依

Example 2:
Cliffs are steep, mountain ridges crowded together,
Islands wind around, sandbars are joined one after another.
White clouds embrace the secluded rocks,
Green bamboos charm the clear ripples.
    (*HLYS*, 26)
岩峭嶺稠疊
洲縈渚連緜
白雲抱幽石
綠篠媚清漣

It is the juxtaposition of comparable things that breaks the normal order of successive time. When two objects stand side by side, the relationship between them will not be one of the sequential, but one of mutual coordination. In Example 1, forest gorges parallel sunset clouds; caltrop and waterlily parallel reeds and rushes. In Example 2, crags are juxtaposed with sandbars, and white clouds with green bamboos. All these parallel images are combined to create an illusion of fullness and completeness, reinforcing the basic conception that the universe is made up of various paired objects.

Hsieh Ling-yün's synchronic description is but a reflection of Chinese traditional cosmology. The Chinese believed that parallelism is an inherent principle of the universe. The poet attempts to discover the correlations already existing in nature, so that he may organize and mold them into poetic parallelism. The following statement by the critic Liu Hsieh sums up this essentially Chinese view:

> Nature, creating living beings, endows them always with limbs in pairs. The divine reason operates in such a way that nothing stands alone. The mind creates literary expressions, and organizes and shapes one hundred different thoughts, making what is high supplement what is low, and spontaneously producing parallelism.[16]
> 造化賦形，支體必雙，神理爲用，事不孤立。夫心生文辭，運裁百慮，高下相須，自然成對。

There can be no doubt that parallelism, understood as an artistic recreation of the universe, is an effective means toward verisimilitude (*hsing-ssu*). Certainly parallelism can never reflect a "formal likeness" of nature in the literal sense of *hsing-ssu*, but no description is completely objective, and a literal representation is rarely welcomed by the Chinese. Describing a scene is like appraising an individual—what is most important is to "communicate the spirit" (*ch'uan-shen*).[17] To Hsieh the function of description is to grasp the spirit of things, and linguistic parallelism seems to come readily as a convenient means of achieving this goal.

Hsieh's greatest achievement lies in his making the mountain/water pivot the basis of his parallelism. His method of alternation is essentially rooted in the art of symmetrical balance, with the mountain and water scenes rotating in regular succession. If we review the two examples of parallelism just cited above, we shall find that indeed the parallel lines are structured according to this particular principle of alternation:

Example 1:
    Couplet 1: mountain scene
    Couplet 2: water scene
Example 2:
    Couplet 1: mountain scene followed by water scene
    Couplet 2: mountain scene followed by water scene

If in parallelism Hsieh seems to have attained the highest achievement of his poetry, it is because nowhere else is the Chinese sense of life energy more beautifully expressed. Often we observe the astonishing relationship between

---

[16] "Li-tz'u," *Wen-hsin tiao-lung*. See Vincent Yu-chung Shih, trans., *The Literary Mind and the Carving of Dragons*, rev. ed. (Hong Kong: The Chinese Univ. Press, 1983), p. 369. Used here with modifications.

[17] For the important function of personality appraisal during the Wei-Chin period, see Ying-shih Yü, "Individualism and the Neo-Taoist Movement in Wei-Chin China," p. 11; Wei-ming Tu, "Profound Learning, Personal Knowledge and Poetic Vision," in *ESP*.

Hsieh Ling-yün
A NEW DESCRIPTIVE MODE

his parallel landscape of *shan-shui* and the cosmic significance of natural growth so central to Chinese belief. A case in point may be found in his "On My Way from South Mountain to North Mountain, I Glance at the Scenery from the Lake," a poem cited in an earlier section of this chapter. The poet stops in the middle of his journey to make the following observation:

> What is the effect of Nature's "deliverance" and "becoming?"
> All things growing are lush and thriving.
>   (*HLYS*, 90)

解作竟何感
升長皆豐容

"Deliverance" (*hsieh*) and "becoming" (*tso*) are important terms borrowed from a chapter of the *I-ching* (*Book of Changes*). They refer to the flourishing state of all things following the cosmic "release" of a thunderstorm. The commentary reads:

> When heaven and earth deliver [*hsieh*] themselves, thunder and rain set in [*tso*]. When thunder and rain set in, the seed pods of all fruits, plants, and trees break open.[18]

This animating force of luxuriant growth is the key to the philosophy of the *I-ching*. Nothing could be more striking than the fact that it is through the device of parallelism that Hsieh manages to recreate this traditional conception so powerfully in poetry:

> Young bamboos are wrapped in green sheaths,
> Fresh rushes embrace their purple flowers.
> Seagulls play by the springtime banks,
> Wild pheasants sport in the gentle breeze.
>   (*HLYS*, 90)

初篁苞綠籜
新蒲含紫茸
海鷗戲春岸
天鷄弄和風

What is important is that through parallelism in poetry Hsieh has turned a philosophical attitude into an aesthetic experience. For the harmonious world in which everything grows according to the Tao is at the same time most beautiful.[19] With Hsieh Ling-yün nature has become a series of alluring

---

[18] From Richard Wilhelm, trans., *The I Ching, or Book of Changes*, rendered into English by Cary F. Baynes (Princeton: Princeton Univ. Press, Bollingen Series 19, 1967), p. 585. See also p. 154 for the "Judgment" of the hexagram *hsieh* (deliverance).

[19] See also Tsung Ping's (375–443) "Introduction to Landscape Painting," in *Sources of Chinese Tradition*, comp. William Theodore de Bary (New York: Columbia Univ. Press, 1960), I, 253–254.

Hsieh Ling-yün
A NEW DESCRIPTIVE MODE

scenes, forever decorated with vivid colors (e.g., green sheaths, purple flowers). And it is in the picturesque description of landscape that the poet's descriptive impulse is best expressed.

We should remember that the device of parallelism is essentially one of selection, not one of enumeration. The impression of a unified, balanced world in Hsieh is only the reflection of a personal interpretation of particular visual experiences. Time and again we see in Hsieh's parallelism an urge to "interpret" things according to a cause-effect reasoning.[20] Consider the following examples in which the second half of a line is consistently viewed as resulting from the first half of the line:

> The sun goes down, valley streams gather more ripples,
> Clouds arise, mountain peaks are piled higher and higher.
> (*HLYS*, 41)
> 日沒澗增波
> 雲生嶺逾疊

> The cliffs are steep—difficult for the sunlight to linger,
> The forest extends far down—the sound echoes easily.
> (*HLYS*, 69)
> 崖傾光難留
> 林深響易奔

> The valley winds around, the stream keeps straying out of sight,
> The forest is distant, the cliffs cluster more and more together.
> (*HLYS*, 34)
> 澗委水屢迷
> 林迥巖逾密

Yet it should be noted that the implied "because" in these lines is never spelled out. And herein lies the power of Hsieh's object-oriented parallelism. On the one hand, such descriptions of landscape imply the existence of an analytical viewer. But, on the other hand, it is the natural objects, not the poet's interpretation, that are kept in the foreground. As a result the causal relationship between things often appear to have an internal quality. There seem to be no "external" relationships, for such parallelism reinforces the impression of a world of total containment.

Hsieh Ling-yün's superb mastery of parallelism contributes a vital quality to his description of "mountains and waters." It should be noted that at the center of parallelism lies the painstaking workmanship required of all practic-

---

[20] See also Konishi Jin'ichi's discussion of a growing "conceptual attitude" in Six Dynasties poetry and its influence on the Japanese *Kokinshū* style, in "The Genesis of the *Kokinshū* style," trans. Helen C. McCullough, *Harvard Journal of Asiatic Studies*, vol. 38, no. 1 (June 1978), 61–170.

Hsieh Ling-yün
A NEW DESCRIPTIVE MODE

ing poets. For this reason, Chinese critics often use the word *ch'iao*, meaning "artistry" or even "artifice," to refer to the craftsmanlike nature of parallelism. Liu Hsieh points out *ching-ch'iao* ("artistic refinement") as the highest aesthetic value of parallel couplets.[21] When Chung Jung praises Hsieh Ling-yün's poetry for its quality of *ch'iao-ssu* ("artistry and verisimilitude"), he certainly has in mind the poet's skillful manipulation of parallelism. And our discussion so far has shown that the interplay of verisimilitude and parallelism is especially important in Hsieh's *shan-shui* poetry.

Here we may observe a very interesting phenomenon in the development of Chinese poetry. With Hsieh Ling-yün *shih* poetry has become more elaborately descriptive, and has never before been so keen about the display of parallel couplets. Yet *shih* poetry as a genre did not at first consider description a major mode, in sharp contrast to the epideictic *fu*, which makes elaborate description its generic trait.[22] One cannot help asking at this point: Is this new awareness of description in *shih* poetry influenced in any way by the *fu* poetics? Or are there any reciprocal influences between *shih* and *fu*?

Let us now begin with the characteristics of *fu*. From Han times the epideictic *fu*, with its tendency toward long and extensive description, had been an ideal literary form for describing the grand spectacles of the natural world.[23] Whereas descriptions in the *Shih-ching* (*Book of Songs*) are based on the method of association—what may be defined as that of "using a few examples to illustrate the whole range" (*i-shao tsung-to*)[24]—the *fu* emphasizes endless cataloging of objects, with the aim of creating an overpowering accumulation of details. Liu Hsieh sums up eloquently the descriptive function of *fu* in his chapter on "The Physical World":

> ... Types of description had multiplied, and it was practically impossible to depict all the aspects of things with faithfulness to their nature. For it had then been found necessary to describe the same things in a variety of forms. So various terms to describe craggy height, or to describe luxuriant growth, come to be collected. Ch'ang-ch'ing [or Ssu-ma Hsiang-ju] and his group adopted a pre-

---

[21] "*Li-tz'u*," in *WHTL*, II, 589.

[22] *Fu* is translated as "rhyme-prose" by Burton Watson (see his *Chinese Rhyme-Prose: Poems in the Fu Form from the Han and the Six Dynasties Periods* [New York: Columbia Univ. Press, 1971],). But most scholars prefer to call it *fu*, as there seems to be no good English equivalent for this poetic genre. (See, for example, Frankel, *The Flowering Plum*, pp. 212–213; Hightower, *Topics in Chinese Literature: Outlines and Bibliographies*, rev. ed. [Cambridge: Harvard Univ. Press, 1971], pp. 26–29.) The *fu* varies in length, prosody, and style. Generally the descriptive *fu* is considered a primary form, and the lyrical *fu* a minor form.

[23] See David R. Knechtges, *The Han Rhapsody: A Study of the Fu of Yang Hsiung (53 B.C.—A.D. 18)* (Cambridge: Cambridge Univ. Press, 1976), pp. 42–43.

[24] See Liu Hsieh's chapter 46, "Wu-se" (*WHTL*, II, 694).

tentious style and extraordinary tonal patterns, and their descriptions of mountains and waters consist of strings of words in rows, like columns of fish....[25]

...觸類而長，物貌難盡，故重沓殊狀，於是嵯峨之類聚，葳蕤之羣積矣。及長卿之徒，詭勢瓌聲，模山範水，字必魚貫。...

Thus, the elaborate schemes of parallelism which resemble "columns of fish" were originally developed by the *fu* poets. Parallelism in *fu* must have provided a good source of inspiration for the Six Dynasties poets, who were just beginning to develop a new descriptive mode in the *shih* genre. Indeed, we witness a growing tendency toward cross-generic influences at this time, as is shown by the fact that the Six Dynasties poets and critics often employed the same critical terms to refer to both genres. Shen Yüeh (441–513), for example, borrows the term "verisimilitude" (*hsing-ssu*) from contemporary *shih* criticism in his comment on Ssu-ma Hsiang-ju's *fu*:

> [Ssu-ma] Hsiang-ju is skillful in inventing expressions of verisimilitude.
> (*SS*, *chüan* 67, VI, 1778)
> 相如巧爲形似之言

All this sharing of critical terms and descriptive techniques between the two genres results in the general impression that the original classic distinction made by the Western Chin poet Lu Chi—i.e., *shih* being primarily suitable for the expression of feelings (*yüan ch'ing*), and *fu* being a perfect medium in which to describe things (*t'i-wu*)—is now no longer valid.[26] In particular, Liu Hsieh begins to claim that both genres must possess the quality of *t'i-wu* ("being descriptive"),[27] a characteristic that formerly had referred exclusively to the *fu*.

It would be wrong, however, to assume that all *fu* are descriptive. In fact, there emerged gradually since the time of Wang Ts'an (177–217) a particular type of *fu* that may be called "lyrical," in direct opposition to the traditional epideictic *fu*.[28] Perhaps this means that to a certain extent the *fu* genre had been affected by the lyrical nature of *shih* poetry. A case in point is T'ao Ch'ien's "*Fu* on Calming the Passions" ("*Hsien-ch'ing fu*"), an intensely lyrical work which has been discussed at length in the previous chapter.[29] But, despite this newly acquired lyrical concern, in the Six Dynasties the *fu* genre is

---

[25] See Yu-chung Shih, trans., p. 350.

[26] See "*Wen-fu*," in *WH*, *chüan* 17, I, 352.

[27] See *WHTL*, 80, 494.

[28] See Wang Ts'an's "Climbing the Tower," in Burton Watson, trans., *Chinese Rhyme-Prose*, pp. 52–54.

[29] T'ao Ch'ien's other *fu* "The Return" ("*Kuei-ch'ü-lai-hsi tz'u*") (*TYMC*, 159) is also a good example. See Hightower, "The *Fu* of T'ao Ch'ien," pp. 213–230.

Hsieh Ling-yün
A NEW DESCRIPTIVE MODE

still primarily descriptive. It is in view of this fact that we regard Hsieh Ling-yün as a vital literary figure who stands at the intersection of reciprocal influences between his description-oriented *shih* and the *fu*.

Before we can say more about the meeting of the two genres, we must first consider Hsieh's representative work in *fu*, "Dwelling in the Mountains" ("*Shan-chü fu*").[30] This *fu* is about the grandiose scenery of Hsieh's famous villa, the Shih-ning settlement in Kuei-chi prefecture (modern Shao-hsing in northern Chekiang), where he stayed in voluntary retirement first during 423–426 and again in 428–431. The Shih-ning estate, covering an enormously large area of scenic sights, was originally designed and mapped out by Hsieh's grandfather, Hsieh Hsüan. Within the confinement of this family estate, there are mountains and lakes, gardens and pavilions, well-cultivated orchards and many animals—indeed a worldly paradise of plenitude. Reading Hsieh's "*Fu* on Dwelling in the Mountains," one marvels at the detailed description that the poet has succeeded in giving. The *fu* is extremely long, obviously modeled after the traditional epideictic *fu*. In addition, the grand scale of the scenery and the exhaustive catalog of trees, flowers, and animals, all remind us of the Han *fu* style.

Yet, upon closer scrutiny, one realizes that Hsieh's *fu*, despite its length, is primarily rooted in the same poetic tradition as his *shan-shui* poetry, namely that of descriptive realism. While the Han *fu* often detail various mythical animals and objects of a fictitious nature, Hsieh's *fu* is based on realistic description of existing objects. Unlike the epideictic *fu* by the Han authors, which are often about the elaborate exhibition of the somewhat artificial palace parks, Hsieh's piece aims at describing the "natural" scenery of mountains and waters, as he declares in his Preface. The result of this new emphasis on "realism" is the creation of a genuinely descriptive *fu* devoid of the hyperbole so often found in the Han *fu*.

Compared with more recent works in the *fu* form, Hsieh's *fu* is also distinguished by its very "realism." For example, it is clearly different from Sun Ch'o's "Wandering on Mount T'ien-t'ai" (*Yü T'ien-t'ai shan fu*), a *fu* which appears to be describing a real journey but is actually inspired by a diagram or something of the sort.[31] Besides, the real subject of Sun Ch'o's *fu* is journeying to the immortal world, with the charioteer of the sun as a guide. The descriptions of the journey are certainly profoundly moving, but they nevertheless represent the *yu-hsien* style, quite different from Hsieh Ling-yun's realistic

---

[30] See *SS*, *chüan* 67, VI, 1,754–1,772. For a complete translation of this piece, see Francis A. Westbrook, "Landscape Description in the Lyric Poetry and '*Fu* on Dwelling in the Mountains' of Hsieh Ling-yün," diss. Yale Univ., 1973.

[31] *WH*, *chüan* 11, I, 223–227; and Burton Watson, trans., *Chinese Rhyme-Prose*, pp. 80–85. For a discussion of this *fu*, see Richard Mather, "The Mystical Ascent of the T'ien-t'ai Mountains: Sun Ch'o's *Yu-t'ien-t'ai shan Fu*," *Monumenta Serica*, 20 (1961), 226–245.

Hsieh Ling-yün
A NEW DESCRIPTIVE MODE

approach. When we begin to read the detailed notes that Hsieh provides for his own piece, we feel that indeed his realism in depth—that is, meticulous research into the geographical conditions as well as aesthetic considerations—is a method heretofore unknown to the Chinese *fu* tradition.

Hsieh's *fu*, like his *shan-shui* poetry, insists on the complementary relationship of mountains and rivers. The whole idea of a family park is by definition one of completion and fullness—of possessing both mountain and water scenes.[32] That Hsieh intends to view his Shih-ning estate as a complete world in miniature is quite clear. He begins his description of the park landscape with the following lines:

> My home is surrounded
> By lakes on the left and rivers on the right,
> Everywhere there are sandbars and islets.
> With mountains in front and hills at the back,
> The homestead is blocked toward the east, verging toward the west.
>   (*Sung shu, chüan* 61, VI, 1757)

其居也
左湖右江
往渚還汀
面山背阜
東阻西傾

Afraid that readers might not understand his idea of a total vision on the basis of the combined existence of "mountains and waters," Hsieh continues to comment in his notes upon the necessity of such physical coordinates:

> "Everywhere there are sandbars and islets" means that there is water in all four directions. "With mountains in front and hills at the back" suggests that there are mountains on both the east and the west, which are again surrounded by water on all sides.
> 往渚還汀，謂四面有水，面山背阜，亦謂東西有山，便是四水之裡也。

The point is that without the alternation of mountain and water scenes, the landscape would be missing its essential quality of being all-encompassing. Hsieh Ling-yün is confident that this aesthetic requisite, so consciously worked out, is his own invention, and it is wholly different from that of the ancient authors. With this in mind, he criticizes Mei Sheng (?–140 B.C.), author of a Han *fu* "*Ch'i fa*," for failing to see the importance of this complementary conception:

[32] See also Plaks, "The Chinese Literary Garden," p. 168.

Hsieh Ling-yün
A NEW DESCRIPTIVE MODE

> Mei Sheng said: "With rivers to the left and lakes to the right, my joy is beyond description...." But although he had rivers and lakes, he still lacked mountains and crags....
> 枚乘曰：" 左江右湖，其樂無有。..."彼雖有江湖而乏山巖。...

Thus Hsieh points out the essential difference between his *fu* on "mountains and waters" and that of the earlier *fu*. And behind this new landscape conception we see the gradual convergence of his *shih* and *fu* poetics.

There is little doubt that Hsieh is the one who takes the first large step to bring the two genres closer. As a result, this combination became an integral part of the current poetics. What holds them together is also the unusual sensory taste of the period—descriptive impressiveness, elaborate coloration, unyielding fascination with the natural world. However, it should be borne in mind that the mutual influences of *shih* and *fu*, at least in this early stage, by no means imply a complete identity between the two.

In the final analysis, *shih* poetry, no matter how descriptive it has become, will never depart from its primarily expressive function. It is important to note that lyrical feeling is a poetic requisite for *shih* poetry, although the same cannot be said of *fu*. This underlies perhaps the most crucial difference between the two genres. So we find in Hsieh's *shih* poetry an emphasis on the momentary "perception" of nature, in contrast to the impersonal description in his *fu*.[33] If description in Hsieh's *shih* poetry appears to be intensive, then the structure of his *fu* may be said to be extensive. The former is grounded on the principle of selection, while the latter on that of exhaustiveness. The distinction between these two descriptive modes will become especially clear if we compare his "*Fu* on Dwelling in the Mountains" with his *shih* on the same subject—i.e., "South of the Field a Garden Was Cultivated, and by the Rapid Currents Trees Were Planted like a Rail Fence" (*HLYS*, 67). For the *shih*, consisting of only twenty lines, calls attention to representative details and stresses the importance of selection based on the lyrical consciousness of the moment. Yet the *fu*, lasting as long as seventeen pages in its modern reprint, pretends to exhaustiveness—indeed is full of apologies for the inadequacy of description:

> All these are the beautiful scenes of the lake. I am afraid that my words do not convey all that is in my mind, and that what I have written captures less than one ten-thousandth of the charms of the place.... (*Sung shu*, *chüan* 61, VI, 1,760, note)
> 此皆湖中之美，但患言不盡意，萬不寫一耳。...

---

[33] For the importance of "perception" in *shih*, see also Stephen Owen, "A Monologue of the Senses," in *Toward a Theory of Description*, ed. Jeffrey Kittay, no. 61 of *Yale French Studies* (1981), p. 249.

Hsieh Ling-yün
A NEW DESCRIPTIVE MODE

Yet there still remains an important similarity between these two types of literature: in both the poet demonstrates that describing beautiful scenery is his main purpose. Hsieh's accomplishment in the *shih* form is particularly important, for the way he wants nature to be seen is quite original. His new *shan-shui* aesthetics entails first of all the enlargement of the scope of *shih* poetry, making his unswerving aspiration toward landscape a new poetic principle.

III. The Lonely Traveler

We should bear in mind that Hsieh Ling-yün's description of landscape, however elaborate, is only a point of departure for his self-realization. Or, more exactly, that Hsieh structures his poem, consciously or unconsciously, as a progressive "narrative"—it starts with the tour, continues with the visual experience, and concludes with an emotional response and revelation. This explains why in most of his *shan-shui* poems there is a distinct method of progression—from the narrative to the descriptive, and then finally to the expressive. The exact order of progression is important here, for the impression created is that it is the visual perception that elicits the strong emotions in the poet, not the other way around. And often the concluding expressions in his poems are a clear break from the descriptive mode of parallelism. The following passage is a typical example of Hsieh's conclusion of a detailed scenic description:

> I imagine seeing a mountain-hermit,
> His fig-leaf jacket and rabbit-floss belt as if before my eyes.[34]
> I gather a handful of orchids, but my effort in tying them is in vain,
> I pluck the hemp, yet there is no one for me to open my heart to....
>   (*HLYS*, 92–93, lines 15–18)
> 想見山阿人
> 薜蘿若在眼
> 握蘭勤徒結
> 折麻心莫展....

We feel that by this statement the poet has come back from description to expression. The world of aestheticism in the descriptive section of the poem is now gone. The poet suddenly awakens, and sees in his lonely soul a burning need for the true friendship in the face of the beautiful scenery. Yet the hope of finding an ideal friend is remote, and his ultimate consolation has to come

---

[34] The phrase "fig-leaf jacket and rabbit-floss belt" was originally used to describe the special clothing of a mountain goddess. (See David Hawkes, *Ch'u Tz'u: The Songs of the South*, p. 43.) Later it became a standard phrase to refer to all recluses.

from an inner grasp of the Tao in the "mountains and waters." So the poem again moves from the intense expression of emotions to a philosophical conclusion that objectifies the personal feelings:

> To appreciate [nature] with a sensitive heart is pleasure,
> But the hidden truth,—who can ever discern it?
> Looking at this scenery I cast off my concern with things,
> Once enlightened, I let everything go its own way.[35]
>   (lines 19–22)
> 情用賞爲美
> 事昧竟誰辨
> 觀此遺物慮
> 一悟得所遣

This final transformation from feeling to reason is a typical Taoist attitude. For Hsieh Ling-yün the mountains and waters are originally the means of emotional indulgence, and yet the end product of his poetry is far from being subjective. This is because Hsieh, more often than not, concludes his poems with Taoist reflections.[36] But, unlike T'ao Ch'ien, who often opens his poems like one who has already acquired Tao, Hsieh Ling-yün is more interested in the "process"—of constant search and changing realizations. Such a process of inner struggle, through the medium of *shan-shui*, is the very heart of Hsieh's poetry.

Of course, not all of Hsieh's poems conclude with a firm resolution. Many of his works end with an unresolved tension, thus reversing the usual sequence of moving from feeling to reason. The following conclusion of a poem is a typical example of this kind:

> My heart is in harmony with the trees of autumn,
> My eyes luxuriate in the buds of spring.
> I live a simple life and wait for my end,
> I follow nature and am content with my destined lot.
> My only regret is that there is no understanding friend
> To climb with me this ladder to the blue clouds.
>   (*HLYS*, 87, 1. 15–20)

---

[35] The line alludes to an important concept in Taoism, *wu so pu ch'ien* (literally, "there is nothing that one cannot let go of"). See also Note 20, in Yeh Hsiao-hsüeh, *Hsieh Ling-yün shih-hsüan*, p. 94.

[36] Some of his concluding statements are Buddhist in nature. For the Buddhist themes in Hsieh Ling-yün, see Richard Mather, "The Landscape Buddhism of the Fifth Century Poet Hsieh Ling-yün," *Journal of Asian Studies*, 18 (Nov. 1958), 67–79. See also Fung Yu-lan, *A History of Chinese Philosophy*, trans. Derk Bodde, II (Princeton: Princeton Univ. Press, 1953), pp. 274–284.

Hsieh Ling-yün
A NEW DESCRIPTIVE MODE

心契九秋榦
目玩三春荑
居常以待終
處順故安排
惜無同懷客
共登青雲梯

The ending couplet betrays a deep sense of unfulfillment. Like T'ao Ch'ien, Hsieh Ling-yün is preoccupied with the thoughts of finding a *chih-yin*, the true friend with whom he may communicate his self-realization. Yet, whereas T'ao Ch'ien succeeds in realizing his *chih-yin* in history and fiction—in Ching K'o, Mr. Five Willow Trees, and the Gentleman in the East, etc.—Hsieh Lin-yün often fails in his endeavor. This sharp contrast between the two poets is especially important here, as it reflects different personalities, different inclinations, different situations in life, and different poetic styles.

It is of particular interest that Hsieh's quest journey, when resolved in bitter loneliness, is almost always modeled after Ch'ü Yüan's poetry. The chief frustration of Ch'ü Yüan, as all readers of "Encountering Sorrow" ("*Li sao*") know, is his unsuccessful search for an ideal ruler to appreciate his worth—a failed attempt symbolized by the failure of the quest for the goddess.[37] It is intriguing to note that this classical theme of pessimism often surfaces to dominate Hsieh's poetry, as can be seen in the many poems in which the desired *chih-yin* appears to be intangible.[38] More important, Hsieh calls his ideal friend "the fair one" (*mei-jen*), obviously under the influence of Ch'ü Yüan:

> The fair one has gone roaming and does not return,
> When shall I ever see him again?
>   (*HLYS*, 69)

美人遊不還
佳期何繇敦

> The fair one does not come,
> In vain have I dried my hair on the Bank of Sunlight.[39]
>   (*HLYS*, 89)

---

[37] See David Hawkes, "The Quest of the Goddess," in Cyril Birch, ed. *Studies in Chinese Literary Genres* (Berkeley: Univ. of California Press, 1974), pp. 42–68.

[38] See, for example, *HLYS*, 39, 41, 69, 87, 89, 109, 112.

[39] This couplet is a direct allusion to a passage in *The Nine Songs* where the speaker sings:
> I will wash my hair with you in the Pool of Heaven;
> You shall dry your hair on the Bank of Sunlight.
> I watch for the Fair One, but he does not come.
> Wildly I shout my song into the wind.
>   (Hawkes, trans., *Ch'u Tz'u*, p. 41)

Hsieh Ling-yün
A NEW DESCRIPTIVE MODE

美人竟不來
陽阿徒晞髮

Once the poet is overcome by this kind of profound frustration, even the landscape cannot put him at ease. In fact, the more he views nature (*lan-wu*), the more he feels troubled, as he confesses in the following lines:

> Not only can I not forget my grief,
> But the more I contemplate nature [*lan-wu*], the more my feeling grows intense.
> (*HLYS*, 39)

非徒不弭忘
覽物情彌遒

> A heart that embraces natural transformations is never bored,
> Yet the more I contemplate nature [*lan-wu*], the more my concerns deepen.
> (*HLYS*, 90)

撫化心無厭
覽物眷彌重

He explains that it is the absence of an understanding friend which makes it impossible for him to enjoy the enduring moments of scenic beauty:

> I do not regret the wind and rain,
> But my innermost feelings: to whom do I tell them?
> If only I had with me a close friend branched off from the same tree,[40]
> This day would be worth a thousand years.
> (*HLYS*, 99)

風雨非攸恡
擁志誰與宣
倘有同枝條
此日即千年

The truth is that Hsieh Ling-yün is a "lonely" traveler, though accompanied by hundreds of attendants. Unlike T'ao Ch'ien, who appears to be always sure of his inner Tao, Hsieh draws his ultimate pleasure from the momentary triumph of landscape over his feelings. Thus beauty for Hsieh is in the instant of perceiving nature, in the feelings that constitute the instant. It is important for him to hold fast to these moments, and to turn them into aesthetic experience. One gets the impression that the poet "leaps" rather than "moves" in the river of time, jumping from one moment of aesthetic duration

---

[40] *T'ung chih-t'iao* (branches grown from the same tree) is a conventional metaphor for good friends.

Hsieh Ling-yün
A NEW DESCRIPTIVE MODE

to another. Beauty is thus a state of mind always challenged and always reaffirmed. To the poet nothing is achieved once and for all. In every poem by Hsieh one seems to see a brand-new process of progression, and a curious feeling that the resolution, however "final," is still momentary.

It is Hsieh's poetic style to postulate simultaneously a basic contradiction between the self-fulfilling sense of aesthetic pleasure and the inevitable feeling of disillusion. Such an opposition arises from the poet's unresolved pathos of loneliness. As has been mentioned, after his uncle Hsieh Hun died as a loyalist of the Eastern Chin, Hsieh Ling-yün was destined to lead a thorny and dangerous political life under the new government of the Liu-Sung. Worse still, Hsieh's patron and friend at court Liu I-chen, the talented Prince Lu-ling, was eventually executed in A.D. 424, a tragic event that destroyed all of Hsieh's hopes and dreams.[41] It was unavoidable that Hsieh should have been at odds with the court of the new dynasty and ultimately meet his own tragic execution. We will see later in the following chapters that tragedies such as this, or fears of one's destiny provoked by contemporary political conditions, play a much greater part than one would normally assume in shaping the style of poetry during the Six Dynasties.

What is certain is that the feeling of loneliness expressed in Hsieh's poetry closely reflects his feeling of alienation in politics. Moreover, we see in both his life and his poetry an unresolved conflict between public service and voluntary retirement, indeed a "tragic flaw" that eventually leads him to his disastrous end. On the one hand, we see in Hsieh a distaste for the routine nature of public service and a genuine love for the recluse's world. But, on the other hand, we get the impression that whether or not he retires, he will always be plagued by the same feeling of loneliness. Hsieh did resign from his office in 424, but his inability to remain a permanent recluse caused him to come back to politics in 428 and again in 431, and to forget the political danger that was eventually to befall him. In his last poem, written on the eve of his execution in 433, Hsieh poignantly expressed his regrets that he had not persisted in being a recluse, and hence could not have died happily in retirement:

> I regret that my gentleman's sense of purpose
> Could not have been fully realized off in the mountains....
> (*CHSK*, II, 654)

恨我君子志
不得巖下泯....

This sense of incompletion felt by Hsieh before his death is very different from T'ao Ch'ien's ready acceptance of his destiny as expressed in his deathbed dirge. We cannot help feeling sorry for Hsieh's inability to achieve the self-

---
[41] See Hsieh's poem on visiting the grave of Prince Lu-ling in *HLYS*, 80.

Hsieh Ling-yün
A NEW DESCRIPTIVE MODE

awareness which he so often came close to realizing.[42] Yet literature has the power of transcending death. Ultimately it is in Hsieh's *shan-shui* poetry, not in his life, that his readers come to find a sense of completion. For the first time the aesthetic appreciation of mountains and waters and the ecstasy of viewing nature so typical of the Six Dynasties attitude is fully expressed in poetry. The T'ang poet Po Chü-i in his poem on Hsieh Ling-yün explains this triumph of poetry over life:

> Master Hsieh's talents were broad,
> But he was at odds with his times.
> His lofty ambitions, sadly, were of no use,
> He needed to vent his feelings,
> Once expressed, they became landscape poetry,
> In which excellent taste harmonized with extraordinary imagination.[43]
> 謝公才廓落
> 與世不相遇
> 壯志鬱不用
> 須有所洩處
> 洩爲山水詩
> 逸韻諧奇趣

So the last word still lies with the enduring value of poetic expression. Most strong poets in China understand this, and aspire to turn their experiences of suffering into immortal pages.

---

[42] See also Mather, "The Landscape Buddhism of the Fifth Century Poet Hsieh Ling-yün," p. 73.
[43] *Po Chü-i chi*, I, 131.

III

Pao Chao

IN SEARCH OF EXPRESSION

In sharp contrast to his relatively short life, Hsieh Ling-yün's poetry exercised a powerful influence long beyond his time, an influence so great that the entire age continued to be nourished by it. It seems that the Six Dynasties poetry had finally encountered someone of Hsieh's stature to define its taste, to refine it, even to redeem it. It was with Hsieh that "descriptive" and "aristocratic" first became the adjectives most appropriately applied to the collective taste. Indeed, one can almost conclude that the poetic style of this period was based mainly on an individual style—a phenomenon rarely seen in any other literary era.

However, as T. S. Eliot puts it, "a man may be a great artist, and yet have a bad influence."[1] No other statement can better describe the inevitable dilemma that the followers of Hsieh Ling-yün were to face for the many decades to come: on the one hand, poets benefited profoundly from the accomplishments of this giant poet who had set the basic aesthetics for their literary standards, but at the same time their poetry had lost the unique flavor that often characterizes all individualistic styles. More specifically, poets in the so-called "Hsieh Ling-yün school" tended to copy only Hsieh's descriptive similitude and extended parallelism without also learning from his poetic dynamism. A century later Hsiao Kang (503–551), who afterward became Emperor Chien-wen of the Liang, could still give witness to the extent of Hsieh Ling-yün's influence:

> Also, at times there are those who try to imitate the style of Hsieh Ling-yün ... and in doing this they are very much misled. Why so? Hsieh creates words like a genius, which all come from natural

---

[1] T. S. Eliot, "Milton, Part I," in his *On Poetry and Poets* (1943; rpt. New York: The Noonday Press, 1961), p. 156.

spontaneity. But sometimes he pays no attention to the rules, and what he produces are mere dregs.... Thus, by imitating Hsieh's writing one does not attain its essential beauty, but rather its verbosity.... (*CKLT*, I, 327)
又時有效謝康樂...者，亦頗有惑焉。何者？謝客吐言天拔，出於自然，時有不拘，是其糟粕。...是爲學謝則不屆其精華，但得其冗長。...

Under such circumstances it is hardly surprising that a poet who sought to be creative would try to deviate from this prevailing current of imitation. And the poet Pao Chao (414?–466) was one of the few, if not the single one, among younger authors who first consciously sought a new literary horizon beyond what was established by Hsieh Ling-yün. For Pao Chao understood that no good poetry can be purely a reflection of a period style, and no poet can set the terms for the way another creative spirit seeks to express his feelings. When Pao Chao was old enough to begin searching actively for his own distinctive voice in poetry, both T'ao Ch'ien and Hsieh Ling-yün were dead—he was thirteen when T'ao died, and nineteen when Hsieh died. The time seemed to him to require a new mode of lyricism.

Pao's creative innovation takes root in a great fascination for the rich variety in literary genres. He displays a love for the unique value of each genre—whether *shih*, *fu*, *yüeh-fu*, or whatever—a love for the harmonious blending of diverse styles in each. It is his enormous poetic energy that helps him experiment with forms continually, so that the very process of writing in new genres becomes a process of finding his own voice. Thus, the voice in which Pao speaks to his readers almost always reflects that key element in his personality: a genuine delight in diversity.

Pao tried his hand in almost all genres—poetic or prosaic, literary or popular. Aside from the multiplicity of styles in his *shih* poetry, his *fu* poetry and prose literature are all characterized by a wide mixture of themes. At a time when the poetic scene was dominated by the five-character-line *shih* (*wu-yen shih*), he boldly experimented with the seven-character-line *yüeh-fu*, a poetic form rooted in the popular song tradition.[2] While the literati poetry was definitely moving in the direction of the "regular line" aesthetics, he deliberately mixed lines of irregular length with those of regular length, thus

[2] For the dominant importance of five-character-line poetry at this time, see Chung Jung's *Shih-p'in*, in which poets are judged and rated according to their accomplishments in the five-character-line *shih*. But note that Pao Chao also produced many poems in another originally popular form: the seven-character-line *yüeh-fu*. It is in Pao Chao that this *yüeh-fu* form first acquired an elite stature, although Ts'ao P'i (187–226) had already written a poem in this form, entitled "*Yen-ko hsing*," two centuries before. See Wang Yün-hsi's article on the development of the seven-character-line poetry, in his *Yüeh-fu shih lun-ts'ung* (Peking: Chung-hua shu-chü, 1962), pp. 165–170.

Pao Chao
IN SEARCH OF EXPRESSION

creating a popular appeal that was both a liberation from and a broadening of the classical horizons.[3] His adoption of the *chüeh-chü* quatrain, a form of *yüeh-fu* song, also produced a new phenomenon in the literary field, mingling the popular style harmoniously with the elite lyricism.

There is little doubt that it is Pao's *yüeh-fu* songs, which constitute about one half of the entire corpus of his work, that are generally recognized as the finest of his literary products. These *yüeh-fu* songs, marked by a straightforward voice, appealed especially to the common people. The striking thing is that this appeal was not limited to the Chinese in South China; the "barbarian" court in the north also celebrated his *yüeh-fu* songs. The following passage from the official history of the Northern Wei records a particularly telling incident that took place around the middle of the sixth century:

> The Emperor [Emperor Hsiao-wu] gave a banquet in the living quarter of the palace. He asked the women to recite poems, and one of them sang a couplet from Pao Chao's *yüeh-fu*:
>
> "The noble palace has nine outer doors, and nine inner chambers,
> I wish to follow the moonlight, and penetrate into your bosom."[4]
>
> 帝〔孝武帝〕內宴，令諸婦人詠詩，或詠鮑照樂府曰：
> 朱門九重門九閨
> 願逐明月入君懷

Thus, it is not surprising that authors in the north would emulate the style of Pao Chao's *yüeh-fu*, treating him as a model poet of the Southern Dynasties.[5]

Yet, ironically, to the southern poets and critics, at least in the beginning, nothing seemed more "alien" or "vulgar" than Pao Chao's *yüeh-fu* songs. Obviously it is Pao's popular *yüeh-fu* that the critic Chung Jung refers to as something "rather lacking in purity and elegance" (*ch'ing-ya*), and flawed by "eccentricity and vulgarity" (*hsien-su*).[6] It seems to me that Chung Jung takes a stand that is largely conditioned by the contemporary poetics of the five-character line, and for this reason Pao Chao's new *yüeh-fu* style would certainly appear to be without aesthetic quality in both form and content. Clearly

---

[3] The most notable examples are the eighteen *yüeh-fu* poems in this form (*PTCC*, 205–216). For a discussion of Pao Chao's contribution to the development of the *chüeh-chü* quatrain, see Shuen-fu Lin, "The Nature of the Quatrain," in *ESP*.

[4] The quote is from Li Yen-shou, *Pei shih, chüan* 5 (Peking: Chung-hua shu-chü, 1974), I, 174. The *yüeh-fu* lines sung by the palace lady are from Pao Chao's poem entitled "*Tai Huai-nan Wang*," though with minor modifications. (See *PTCC*, 246.)

[5] See Tseng Chün-i, "Pao Chao yen-chiu," in *Wei Chin Liu-ch'ao lun-wen chi* (Hong Kong: Chung-kuo yü-wen hsüeh-she, 1969), p. 135.

[6] See *SPC*, 47.

this is why Chung Jung criticizes those worshipers of Pao Chao as "frivolous people" (*ch'ing-po chih t'u*).[7] With this background information in mind, we will not be surprised to see that Liu Hsieh ignores Pao Chao completely in his *Wen-hsin tiao-lung*, while elevating the positions of Hsieh Ling-yün and Yen Yen-chih.[8] Nor are we surprised to find that, in the critical atmosphere of his time, Pao had not emerged as a "first ranking" poet or acquired a group of literary followers like Hsieh Ling-yün, though in general esteem and influence he was no less than Hsieh's equal.[9]

However, it would be wrong for us to assume that all of Pao Chao's literary products were poorly received by the literati poets and critics. It would be more exact to say that, whereas his *yüeh-fu* songs seemed unacceptable to contemporary taste, his *shih* poems in the five-character-line form were generally in keeping with current literary trends. It is in this sense that Pao Chao was both an innovator and a conventionalist. I have observed that while his lyrical feelings are largely, or rather best, expressed in the *yüeh-fu* form, his description of landscape is almost always written in the five-character *shih* form. In other words, Pao appears to be more individualistically lyrical in his *yüeh-fu* songs, but more inclined to slip into the description-oriented poetics in fashion when composing his *shih* poetry. Not surprisingly, a conventional critic like Chung Jung could approve of Pao's descriptive techniques in his *shih* poetry:

> [Pao Chao] is skillful at creating expressions which capture the shape of things. His poetry has inherited Ching-yang's [Chang Hsieh's] crafty style and Mao-hsien's [Chang Hua's] adorned images.... He prefers artistic similitude (*ch'iao-ssu*). (*SPC*, 47)
> 〔鮑照〕善製形狀寫物之詞，得景陽之諔詭，含茂先之靡嫚。...貴尚巧似。

Indeed it is the "artistic similitude" in Pao's landscape *shih* poetry—the particular quality that reminds one of the *shan-shui* poetry of Hsieh Ling-yün and Yen Yen-chih—that earns him respect in the literati circle, and ranks him among "the three literary giants of the Yüan-chia reign." True enough, the art of verisimilitude is by no means contrary to Pao's temperament, and in fact it satisfies part of his creative instinct—namely, a love for visual excitement and

---

[7] *SPC*, 47.

[8] See Liu Hsieh's chapter on "Literary Development and Time" (*Shih-hsü*), in which he praised Yen and Hsieh for producing "works as wondrous as colors of phoenixes" without even mentioning Pao's name. (in Vincent Yu-chung Shih, trans., p. 471).

[9] Pao is rated as a "second-ranking" (*chung-p'in*) poet by Chung Jung (See *SPC*, 47). For information about the literary group that Hsieh gathered—the so-called "Four Friends" (*ssu-yu*)—see *SS*, *chüan* 67, VI, 1,774. See also Hsieh's own poem entitled "Written After Climbing Ling-hai Mountain and Before Leaving for Chiang-chung, A Poem in Response to My Cousin Hui-lien, and My Friends Yang and Ho" (*HLYS*, 106).

graphic directness. This descriptive aspect, if anything, provides a delightful variation for his lyrical freedom. Even on purely practical grounds, this diversity is especially suitable for Pao Chao, as it permits him to acquire the necessary apprenticeship in conventional genres, without which a truly creative poetry may not be realized. The express confirmation of this conviction can be found in Pao's wholehearted appreciation of Hsieh Ling-yün's five-character-line poetry—a poetry that obviously serves as his model of description: "Hsieh's five-character poems are like newly opened lotus flowers, spontaneous and lovely...." [10]

謝五言如初發芙蓉，自然可愛。...

There are about thirty some *shih* in Pao Chao's collection that can be categorized as poems of "mountains and waters." [11] In many aspects these poems, including their titles, bear a striking stylistic resemblance to Hsieh's landscape poetry. The orderly progression of a journey gradually moving to a visual experience, the display of colorful images, the parallel juxtaposition of mountain and water scenes, and the frequent description of a traveler constantly seeking the cause-and-effect relationship between things—all these reflect Hsieh Ling-yün's influence. Perhaps it is because Pao does not seem to be particularly innovative in these areas that the Ch'ing poet and anthologist Shen Te-ch'ien (1673–1769) judges Pao's five-character-line *shih* to be inferior to Hsieh's.[12] To some extent this criticism is fair, but the real power of Pao Chao's landscape poetry lies in those other areas where he produces an entirely new poetic mode by mingling conventional devices with his innovative vision, or more specifically by exaggerating some poetic elements that are particularly consonant with his creative temperament and personal experience. The following discussion will begin with this very subject.

I. From Landscape to Objects

Like Hsieh Ling-yün, Pao Chao spent much of his life traveling from place to place.[13] But, while Hsieh made his journeys usually for the purpose of sightseeing, Pao traveled on official duties. As a military officer, Pao Chao was

---

[10] The quotation is from the "Biography of Yen Yen-chih," in Li Yen-shou, *Nan shih*, *chüan* 34, III, 881. A similar passage can be found in Chung Jung's *Shih-p'in*, where the comment on Hsieh Ling-yün is said to have been made by T'ang Hui-hsiu, a contemporary of Pao Chao. (See *SPC*, 43.) The *Nan shih* version is generally believed to be the more reliable one. Yet the *Shih-p'in* version may also be correct in its own way—being a good friend of Pao's, T'ang might very well have shared with Pao an idea about Hsieh Ling-yün.

[11] See *chüan* 5 of *PTCC*, 255–320.

[12] See Shen Te-ch'ien's comment on Pao Chao in *Ku-shih yüan*, as cited in *PTCC*, 450 and 454.

[13] See Ch'ien Chung-lien, "Pao Chao nien-piao," in his *PTCC*, 431–442.

Pao Chao
IN SEARCH OF EXPRESSION

obliged to join military campaigns when required, and had to accompany his superiors on official tours. The following poem written while he was serving Liu I-ch'ing, the famous Lord of Lin-ch'uan and author of *Shih-shuo hsin-yü* (*A New Account of Tales of the World*), is typical of his landscape poetry.

SETTING OUT FROM HOU-CHU

On the river the air turns cold before its time,
Now in mid-autumn, frost and snow have begun to appear.
Going to join the army, I lack clothes and food,
Winter is coming, I bid farewell to my family.   4
Desolate, I try to put thoughts of home behind me,
Gloomy, I go out from the clear and bright sandbars.
Cold dust clouds over the lowlands,
Spume from the waves obscures the tall trees.   8
One lonely ray of light alone lingers,
I see the empty mist ascending and vanishing.
The road going toward the mountain peaks ahead is far,
My feelings, along with the clouds left behind,   12
    are knotted together.
My great ambition crumbles through the fleeting years,
My youthful face is gloomy, startled by the changes of seasons.
I pluck the zither and sigh three times,
"This song breaks off for you."   16
    (*CHSK*, II, 692)

發後渚

江上氣早寒
仲秋始霜雪
從軍乏衣糧
方冬與家別
蕭條背鄉心
悽愴清渚發
涼埃晦平皐
飛潮隱脩樾
孤光獨徘徊
空煙視昇滅
途隨前峯遠
意逐後雲結
華志分馳年
韶顏慘驚節

Pao Chao
IN SEARCH OF EXPRESSION

推琴三起歎
聲爲君斷絕

The opening lines of the poem are marked by a description of a military campaign ready to start in cold winter, the worst season for traveling.[14] With a stoical determination and perseverance, the sad traveler finally bids farewell to his family and embarks upon the official venture (lines 3–6). Any reader familiar with the conventional themes in *shan-shui* poetry would pause here for a moment and think of the sharp difference between Pao's poetic setting and that of his predecessors. Is it not true that *shan-shui* poetry, which traditionally implies visual delights and an attitude of landscape for landscape's sake, would always have to be a product of sightseeing? How can one possibly take Pao's piece to be a *shan-shui* poem when it is full of descriptions of less than desirable, if not miserable, human conditions?

Yet the essential thing about Pao's landscape poetry is precisely that he attempts to create a less than perfect landscape, where human fears, agitations, and hopes are to be reflected. It is something simultaneously beautiful and mournful, permanent and passing—indeed a living semblance of the world itself. To Pao Chao such is the true definition of *shan-shui*. When we examine the details of the scenic description in the poem above, we feel that what the poet has given us is a true impression of his mental perception of the landscape. For example, the following descriptive passage:

> Cold dust clouds over the lowlands,
> Spume from the waves obscures the tall trees.
> One lonely ray of light alone lingers,
> I see the empty mist ascending and vanishing.
>   (Lines 7–10)
> 涼埃晦平皋
> 飛潮隱脩樾
> 孤光獨徘徊
> 空煙視昇滅

Cold, lonely, and empty—such are the adjectives that the poet employs to depict the appearances of the dust, the sunlight, and the ascending mist. And the verbs that he uses are no less suggestive of dispirited isolation: to cloud over (line 7), to obscure (line 8), to linger alone (line 9), to vanish (line 10)—all these rather "expressive" natural movements convey an unmistakably melancholy mood. One gets the impression that somehow the landscape is

---

[14] Many of his poems record the same winter setting. See, for example, *PTCC*, 317, 319, 325, 406, 407.

Pao Chao
IN SEARCH OF EXPRESSION

distorted or exaggerated to express the lonely feeling of the poet at the moment of perceiving nature.

The transference of human loneliness to the things perceived is a characteristic of Pao's descriptive style in *shih*. In the previous chapter I have demonstrated that Hsieh Ling-yün's *shan-shui* poems often close with the image of a lonely traveler. Yet it is important to note that the descriptive section in Hsieh's poem, which comes prior to the expressive conclusion, is generally a representation of a perfect world made up of harmonious and flourishing things. The persona in Hsieh's poetry becomes sad only after he awakens from this suspended moment of aesthetic rapture, from the parallel juxtaposition of things. Not so in Pao Chao. For, although his description of landscape is also governed by parallelism, his parallelism often presents the paired images of imperfection rather than perfection in the world. As in the passage cited above, the lonely sunlight parallels the empty mists, and altogether the lines create through parallelism an illusion that the world is full of things that are equally isolated. When the poet starts to project this sense of loneliness onto birds and animals, the fusion of feeling and scenes becomes symbolic:

> The lonely beast cries for his mate at night,
> The wandering swan calls to his companions, cold with frost.
> When these creatures grieve, my heart is in turmoil,
> As they cry out bitterly, my thoughts are tangled.
> (*PTCC*, 307)

孤獸啼夜侶
離鴻噪霜羣
物哀心交橫
聲切思紛紜

> Graceful swans play by the rivers and lakes,
> Lonely geese gather on the sandy islets....
> Their wings are too weak to fly,
> Aimlessly they wander in the mist.
> (*PTCC*, 297)

輕鴻戲江潭
孤雁集洲沚....
短翮不能翔
徘徊煙霧裡

It is quite obvious that Pao Chao is consciously projecting his feelings into his visual experience. Yet, unlike T'ao Ch'ien, who creates symbolic images like green pines, clouds, and homing birds as though they are fixed allegories of the self, Pao Chao is more interested in the metaphorical meaning of changing scenes. Light, colors, action, all strike the imagination of the visual exploration. And Pao Chao is especially successful in imparting energy to the landscape, as may be seen in his favorite imagery of surging tides. The billowy waves, forever rolling, seem to provide the best kind of visual variety and energy that equal the convulsions and dynamism of life:

> The turbid waters surge forth in spume,
> The whirlwind rises from the riverbank.
> (*PTCC*, 307)

急流騰飛沫
回風起江濆

> In flying sand, darkening yellow mist,
> Among surging waves, fluttering white gulls.
> (*PTCC*, 310)

騰沙鬱黃霧
翻浪楊白鷗

Yet Pao achieves his fullest imaginative response to landscape only by applying *shan-shui* aesthetics to the context of prose literature. On the whole the most important techniques and motifs in the *shih* poetry of "mountains and waters" had already been explored by Hsieh Ling-yün. To express a new perspective on landscape most fitting to his temperament, Pao Chao would need to design a new form. And his choice in this case is the prose form, or more precisely the form of lyric prose called "*shan-shui wen*" (prose on mountains and waters). Although he has left us in this genre only one piece, entitled "A Letter to My Sister after Arriving at Ta-lei Riverbank" (*PTCC*, 83), its impact on literary posterity outweighs his accomplishments in *shan-shui* poetry.[15]

That Pao's essay is primarily a personal letter deserves our special attention. From the time of Ts'ao Chih (192–232), the letter had become a means of communicating one's innermost feelings and is thus most lyrical in the true sense of the word.[16] And this necessarily implies that Pao's letter to his sister Pao Ling-hui, a person who could best share his literary and private interests, must be in intent primarily lyrical.[17] With regard to lyricism, Pao's letter seems rather conventional. But his emphasis on the description of "mountains and waters" signifies the beginning of an important practice in the tradition of

---

[15] For example, the Ch'ing poet T'an Hsien praises Pao's piece as "the poet's essay." And another scholar, Liu Shih-p'ei, regards Pao's essay as "the model of travel literature." See *PTCC*, 94; Pei Yüan-ch'en and Yeh Yu-ming, eds., *Li-tai yu-chi hsüan* (Hunan: Jen-min ch'u-pan-she, 1980), p. 411.

[16] Ying-shih Yü, "Individualism and the Neo-Taoist Movement in Wei-Chin China," p. 16.

[17] Pao Ling-hui was a famous poetess whose collected work *Hsiang-ming fu chi* is no longer extant. See Chung Jung's comments on Pao Ling-hui, in *SPC*, 69–70.

letter-writing—that is, an admixture of the lyrical voice with landscape description. Nothing of this sort is to be found in earlier authors, not even in Hsieh Ling-yün. Of course, Hsieh has been regarded as the founding father of the *yu-chi* travel literature. But his essays focus on geographical details without a strong lyrical power of expression, as may be seen from the extant portions of his "Travels to Famous Mountains" (*Yu ming-shan chih*). It is Pao's innovative combination of the lyrical and the descriptive in prose that seems to be especially favored by later *yu-chi* authors. The enormous impact of Pao's influence can be seen in the sudden flowering of epistolary literature only one or two decades following his death.[18]

Pao Chao was only twenty-five years old when he wrote his famous letter in A.D. 439. The letter was written on his way from Nanking to Kiangsi Province, where he was to assume a position as assistant to Liu I-ch'ing, the Lord of Lin-ch'uan. When Pao Chao stopped by Ta-lei Riverbank in Anhwei Province, he was suddenly overcome with loneliness and felt impelled to write a letter to his sister. He opens his letter with a description of his journey:

> Since I set out there has been cold rain, and few of the days have been spent entirely in travel. Moreover, the autumn rains fall in torrents, and the mountain streams overflow. I cross the boundless waters against the current, and travel along dangerous paths. On the cliff-side roads I eat my meals under the stars; I spend my nights on lotus beds by the water. As a traveler, I am distressed and toil-worn. The rivers and roads are broad and immense. Thus, by mealtime today, I had only reached Ta-lei. I have traveled on this road for a thousand *li*; my journey has taken more than ten days. There is severe frost in this merciless season; the grievous wind bites my flesh. To be parted from the loved ones and to become a wanderer—what, oh what, can be done? (*PTCC*, 83)
> 吾自發寒雨，全行日少，加秋潦浩汗，山溪猥至，渡浉無邊，險徑遊歷，棧石星飯，結荷水宿，旅客貧辛，波路壯闊，始以今日食時，僅及大雷。塗登千里，日逾十晨，嚴霜慘節，悲風斷肌，去親爲客，如何如何。

No passage expresses more vigorously than the above lines the misery and the hardships of traveling in cold weather. It seems that in suffering and struggle the impassioned poet once again finds himself in isolation and helplessness. He wishes that he need not leave home for public service, certainly not for such a minor post. But the curve of his destiny is difficult to control, and all this

---

[18] For example, T'ao Hung-ching's (456–536) "A Reply to Hsieh Chung-shu" ("*Ta Hsieh Chung-shu shu*," and Wu Yün's (469–520) "A Letter to Sung Yuan-ssu" ("*Yü Sung Yüan-ssu shu*"). See Pei Yüan-ch'en and Yeh Yu-ming, *Li-tai yu-chi hsüan*, pp. 423–426.

moving around has made his existence one of perpetual "exile." This is the feeling that he attempts to communicate to his sister.

Yet suddenly Pao Chao's attention is no longer on his own feelings; he discovers himself at the center of an all-encompassing sunset scene:

> Looking far away to the clear and bright sandbars, I let my eyes wander at dusk. To the east I see the Five Islands' straits; to the west I gaze at the Nine Streams' parting. I spy the extraordinary scenery of the earth's gateway; I view the lone clouds at the sky's edge.
> (*PTCC*, 83–84)

遨神清渚，流睇方曛，東顧五洲之隔，西眺九派之分，窺地門之絕景，望天際之孤雲。

What follows is a most unusual description of mountains and waters, one whose colorful variety and powerful energy mirror the intense extremes in Pao's feelings:

> To the southwest I look at Mount Lu,
> Again I am struck by how extraordinary it is.
> Its base presses down on the river's tide,
> Its peaks touch the stars and the Milky Way.
> Above it, rosy clouds often gather,
> Wrought into an ornamental tapestry.
> Evening radiant as the flowers of the *jo* tree,
> Mists pass between cliffs and marshes.
> The emerging light scatters varicolored silk,
> So red, it seems to redden the sky.
> To the left and right, blue vapors
> Form a complement to the Purple Sky Peak.
> From the ridges up,
> Mists are full of golden brilliance.
> At the bottom half of the mountain,
> It is completely sea blue . . .
> In it soaring billows leap up to touch the sky,
> High waves pour onto the sun.
> They swallow and disgorge a hundred rivers,
> Rushing and churning up ten thousand ravines.
> Light mists lingering,
> Water boiling in the splendid cauldron . . . .
> Swirling foam caps the mountains,
> Rushing billows empty the valleys.
> Hard rocks are smashed by them,
> Curving banks are crushed and collapse . . . .
> (*PTCC*, 84)

7. A scene of Mount Lu: "In it soaring billows leap up to touch the sky,/High waves pour onto the sun" (Pao Chao).

西南望廬山
又特驚異
基壓江潮
峯與辰漢相接
上常積雲霞
雕錦縟
若華夕曜
巖澤氣通
傳明散綵
赫似絳天
左右青靄
表裡紫霄
從嶺而上
氣盡金光
半山以下
純爲黛色....

Pao Chao
IN SEARCH OF EXPRESSION

其中騰波觸天
高浪灌日
吞吐百川
寫泄萬壑
輕煙不流
華鼎振渚....
回沫冠山
奔濤空谷
磕石爲之摧碎
碕岸爲之蟦落....

It is important to note that Pao begins his description with details about the shades of color and light as they play against the multiple forms of clouds and mountain peaks. The description, so full of visual richness, is almost charged with a dreamlike quality. And as if to remind himself of the treacherous nature of all beautiful things, he finally builds the climax of his description around the image of the tossing and reckless waves that seem to threaten the entire universe. This procedure of description seems to be most satisfying for Pao Chao, since he prefers to view landscape as an energetic visual exploration. More specifically, the whirling tides seem to correspond to his feeling of excitement, as he describes to his sister quite vividly:

> I look at the Big Fire Star above,
> And listen to the sound of the waves below.
> Shivering, I hold my breath,
> My heart is startled.
> (*PTCC*, 84)

仰視大火
俯聽波聲
愁魄脅息
心驚慓矣

Yet Pao cannot remain a spectator of the landscape; he has to move on, however difficult the journey may be. He ends his letter by promising his sister that, despite all the hardships and adversities that he may yet experience in this trip, he will be sure to take good care of himself until reaching his destination:

> The wind blows in the thundering gale, and I shall be very careful on the road at night. Around the time of the half-moon, I hope I will have arrived at the appointed place. It is difficult to adjust to changes of climate; you must take special care of yourself. Guard yourself well morning and night, and do not worry about me....
> (*PTCC*, 85)

Pao Chao
IN SEARCH OF EXPRESSION

風吹雷颼，夜戒前路，下弦內外，望達所屆。寒暑難適，汝專自慎。夙夜戒護，勿我為念。...

Thus the combination of an expressive voice and an impressive description is most successfully achieved in Pao's prose. I do not wish to imply, however, that all of Pao's five-character *shih* are inferior to his prose in terms of scenic description. Rather, I would like to make an important qualification: whereas his description of large-scale landscape appears to be most innovatively effective in his prose, his five-character *shih* excels in the microscopic details of things. In other words, we seem to witness in his *shih* poetry a shift of focus new to the age—from large and general appearances of mountains and waters to small and particular objects. This new tendency, however, is by no means opposed to traditional literary criteria. For it is rooted in the same aesthetic orientation that governs the original *shan-shui* poetry, namely that of verisimilitude.

For an illustration, we may take the following poem entitled, "I Met a Lonely *T'ung* Tree on My Journey to the Mountain":

> A *t'ung* tree grows amidst a cluster of rocks,
> Its roots are buried alone beneath the cold, dark earth.
> Above, it leans against the receding bank,
> Below, it reaches deep into the cave. 4
> Rapid torrents shoot forth violently in the winter,
> Fog and rain are incessant in the summer.
> Before the autumn frost its leaves are already withered,
> Even without wind its branches moan by themselves. 8
> At dusk and in broad daylight sad thoughts pile up,
> Day and night, sorrowful birds call.
> The abandoned woman, looking at it, will cover her face and weep,
> The exiled official, facing it, will press his heart and sigh. 12
> Though it gives comfort to solitary and brave souls,
> Its own grief and loneliness cannot be borne.
> "I wish to be carved and hewn,
> To become a zither in your hall." 16
>   (*PTCC*, 410)

桐生叢石裡
根孤地寒陰
上倚崩岸勢
下帶洞阿深
奔泉冬激射
霧雨夏霖霏

Pao Chao
IN SEARCH OF EXPRESSION

未霜葉已肅
不風條自吟
昏明積苦思
晝夜叫哀禽
棄妾望掩淚
逐臣對撫心
雖以慰單危
悲涼不可任
幸願見雕斲
爲君堂上琴

We find that all the descriptions in the poem are about the *t'ung* tree itself—about its location, its shape, its mournful sound, even its practical use. Instead of moving from scene to scene like a camera eye, the poet concentrates on the various aspects of one thing. The impression is one of the intense focus not unlike that of a closeup. The author's projection of feeling into the tree is also striking, since it is a projection that comes from the very process of concentration. We know from experience that when we look long and steadily upon an object, we tend to identify ourselves with it. There is always something calm and static about such an experience, and this characterizes precisely the descriptive style of Pao's poems on objects.[19]

This technique of concentrated elaboration was by no means new; it had already been developed by authors in the *fu* genre, the so-called *yung-wu fu*.[20] Since Han times these "*fu* on objects" were regarded as parallel to the epideictic *fu*, with the one focusing on individual objects and the other on large-scale landscapes. Between these two types of *fu* Pao obviously favored the one on *yung-wu*, as may be seen from the fact that although he had produced many *fu* on objects (*PTCC*, 24–49), so far as we can know he had not written a single epideictic *fu*. Nothing could be more striking than the differences between Pao and Hsieh in their descriptive preferences in *fu*. It may be that each poet seized upon a particular stylistic tendency in *fu* and developed it into a *shih* style to his own taste. In any case, the concept of verisimilitude in *shih* is originally based upon the aesthetic principle of the descriptive *fu* in general.

Here again, Pao's innovation lies in his search for variety. His is a visual approach to life, one based on the descriptive mode of presentation so typical of his time. As is only natural in a poet of great vitality, he is not satisfied with the mere description of natural objects learned from his predecessors. Yet the very impulse that enables him to concentrate on things, the very energy that makes it possible for him to perceive life in its interrelations—all these same

---

[19] For other *shih* poems on "objects," see *PTCC*, 392–397, 409, 411.
[20] See, for example, *WH*, *chüan* 13 and 14, I, 270–290.

Pao Chao
IN SEARCH OF EXPRESSION

forces he now applies to the creation of a human world in poetry. Thus, we find that his *yung-wu* techniques ultimately serve to express his aesthetic appreciation of human qualities; the elaborate description of natural objects becomes now the sensory depiction of female beauty.

II. Description and Narration

In one of his *shih* poems Pao Chao tells of a chance encounter with two beautiful women:

IMITATION OF THE OLD STYLE

North wind in the twelfth month,	
Snow falls like scattering kerchiefs.	
This is truly a miserable season,	
In heavy spirits I think of my loved ones.	4
By chance I met two young women,	
Like me, they are both from Lo-yang.	
Beautiful and pleasing, they have good-looking eyes and brows,	
Graceful and refined, their wastelines are delicate.	8
Their fine complexions are as white as snow,	
Bright and radiant, they appear like goddesses.	
From their long glances emerge enticing looks,	
From their red lips comes a seductive voice.	12
Their lapels and garments are rich in colorful designs,	
Their jewelry replete with precious stones.	
Striking a chord, they both began to dance,	
And sing for me songs to shake the rafters:	16
"What's important in life is to realize our goals,	
Our long cherished hope will be achieved through you.	
Luckily in this severe winter evening,	
The night is deep, it is not yet dawn.	20
We have already put out two colorful quilts on the bed,	
With two decorated pillows side by side.	
We hope you rest early,	
We will save our songs for the spring."	24

    (*PTCC*, 355)

學古

北風十二月
雪下如亂巾

Pao Chao
IN SEARCH OF EXPRESSION

實是愁苦節
惆悵憶情親
會得兩少妾
同是洛陽人
嬽綵好眉目
閑麗美腰身
凝膚皎若雪
明淨色如神
驕愛生盼矚
聲媚起朱脣
衿服雜緹繢
首飾亂瓊珍
調弦俱起舞
爲我唱梁塵
人生貴得意
懷願待君申
幸值嚴冬暮
幽夜方未晨
齊衾久兩設
角枕已雙陳
願君早休息
留歌待三春

In this poem we have a world of personal experience: a rather romantic encounter and a delight in the sensual play of life. What is unusual is a spontaneously sensory style, marked by ornate images and flowing narrative. There is an element of romance and adventure, which seems to be dramatically opposed to his poems on objects.

Yet, upon closer scrutiny, we realize that the descriptive approach employed in this poem is none other than that which Pao Chao uses to describe his natural objects, namely, a concentrated focus on details. The only changes are in the nature of the object and the setting of description, for the poem's focus now is the beauty of women: their eyebrows (line 7), their waists (line 8), their rosy lips and charming voices (line 12), their elegant attire (line 13), their jewelry (line 14). It is not surprising that Pao Chao's distinctly sensory approach would bring about a new realism of description. What he has created is an intermediate style in which natural realism and ornate sensualism are combined. From the beginning he prefers the mixed rather than the pure landscape description. And it should be remembered that his natural bent is to combine the landscape-oriented description typical of the Chang Hsieh tradition and the elegant sensuality typical of Chang Hua's style, as is pointed out by Chung Jung in his *Shih-p'in*.

Pao Chao
IN SEARCH OF EXPRESSION

In Pao Chao's case, however, the literary impact is more than that of the descriptive. As can be seen from the poem cited above, the narrative structure is equally, if not more, impressive. It focuses on the world of reality and deals with both the inner and outer movements of a particular event. The story is relatively simple: a lonely traveler, suffering from cold and a yearning for home, has found a temporary refuge in the sensual pleasure provided by two beautiful and cultivated ladies coming originally from his home town, Loyang. What is striking is the combination of visual and aural phenomena in this poem, as in a great majority of Pao's poems. For it is the temporal nature of music that effectively conveys the intrinsic value of the moments and intensifies the narrative tempo. The man and the women meet unexpectedly at one point in their lives, and will again proceed to lead their individual lives as soon as the night is over. The brevity of their communication is made more poignant by the affecting power of the music played by the beauties.

Yet the meeting of these people is more than one of physical attraction—it is rather a meeting of minds. Women in Pao's poetry are much more alive and communicative than the female personages in earlier poetry. Quite evidently there is in Pao a basic trust in the female capacity; he seems to understand the individually human and concrete in women. The result is that he has presented an image of women that has not been explored previously in poetry—that is, an image of woman as *chih-yin*, the ideal understanding friend of men.[21]

As *chih-yin* in Pao's poetry, women are almost always musicians who express their innermost feelings through lyrical songs. Reading Pao Chao one is often struck by the frequency with which music comes to dominate the poetic situation. Yet the value of music played by his women—who possess sensitivity, taste, and understanding—lies rather in the intent of the musician. For at the root of the musical expression there are cultural refinements and tender feelings. The more one penetrates into the musician's emotional intent, the more one can appreciate the beauty of her musical notes. In other words, true music is beyond sounds. In the following poem Pao Chao attempts to communicate this view:

> The winter night is deep; deep in the night you sit and chant,
> Before you begin to sing, I already know your feeling.
> Frost entering the curtain,
> The wind blowing round the trees.   4
> The rosy lamp is extinguished,
> Your rosy face I seek,

---

[21] Of course, one might argue that the image of the woman in T'ao Ch'ien's "*Fu* on Calming the Passions" (*Hsien-ch'ing fu*) is quite similar to this, but T'ao does not develop such an idea elsewhere. However, with Pao Chao the image of women as *chih-yin* is a predominant one.

Pao Chao
IN SEARCH OF EXPRESSION

> I understand your song,
> I follow your voice,   8
> Not valuing the sound,
> But valuing its deep meaning.
>   (*PTCC*, 252)

冬夜沈沈夜坐吟
含聲未發已知心
霜入幕
風度林
朱燈滅
朱顏尋
體君歌
逐君音
不貴聲
貴意深

With this idea of women as *chih-yin* is connected Pao Chao's creative treatment of the theme of separation, particularly the anguished separation from one's wife. As has been mentioned previously, Pao Chao himself had to leave home for prolonged public, especially military, service. The harsh circumstances of conscription that took place frequently in China at his time—marked often by long separations and death—were thus quite real to him. This personal experience gives his social poetry, which constitutes a great majority of his works, a more human approach and a popular appeal to the common people, so that even people in China today grant him the prestigeous title: "the people's poet."[22]

From the viewpoint of the literary development, Pao's "social realism" is not the only reason that sets him apart from his predecessors. The theme of separation with regard to the unmerciful conscription system is as old as the *Book of Songs*. And the longing for one's husband, participating in faraway frontier battles, had been a favorite theme in the tradition of *yüeh-fu* from the times of Eastern Han. In my opinion, Pao's innovation lies in his transforming the conventional inner-chamber lament into one with a male perspective. Now it is the husband himself, not the wife, who expresses his intense yearning for home. We see that again the female image, through the detailed description by the male persona, emerges at the center of interest. Only a poet who truly appreciates the qualities of women could write a poem such as the following:

---

[22] J. D. Frodsham and Ch'eng Hsi, trans., *An Anthology of Chinese Verse: Han Wei Chin and the Northern and Southern Dynasties* (Oxford: Clarendon Press, 1967), p. 142.

Pao Chao
IN SEARCH OF EXPRESSION

Dreaming of Returning Home

With streaming tears I leave the outer city gate,
Holding my sword, I set out on the empty road.
The desert wind arises out of the dark sky,
My nostalgic heart longs for my home town.   4
At midnight, I sleep on a solitary pillow,
I dream that for a moment I have returned home:
My widowed wife sighs at the door,
She draws silk from cocoons, or else clacks her loom.   8
Joyfully reunited we speak of the long separation,
Together we return to the beautiful bedchamber.
Chilly, the cold air beneath the eaves;
Hazy, the moon beams through the curtains.   12
Cut orchids vie with her for fragrance,
Picked chrysanthemums compete with her beauty.
She opens her toilet case, more fragrant than sweet-smelling
    herbs;
I tug at her sleeve, and untie her tasselled belt.   16
In my dream the road far away was near,
After awakening the great river blocks my way.
Startled, I get up and sigh in vain,
In confusion, my spirits flies away.   20
The white water is vast and boundless,
The high mountains are lofty and majestic.
Billows ebb and flow, forever changing,
Wind and frost turns the flourishing to decay.   24
This land is not my land;
My heart is full: to whom, now, do I tell it?
    (*PTCC*, 384)

夢還鄉

銜淚出郭門
撫劍無人逵
沙風暗空起
離心眷鄉畿
夜分就孤枕
夢想暫言歸
孀婦當戶歎
繰絲復鳴機
慊款論久別
相將還綺闈

Pao Chao
IN SEARCH OF EXPRESSION

歷歷簷下涼
朧朧帳裡暉
刈蘭爭芬芳
探菊競葳蕤
開奩奪香蘇
探袖解纓微
夢中長路近
覺後大江違
驚起空歎息
恍惚神魄飛
白水漫浩浩
高山壯巍巍
波瀾異往復
風霜改榮衰
此土非吾土
慷慨當告誰

The most disheartening reality revealed in this poem is that the lonely soldier's communication with his wife can be sought only in dreams. His dream-search for his wife, a search which would inevitably fail in reality, is a poignant reminder of the helpless situation in which he finds himself. Yet the important thing is that the author's deep urge for social justice is not expressed through direct criticism; rather, it gives expression to a moving narrative that details the reunion scene in a dream. Most importantly, the narration of the dream is done in the same spirit as the descriptive closeup with the wife's action in focus (lines 8–16). The speaker of the poem makes sure even to include one decisive bedroom scene which tells of the details of the couple's intimacy (lines 15–16). Clearly Pao's visual imagination has given his narrative a concrete and imagistic appeal.

Sometimes it is the device of dialogue or direct discourse that serves as the focus of the narration. With such a device, the dramatic tension of the moment is emphasized and different points of view introduced. What follows is a pertinent example from his famous *yüeh-fu* series, "Imitation of 'the Hardships of Travel'" ("*Ni hsing-lu nan*"):

> Spring birds are chirping days and nights,
> They most afflict a worthy's troubled thoughts.
> When I first left home to join the army,
> My glorious ambition, my zealous spirits, reached as high as the   4
>   clouds.
> Three years have drifted by slowly since we wandered from
>   place to place,
> Suddenly I found my hair and beard turning white.

Pao Chao
IN SEARCH OF EXPRESSION

In the evening by the riverside I had plucked out all the white hair,
But the next day in the mirror, I saw it thick again. 8
I feared I would die on the road and be a wandering ghost,
My mind disappearing into Nothingness, reduced to Essence in the Great Void.[23]
Whenever I thought of my homeland,
I groaned with dismay as I remembered my old acquaintances. 12
Suddenly there came a passing stranger, asking me who I was.
"Can it be that you know my family back in Southern Town?"
He answered: "I once lived in your town,
And knew you were serving in office here. 16
I have traveled thousands of miles from that city,
And still I am on the road to distant assignments.
Before I set out I heard that your wife
Lived alone in her chamber like a widow, her chastity well-known. 20
Some said she wept bitterly in her quiet room in the morning,
Others told how she grew mournful at night, her tears soaking her robes.
Her face was haggard, unlike her former cheerfulness,
With her hair disheveled, her face grown thin, she never again adorned herself. 24
Looking at her makes one sad,
I hope you will never forget her."
(*PTCC*, 239)

春禽喈喈旦暮鳴
最傷君子憂思情
我初辭家從軍僑
榮志溢氣干雲霄
流浪漸冉經三齡
忽有白髮素髭生

[23] See also Chapter 21 of Lao Tzu's *Tao-te ching*:
... As a thing the way is shadowy, indistinct.
Indistinct and shadowy,
Yet within it is an image;
Shadowy and indistinct,
Yet within it is a substance.
Dim and dark,
Yet within it is an essence. ...
(D. C. Lau, trans., *Tao Te Ching: Tao Te Ching*, 1962; rpt. 1983, New York: Penguin Books, 1983, p. 78)

Pao Chao
IN SEARCH OF EXPRESSION

今暮臨水拔已盡
明日對鏡復已盈
但恐羈死爲鬼客
客思寄滅生空精
每懷舊鄉野
念我舊人多悲聲
忽見過客問何我
寧知我家在南城
答云我曾居君鄉
知君遊宦在此城
我行離邑已萬里
今方羈役去遠征
來時聞君婦
閨中孀居獨宿有貞名
亦云朝悲泣閒房
又聞暮思淚霑裳
形容憔悴非昔悅
蓬鬢衰顏不復妝
見此令人有餘悲
當願君懷不暫忘

One cannot fail to notice an interesting shift in the middle of the poem: a shift from monologue to dialogue, marked by a sudden rhythmic change in line 11.[24] Thus the poem begins with a lyrical expression and moves on to a dramatic interplay between the speaker and the stranger. The dramatic shift is important: on the one hand, we see the lonely soldier living in total despair in separation, and at the same time we come to learn that his poor wife at home suffers equally from social injustice.

The change of the poet's viewpoint is a conventional device frequently used in the *yüeh-fu* songs since the Han.[25] But what is most important in Pao Chao's poem is still the lyrical voice that introduces the poet's innermost feelings at the outset. Dramatic elements no doubt intensify the impression that the suffering individual must eventually be seen as the product of the world, but it is the lyrical center that unifies the self and the world. The lyric self seems to speak from the middle of life, letting us feel his presence amidst all human encounters. It might be more exact to say that for Pao Chao it is always the lyrical blending of the narrative, the descriptive, or the dramatic

---

[24] Perhaps this is why some scholars considered this poem to be originally two poems. See Chung Ch'i, *Chung-ku shih-ko lun-ts'ung* (Hong Kong: Shanghai Book Co., 1965), pp. 97–99.

[25] See Hans Frankel, "Six Dynasties *Yüeh-fu* and Their Singers," *Journal of the Chinese Language Teachers Association*, 13 (1978), 192–195.

that seems most powerful. Significantly, this literary accomplishment is rooted in his profound consciousness of widely varying human conditions.

III. The Lyrical Self and Its World

Pao Chao's poetry has become a link between the external world and his private world: he is most skillful in reflecting his own experiences in poetry, while at the same time objectifying himself in the diverse phenomena of life. He always asks questions about the relationship between the self and its world: How should the self-reflecting individual react to the external world? Should one accept one's fate without question, or rebel against the injustice of society? To these questions Pao Chao does not seem to have satisfactory answers, but he feels confident that there are important lessons to be drawn from his own experience which he wants to share with his readers. What is particularly interesting is that he hopes not only to talk to them but to sing to them the message of his heart. Thus, in the opening poem to his *yüeh-fu* series "Imitation of 'the Hardships of Travel,'" Pao sings to the reader in an impassioned tone:

> ...I wish you would stop grieving and brood no more,
> And listen to my songs of "the Hardships of Travel."
> Have you not seen the Cypress Beam Tower and the Bronze Bird Tower?[26]
> Where can you find the pure music of these ancient flutes now?
> (*PTCC*, 224)
> ...願君裁悲且減思
> 聽我抵節行路吟
> 不見柏梁銅雀上
> 寧聞古時清吹音

It is most fitting that it is through the *yüeh-fu* form that these lines are delivered. *Yüeh-fu* were essentially "song words," to which musical notes were assigned. That music is an analogue for lyric poetry is a long-accepted belief since early antiquity in China. The lyrical impact of music comes largely from its power to "affect" the listener, the *chih-yin* who "knows the tone." If there is any form that Pao Chao should find to be most effective in

---

[26] The Cypress Beam Tower in Ch'ang-an was built by Emperor Wu of Han in 108 B.C. The name of the tower became famous because of a poetic form called "the Cypress Beam style," which is said to have been invented by the Emperor and his officials during one of their literary gatherings on the Cypress Beam Platform. For a history of the Bronze Bird Tower, see Section IV of Chapter Four in this book.

delivering his innermost feelings to an understanding audience, it must be this important song form called *yüeh-fu*.²⁷

Yet, even if we ignore the musical aspect of Pao's *yüeh-fu*—as indeed we must, due to the loss of the music—we can still see that Pao Chao's choice of the genre is an ingenious one. Judged by the *shih* standards, the *yüeh-fu* style, both in diction and syntax, is overly colloquial. In particular, the lines of irregular length often used in *yüeh-fu* permit one to express innermost feelings without restraint. For these reasons the power of Pao's lyrical directness is most strongly felt in his *yüeh-fu* songs. Perhaps, as some traditional critics pointed out, this was why the T'ang poet Tu Fu praised Pao Chao so highly.²⁸

At this point we should note one very interesting phenomenon about Pao's poetic style: while his descriptive *shih* of "mountains and waters" are basically rooted in the tradition of Hsieh Ling-yün, his *yüeh-fu* poetry—in terms of its lyrical forcefulness—rather resembles the *shih* poetry of T'ao Ch'ien. As has been mentioned earlier, the concept of verisimilitude was fashionable during this time, and it was only natural for Pao Chao to model some of his works on Hsieh Ling-yün, the famed master of landscape poetry. However, T'ao Ch'ien's poetry was long ignored in the literary circles, let alone treated as a literary model.²⁹ Did Pao Chao in any sense inherit poetic techniques from T'ao Ch'ien? If so, what was his connection with this earlier author?

Based on the sources available today, Pao indeed was the first poet known to have looked up to T'ao Ch'ien as a precursor. In A.D. 452, when Pao Chao was thirty-eight years old, he produced a *shih* poem entitled "An Imitation of T'ao Ch'ien's Style" (*PTCC*, 362), expressing openly his respect for T'ao Ch'ien's literary greatness. While Pao Chao also wrote other poems in imitation of the works of such famous authors as Ts'ao Chih, Juan Chi, and Lu Chi (*PTCC*, 172, 361, 165), his poem on T'ao Ch'ien must have created a great, if not sensational, impact. For some years later a younger poet Chiang Yen (444–505) also wrote a poem on T'ao Ch'ien (*CHSK*, II, 1047), following in the footsteps of Pao Chao. Viewed from the perspective of literary history, Pao Chao's radical role at the time as the first sympathetic revisionist of the evaluation of T'ao Ch'ien was an extremely crucial one.

Many stylistic features of T'ao Ch'ien's *shih* can be found in Pao Chao's

---

²⁷ So far as we know, Juan Chi, Tso Ssu, Kuo P'u, and T'ao Ch'ien did not produce any *yüeh-fu* songs. Although Hsi K'ang, Lu Chi, and Hsieh Ling-yün all wrote *yüeh-fu* songs, their *yüeh-fu* are much inferior to their *shih* poems. Unlike his predecessors, Pao Chao best excelled in the *yüeh-fu* form. For a more detailed discussion of this subject, see Lee Chik-fong, *Hsieh T'iao shih yen-chiu*, printed with *Hsieh Hsüan-ch'eng shih-chu* (Hong Kong: Universal Book Co., 1968), p. 4–5.

²⁸ This refers to Tu Fu's line, "How great and outstanding Inspector Pao's [Pao Chao's] poetry is," in his poem entitled "Thinking of Li Po on a Spring Day." For the views of later critics on this comment, see *PTCC*, 281.

²⁹ It is interesting to note that Hsieh Ling-yün did not mention T'ao Ch'ien's name even once in his extant writings.

Pao Chao
IN SEARCH OF EXPRESSION

yüeh-fu—chief among them a preference for flowing syntax, a deliberate use of colloquial diction, a frequent play of rhetorical questions and dialogue. As has been mentioned in Chapter One, these are just the qualities that are played down as unpoetic by poets in fifth-century China. Certainly there is at the same time in Pao Chao's poetry a strong sensory dimension created by the imagistic description of objects, which seems to be opposed to T'ao Ch'ien's unadorned imagery. Yet, in regard to rhetoric, Pao Chao definitely prefers T'ao Ch'ien's style to the currently predominant ones. Even in terms of thought, Pao's poetry often echoes the same kinds of philosophy and reasoning that are typical of T'ao Ch'ien's. Compare the following examples:

T'ao Ch'ien:

> Heaven and earth last without end,
> Mountains and rivers never change.
> Grass and trees keep the natural rhythm—
> Frost and dew make them flourish or wither.
> I say man is the most sentient and wisest of all,
> Yet he alone is not like this.
>   (*TYMC*, 35)

天地長不沒
山川無改時
草木得常理
霜露榮悴之
謂人最靈智
獨復不如茲

Pao Chao:

> Have you not seen the grass by the riverside?
> In winter it withered and died; in spring it filled the roads.
> Have you not seen the sun above the city wall?
> At night it retreats, and vanishes from sight,
> Yet, next morning, it comes out again.
> How can I ever be like them?
> Once I die, I shall descend to the Yellow Springs forever.
>   (*PTCC*, 230)

君不見河邊草
冬時枯死春滿道
君不見城上日
今暝沒盡去
明朝復更出
今我何時當得然
一去永滅入黃泉

Pao Chao
IN SEARCH OF EXPRESSION

Both passages offer a sharp contrast between the ceaseless renewal of nature and the transience of human life. Both poets are concerned with the problem of death, of how to accept the inevitable end of life. In his deathbed dirge T'ao Ch'ien writes about the fact that "once the dark tomb is closed/I shall never see the sunlight again for a thousand years" (lines 9–10). And Pao Chao conveys the same feeling in his *yüeh-fu*:

> Once gone, we can never return,
> A thousand autumns, ten thousand years,
>   there will be no word from us.
>   (*PTCC*, 237)
> 一去無還期
> 千秋萬歲無音詞

It should be noted that the idea about the finality of death became conventional in dirge literature as early as the third century.[30] But T'ao Ch'ien and Pao Chao were the two major poets around the fifth century who made an effort to revive this old theme in poetry, and attempted to give it a new meaning. Pao Chao seemed to be particularly influenced by T'ao Ch'ien in his treatment of the topic. For example, to the problem of death Pao offers a solution similar to T'ao Ch'ien's—that is, "since life is short, enjoy drinking while you may." Pao Chao concludes his "Imitation of 'the Hardships of Travel'" with the following advice:

> With wine before us, we compose long verses,
> Leave our miserable lot with heaven.
> Let us fill our goblets with the best brews,
> And not grudge the hundred cash lying at our beds....
>   (*PTCC*, 243)
> 對酒叙長篇
> 窮途運命委皇天
> 但願樽中九醞滿
> 莫惜牀頭百個錢....

What really sets Pao Chao apart from T'ao Ch'ien's influence is a different attitude toward society. Unlike T'ao Ch'ien, who is primarily interested in realizing his self-conception through a reconciled acceptance of nature, Pao Chao's target is society. While T'ao Ch'ien talks mostly to himself, Pao Chao addresses, or rather sings, to his fellow men—especially to those who adopt the pose of social outcasts. As a result, Pao's lyricism has acquired a new dramatic quality with a direct rhetorical impact. He confesses to the reader

---

[30] For a discussion of this subject, see Susan Cherniack, "The Eulogy for Emperor Wen, and Its Generic and Biographical Contexts" (draft, 1984).

Pao Chao
IN SEARCH OF EXPRESSION

that he wishes to give full expression to his feelings, but dares not do so—a subtle complaint about the lack of freedom in Chinese society:

> My heart is not made of wood or stone—how can I have no feeling?
> Yet I repress my anger, hesitate, and dare not speak.
>   (*PTCC*, 229)
> 心非木石豈無感
> 吞聲躑躅不敢言

It will not be surprising to see that Pao Chao's frequent complaints against fate are in fact veiled criticisms of society. Let us take a close look at his famous *yüeh-fu* series, "Imitation of 'the Hardships of Travel.'" Its title, borrowed from an ancient tune title "The Hardships of Travel" ("*hsing-lu nan*"), serves clearly as a metaphor for life's troubles. There are eighteen poems in this series, each focusing on a particular aspect of life's misery. According to the poet, the most tormenting situations in life, namely, separation and poverty, are caused largely by social injustice. Soliders are forced to undergo all kinds of adversity on the frontier without reward, virtuous wives are abandoned, members of poor families have no hope of promotion. Living in the Six Dynasties society, where the future of an individual was practically class-determined, Pao Chao understood only too well the evils of such a society. It was only natural that he emerged as a silent questioner of the social values, if not an open dissenter. In the following lines we see the merging of the poet's voice and that of a frustrated official:

> Facing the table, I cannot eat,
> I draw my sword, strike the pillar, and heave a long sigh.
> How long can a man live?
> How can I allow myself to stumble about with folded wings?
> Let me give up all this, leave my post and go,
> Back to my family to take my rest....
>   (*PTCC*, 231)
> 對案不能食
> 拔劍擊柱長嘆息
> 丈夫生世會幾時
> 安能蹀躞垂羽翼
> 棄置罷官去
> 還家自休息....

Yet all these criticisms he dares not voice openly against society, let alone against the government. The numerous instances of execution which had befallen the major poets after the Wei-Chin period—Hsi K'ang, Chang Hua, P'an Yüeh, Kuo P'u, Hsieh Ling-yün—were enough to warn him against any outspoken judgment. But surely it is harmless to attribute the individual's sufferings to fate, and this last consideration has a bearing upon the poet's rather disillusioned yet ironic tone of voice:

> Our life is guided by Fate,
> Why should we sigh as we walk, grieve as we sit?
>   (*PTCC*, 229)
> 人生自有命
> 安能行嘆復坐愁

> Gentlemen, do not sigh over your poverty,
> Wealth and high position are not man's to decide.
>   (*PTCC*, 243)
> 諸君莫嘆貧
> 富貴不由人

Pao Chao's social criticism, implicit or explicit, reminds one of the Western Chin poet Tso Ssu, whom the critic Chung Jung refers to as one of T'ao Ch'ien's precursors.[31] Like Pao Chao, Tso Ssu came from a poor family and often revealed his bitterness against the injustice of society. From the Han Dynasty the Chinese social system was such that good family background, rather than personal accomplishments, became the key to success. In one of his "Poems on History" (*Yung-shih shih*), Tso Ssu openly criticizes this class-determined system through a metaphorical device:

> Lush and green, the pine trees at the valley's depths,
> Drooping down, the small sprouts atop the mountain.
> Though their stalks are only one inch thick,
> They overshadow the hundred-foot pines.   4
> Sons of prominent families mince their way to the top,
> While brilliant men sink to lowly offices.
> The terrain of the earth brings this about,
> It is not the work of one day.   8
> The Chin's and the Chang's rely on their ancient heritage,
> For seven generations they wore the official sable of the Han.
> Master Feng, was he not great?
> Though his hair had turned white, he was still not summoned.[32]   12
>   (*CHSK*, I, 385)
> 鬱鬱澗底松
> 離離山上苗

[31] See *SPC*, 41. Chung Jung points out that T'ao Ch'ien derives his "lyrical forcefulness" (*feng-li*) from Tso Ssu.

[32] This refers to Feng T'ang, who lived from the reign of Emperor Wen to that of Emperor Wu of Han.

Pao Chao
IN SEARCH OF EXPRESSION

以彼徑寸莖
蔭此百尺條
世冑躡高位
英俊沈下僚
地勢使之然
由來非一朝
金張藉舊業
七葉珥漢貂
馮公豈不偉
白首不見召

We have no way of proving whether Pao Chao knew of this particular poem by Tso Ssu, but the important point is that Pao Chao did compare himself to this earlier poet, who came from a similar family background and who understood what it meant to work his way up from a lower level of the social strata. This can be attested to by the fact that when Emperor Hsiao-wu (Sung Hsiao-wu ti) asked Pao Chao about his sister Pao Ling-hui, Pao responded with a most interesting answer that obviously came from the poet's unconscious, or rather conscious, affinity to Tso Ssu:

> My younger sister's talent is of course not as great as Tso Fen's, and my ability is inferior to T'ai-ch'ung's [Tso Ssu's].[33]
> 臣妹才自亞於左芬，臣才不及太沖爾。

Pao Chao did not withdraw from the reality of society, did not abandon it, did not keep aloof from it—instead, he attempted to face it. Reading Pao's poetry, one gets the impression that the events of contemporary history seemed to affect him much more strongly than they did the earlier poets. And nothing can demonstrate more poignantly and directly Pao's devotion to history than his "*Fu* on the Desolate City" ("*Wu-ch'eng fu*"). This *fu* represents the moment in poetry when the poetic act of self-definition parallels historical movements. It is about the tragic fall of the city Kuang-ling, on the site of Yangchow in today's Kiangsu. The city had been the center of a region of wealth and a vital strategic point between the north and south since the Han dynasty. Suddenly in A.D. 459 the Lord Ching-ling (Liu Tan), a brother of the Emperor and a feudal lord whose troops garrisoned the city of Kuang-ling, took up arms against the Liu-Sung government. In a fit of anger Emperor Hsiao-wu ordered that the rebels be annihilated right away and the entire city destroyed. More than three thousand innocent residents were killed in the massacre, and overnight Kuang-ling became a deserted wasteland. Pao Chao revisited the city some months after the incident, where he witnessed the extent of the destruction:

[33] Tso Fen, a known poetess, was Tso Ssu's younger sister. This passage is cited in *SPC*, 69–70.

Pao Chao
IN SEARCH OF EXPRESSION

Damp mosses cling to the well,
Tangles of kudzu vine snare the path;
Halls are laced with vipers and crawling things,
Musk deer and flying squirrel quarrel by the stairs....
The painted doors, the gaily stitched hangings,
Sites where once were halls of song, pavilions of the dance,
Jasper pools, trees of jadeite,
Lodges for those who hunt in woods, who fish the shores,
Music of Wu, Ts'ai, Ch'i, Ch'in,
Vessels in shapes of fish and dragon, sparrow and horse—
All have lost their incense, gone to ash,
Their radiance engulfed, their echoes cut off.
Mysterious princess from the Eastern Capital,
Beautiful lady from a southern land,
With heart of orchis, limbs of white lawn,
Marble features, carmine lip—
None whose soul is not entombed in somber stone,
Whose bones do not lie dwindling in the dust....[34]

澤葵依井
荒葛胃塗
壇羅虺蜮
階鬥麝鼯....
若夫藻扃黼帳
歌堂舞閣之基
璇淵碧樹
弋林釣渚之館
吳蔡齊秦之聲
魚龍爵馬之玩
皆薰歇燼滅
光沈響絕
東都妙姬
南國麗人
蕙心紈質
玉貌絳脣
莫不埋魂幽石
委骨窮塵....

Pao Chao's descriptive realism is a product of his period, for the mixing of detailed description and social realism is itself a part of the contemporary atmosphere. In sharp contrast to the many Han *fu* masterpieces which elabo-

---

[34] Translation taken from Burton Watson, trans., *Chinese Rhyme-Prose*, pp. 93–94.

Pao Chao
IN SEARCH OF EXPRESSION

rate on, or rather exaggerate, the splendor and prosperity of cities,[35] Pao Chao's *fu* is deliberately realistic about scenes of devastation and horror. His realism is also different from Tso Ssu's—while Tso Ssu's "*Fu* on Three Capitals" advocates historical and geographical accuracy,[36] Pao's *fu* is based upon visual impression and an emotional response to the scene. If anything, "*Fu* on the Desolate City," with its lyrical focus on the moment of perception, has become more a *shih* poem than a *fu*.

Pao's indirect criticism of Emperor Hsiao-wu's ruthless massacre of the common people is perhaps even more important. If there was anyone who was most familiar with the thriving atmosphere of Kuang-ling city of the past, it was Pao Chao himself. All his former superiors—the Lord of Lin-ch'uan, the Lord of Heng-yang, the Lord of Shih-hsing—had from time to time taken charge of the city. As an official attendant to these lords, Pao Chao had an opportunity to become acquainted with the city and its people. Now, following the outbreak of the rebellion, there was hardly a soul left. It is indeed an irony that the people in Kuang-ling died not from any invasion from the northern "barbarians"—of whom they had been most apprehensive—but from a power struggle within the Chinese ruling class. Given his sympathetic involvement with the people, Pao Chao must certainly have been heartbroken to witness this tragedy:

> Dwell on it, listen in silence—
> It wounds the heart, breaking it in two.[37]
> 凝思寂聽
> 心傷已摧

Yet throughout his *fu* Pao dares not mention the name of the city "Kuang-ling," let alone the names of the Emperor and the rebel. Again, his realistic impulse to tell all has been thwarted. So he makes Heaven responsible for the merciless killing of the people:

> What is Heaven's way
> That so many should swallow their hatred?
> (*PTCC*, 13)
> 天道如何
> 吞恨者多

Then, as if to sound his protest against Heaven, the poet concludes his *fu* with a song of "the Desolate City":

---

[35] See, for example, the *fu* on metropolises and capitals by Pan Ku (A.D. 32–92) and Chang Heng (A.D. 78–139). In Knechtges, trans., *Wen xuan*, pp. 93–336.

[36] See Knechtges, trans., *Wen xuan*, pp. 337–477.

[37] Translation taken from Burton Watson, trans., *Chinese Rhyme-Prose*, p. 94.

Pao Chao
IN SEARCH OF EXPRESSION

> A thousand ages, ten thousand generations,
> All perish together like this—
> > What more is there to say?
> > (*PTCC*, 14)

千齡兮萬代
共盡兮何言

It could not be more of a coincidence that not long after Pao wrote this *fu* he was killed in the frantic tumult of a rebellion.[38] He finally perished with the destruction of a city, as if to fulfill the prophecy made in his poetry.

---

[38] The rebellion, which took place in Ching-chou in A.D. 466, was started by the Lord of Linhai under whom Pao then served.

IV

Hsieh T'iao

THE INWARD TURN OF LANDSCAPE

After the Liu-Sung Dynasty ended in 479, the capital, Chien-k'ang (i.e., today's Nanking), seemed somewhat different. Politics in Chien-k'ang now found a surprising balance with culture. In Chinese literature, this was the beginning of the Ch'i-Liang Era, the era in which the palace gradually became the literary as well as the political center in the south.[1] It was not that Chien-k'ang, the capital since 317, did not acquire its grandeur until this time. For the rich palaces in the capital had been the center in which the ruling clan enjoyed its luxurious life regardless of outside political turmoil. But with Emperor Wu of the Ch'i Dynasty (Ch'i Wu-ti), Chien-k'ang began to acquire a new quality of refinement through its sudden flowering of literary activities. The Emperor and two of his sons, namely, Hsiao Tzu-liang (460–494, Prince Ching-ling) and Hsiao Tzu-lung (474–494, later Prince Sui of Ching-chou), were all distinguished by an unusual poetic sensitivity and were largely responsible for this new phenomenon. Prince Ching-ling was especially known for his literary salon, to which practically all the aspiring poets at the time belonged. The meetings of the poets were frequently held in his grandiose West Residence (*hsi-ti*), which he built on the scenic Chi-lung Mountain in the capital district. It is only natural that under his patronage a great many literary talents were bred and aesthetic taste cultivated. The most eminent members of the salon were called "the eight friends of Prince Ching-ling" (*Ching-ling pa-yu*), who were at the center of the contemporary literary scene.[2]

---

[1] This refers only to the Ch'i and Liang periods in the Six Dynasties. The development of Nanking in Late Imperial China was quite different. See, for example, F. W. Mote, "The Transformation of Nanking: 1350–1400," in *The City in Late Imperial China*, ed. G. William Skinner (Stanford: Stanford Univ. Press, 1977), pp. 101–153.

[2] For the names of these poets, see Li Yen-shou, *Nan shih*, chüan 6, I, 168.

Hsieh T'iao

THE INWARD TURN OF LANDSCAPE

Hsieh T'iao (464–499), a poet who had become famous in the metropolitan court circle from the young age of fifteen, was the greatest talent among the "eight friends." He seemed to be born for this era of poetic renaissance and cultural gaiety. No other literary figure of the period had a better aristocratic lineage than he. His father came from the same family as Hsieh Ling-yün, his grandmother was a sister of the noted historian Fan Yeh, and his mother was Princess Ch'ang-ch'eng (Ch'ang-ch'eng kung-chu) of the Liu-Sung. And, as if literary history was purposely providing its own *raison d'être* for the new metropolitan culture, Hsieh T'iao was born right in the city of Chien-k'ang and certainly knew the flavor of palace life.

Most important, however, is that Hsieh T'iao's poetry comes to represent an awareness of self-containment surrounding the new literary salon to which the contemporary life and arts seemed to aspire. More exactly, the artistic consciousness begins to retreat into the literary garden, into the realm where life is the equivalent of art. In his "*Fu* on Visiting a Private Garden" ("*Yu hou-yüan fu*'"), Hsieh T'iao writes convincingly about the artistic nature of salon life:

Dense flowers, choice trees,
Secluded orchids, verdant bamboos.
Above, their lushness makes ample shade,
Below, row on row, they cover the valley.   4
To the left, fields of fragrant plants as far as the eye can see,
To the right, plains of aromatic grasses fill the view.
Mountains rise like rosy clouds, and are sheered off,
Waters are brilliant, they ebb and flow.   8
Now the dimness of the spacious open-air chambers,
And the loftiness of the cloud-high lodge.
Wandering around winding corridors up and down,
Facing the deep, wide jade halls,   12
I ponder hot summer's end,
I look for the first breezes on clear autumn days.
His special favor lets us wander freely,
Meeting, talking, and strolling about at leisure here.   16
Now the morning sun rests on elms and willows,
Rosy clouds reflect the setting sun.
Lonely cicadas disperse,
Departing birds fly in rows.   20
Gentle breezes abound, the curtained hall is quiet,
Soothing shadows rise, the water pavilion is cool.
Ivory utensils are laid out, along with jade ornaments,
We eat with orchid-patterned wares and drink cassia wine.   24

Hsieh T'iao
THE INWARD TURN OF LANDSCAPE

I look up at his noble bearing, beautiful beyond measure,
I revere his distinguished manner, as fine as jade.
Relying on his lofty command of literature, we engage in pure conversation,
As we prepare to chew our brushes and hold our pens.
This is as rich as looking at the boundless sea,
To visit the sage is to know our direction.
    (*HHCC*, 64)

積芳兮選木
幽蘭兮翠竹
上蕪蕪以蔭景
下田田兮被谷
左蕙畹兮彌望
右芝原兮寫目
山霞起而削成
水積明以經復
於是敞風閨之藹藹
聳雲館之苕苕
周步欄以升降
對玉堂之沈寥
追夏德之方暮
望秋淸之始飆
藉宴私而遊衍
特晤語而逍遙
爾乃旦棲楡柳
霞照夕陽
孤蟬以散
去鳥成行
惠氣湛兮惟殿肅
清陰起兮池館涼
陳象設兮以玉瑱
粉蘭藉兮咀桂漿
仰微塵兮美無度
奉英軌兮式如璋
藉高文兮淸談
預含毫兮握芳
則觀海兮爲富
乃遊聖兮知方

The subject of the *fu* is believed to be the garden in Prince Ching-ling's West Palace, where sumptuous parties, musical performances, and meetings of poets were held during the Yung-ming period (483–493).[3] Reading the opening lines of Hsieh T'iao's *fu*, one is inevitably reminded of Hsieh Ling-yün's "*Fu* on Dwelling in the Mountains." Despite its much shorter length, Hsieh T'iao's piece is also about an enclosed landscape where the quality of self-containment is valued. Like Hsieh Ling-yün, Hsieh T'iao employs the basic mode of descriptive similitude, with an attempt to present scenes in all directions and positions—"above," "below," "on the left," "on the right" (lines 3–6). The juxtaposition of mountain and water scenes in lines 7–8 is particularly familiar. But at this point the comparison stops. We are gradually led into winding corridors and jade halls (lines 11–12), slowly approaching the inner compound of the palace, where the rich and the well-born will have their party (lines 15–22). Everywhere there is a display of aristocratic plenitude—the jade utensils, the cassia wine, and finally the dazzling figure of the prince (lines 25–26). Not until the end of the *fu* do we come to the realization that the occasion is for a meeting of poets.

These cultured guests were called the Yung-ming poets, named after the reign title of Emperor Wu, the father of Prince Ching-ling. These poets had the privilege of touring the prince's garden with a kind of exuberance not unlike Hsieh Ling-yün's experience of long-distance excursions. In such a context it does not come as a surprise that Hsieh T'iao borrowed Hsieh Ling-yün's favorite term *yu-yen* ("strolling about merrily") to describe his sightseeing experience in the prince's garden (line 15).[4] However, in Hsieh T'iao's case, the happy excursion takes place in a different environment. Unlike Hsieh Ling-yün's family park, where various kinds of animals and plants are assembled to create a natural impression, Hsieh T'iao's garden is characterized by an artistic high-life atmosphere. This garden, which serves as the stage of Prince Ching-ling's literary salon, is a miniature of nature and culture combined. There is nothing more artificial than the symbolic "retreat" to the garden. Indeed, it is no longer a retreat but a center of aesthetic cultivation.

I. The Literary Salon and Poetic Formalism

It was no coincidence that poetic formalism also came onto the literary horizon at this time. Like the salon garden which contains everything aes-

---

[3] See Prince Ching-ling's poem on his own garden, with the same title as Hsieh T'iao's, in *CHSK*, II, 753. See also the Biography of Liu Yün in Yao Ssu-lien, *Liang shu*, *chüan* 21 (Peking: Chung-hua shu-chü, 1973), II, 331. Not all scholars agree about the location of this garden, however. For example, Wu Shu-t'ang believes that Hsieh's *fu* refers to Prince Ching-ling's garden. But the Japanese scholar Ami Yūji thinks that the piece is about the garden in Prince Sui's palace in Ching-chou, where Hsieh T'iao was to enjoy a similar salon life from 490 to 493 (see *HHCC*, 65 and 69). The controversy about the location is not our major concern here, for what is important is the description of this type of garden in poetry.

[4] For Hsieh Ling-yün's use of the term, see, for example, *HLYS*, 58.

Hsieh T'iao
THE INWARD TURN OF LANDSCAPE

thetic, so literature itself is potentially a self-regulating world of completion. The poets, knowing the privileged character of their poetry, went further to define the boundaries of the genre: that which employs rhyme is *wen* (belles-lettres); that without it is *pi* (plain writing).[5] The main purpose of this distinction was to narrow down the meaning of the classical term *wen* (patterns), which originally had a broader meaning applied to both *wen-hsüeh* (literature) and *wen-chang* (composition) in general.[6] A formal criterion seemed to the Yung-ming poets best for defining the normative boundary of their new concept of *wen*. Their formalist movement, at first an expression of aesthetic sophistication, became eventually a conscious literary reform which came to influence almost every aspect of Chinese literature. The extent of controversy provoked by this formal revisionism was something similar to, if not greater than, the European Renaissance debate over poesy.

To Hsieh T'iao a formal distinction of belles-lettres defined by the use of rhymes was not at all new. He grew up in a family where rhyming was long considered the poetical requisite of *wen*. Hsieh Ling-yün's meticulous attention to tonal and rhyming effects in poetry must have provided him with a living inspiration. Moreover, his grand-uncle Fan Yeh, author of the *History of Latter Han* (*Hou-Han shu*), was known especially for his sensitivity to tonal distinctions. The letter that Fan Yeh wrote to all his nephews from prison must have become a sort of family instruction in the Hsieh clan:[7]

> It is only natural that we have the inborn ability to discriminate between the musical notes of *kung* and *shang* and to recognize clear and turbid sounds. But I have observed that most of the ancient and present authors do not completely comprehend this point. Even if there are some who understand this, they do not always follow the fundamental rules. All of my words can be proved by concrete examples, and are not empty talk.... When writings are inferior, it is because they do not obey the rules of rhymes. (*Sung shu, chüan* 69, VI, 1830)
> 性別宮商，識清濁，斯自然也。觀古今文人，多不全了此處。縱有會此者，不必從根本中來。言之皆有實證，非爲空談。...手筆差易，文不拘韻故也。

---

[5] I have borrowed these translated terms from James J. Y. Liu. See his *Chinese Theories of Literature* (Chicago: Univ. of Chicago Press, 1975), p. 8. See also Liu Hsieh's statement on *wen* and *pi* in his *Wen-hsin tiao-lung*, Vincent Yu-chung Shih, trans., p. 327. For a more detailed discussion of this subject, see Lo Ken-tse, *Chung-kuo wen-hsüeh p'i-p'ing shih* (Shanghai: Ku-tien wen-hsüeh ch'u-pan-she, 1957–1961), pp. 140–144; Kuo Shao-yü, *Chung-kuo wen-hsüeh p'i-p'ing-shih* (1956; rpt. Hong Kong: Hung-chih shu-chü, 1970), pp. 58–65.

[6] James J. Y. Liu, *Theories of Literature*, p. 8.

[7] While he was Magistrate of Hsüan-ch'eng, Fan Yeh was put to prison and finally executed in 446 for his involvement in a revolt (See *SS, chüan* 69, VI, 1,825–1,828).

Hsieh T'iao
THE INWARD TURN OF LANDSCAPE

It goes without saying that when Hsieh T'iao joined Prince Ching-ling's salon he was immediately attracted to the tonal and rhyming innovations advocated by its members.

The foremost leaders of the tonal formalism were Wang Jung (468–494) and Shen Yüeh (441–513). Shen Yüeh, who was at the center of Ch'i and Liang literary circles for more than thirty years, was especially important as a lifelong advocate of the salon's formal theories. His newly prescribed prosodic rules were summed up in the so called "four tones, eight prohibitions" (*ssu-sheng pa-ping*). The "four tones" refer to the "level" tones and three "oblique" tones ("rising," "parting," "entering" tones), which the poet must distinguish in composing poetry.[8] The "eight prohibitions" are eight specific points concerning some tonal and rhyming violations.[9] The entire prosodic system may be said to be based on one main idea: the correlation of "level" and "oblique" tones within a line and between lines. Shen Yüeh and his fellow poets certainly could not have imagined that by their formulation of this new canon they would indeed launch the first important step in the direction of T'ang Regulated Verse, a form that was to represent the ideal model of Chinese poetry down to the turn of our century. Yet these Yung-ming poets and their followers believed that what they had invented had an unprecedented importance, and were truly "innovations" (*hsin-pien*).[10]

The widespread influence of their theory of "four tones, eight prohibitions" was such that it immediately met with some critics' resistance. Chung Jung, who went to the trouble of discussing poetry with Hsieh T'iao in 488,[11] was

---

[8] The "level" tone corresponds to the first and second tones of today's northern or standard Mandarin, while the "rising" and "falling" tones are the third and fourth tones, respectively. The "entering" tone no longer exists in modern Mandarin, as it has long been redistributed to the other three catagories, some going to "level" and some to "oblique" classes. Today it is not difficult for most Chinese to distinguish the differences among these tones. But in Shen Yüeh's time, when the idea of the "four tones" was first proposed, it did not seem at all easy for some. Even Hsiao Yen, the future Emperor Wu of the Liang and one of the "Eight Friends of Ching-ling," was said to be unable to discriminate between the second and the third tones. (See Kūkai, *Bunkyō hifuron*, pp. 31–32; Yao Ssu-lien, *Liang shu*, *chüan* 13, I, 243). The "four-tone" system seems to have been based on the southern version of the northern Lo-yang dialect, an official language used in the southern court, upon which the literary language was based. See Richard B. Mather, "A Note on the Dialects of Lo-yang and Nanking During the Six Dynasties," in *Wen-lin*, *Studies in the Chinese Humanities*, ed. Tse-tsung Chow. (Madison: Univ. of Wisconsin Press, 1968), pp. 247–256. Also consult Ch'en Yin-k'o, "Tung-Chin Nan-ch'ao chih Wu-yü," in *CYK*, II, 143–148.

[9] See Kūkai, *Bunkyō hifuron*, pp. 179–197. There is a possibility that not all of these eight prohibitions were invented by Shen Yüeh. (See Feng Ch'eng-chi, "Lun Yung-ming sheng-lü—pa ping," in *CKWH*, 637–649.) It may be of interest to note that even Japanese poetics was influenced by these "prohibitions." See, for example, *Kakyō hyōshiki* (dated 722), by Fujiwara no Hamanari. I am indebted to Judith Rabinovitch for this point.

[10] See biography of Yü Chien-wu in Yao Ssu-lien, *Liang shu*, *chüan* 49, III, 690.

[11] See "Preface" to *HHCC*, 5–6; and *SPC*, 48.

Hsieh T'iao
THE INWARD TURN OF LANDSCAPE

apparently not impressed with the self-proclaimed innovators in the salon. For he rigorously attacked Shen Yüeh, Wang Jung, and Hsieh T'iao in his Preface to *Shih-p'in*. In the view of Chung Jung, the auditory effects that came from natural harmonies of sound were the best: "Simply allow the sounds to flow smoothly, and the mouth and lips to work harmoniously together—that is sufficient."[12] He wondered why it was necessary to design the new prosodic rules.

Why did the innovators suddenly advocate the system of "four tones," anyway, if the traditional methods of creating musical effects in poetry seemed satisfactory? This is an extremely important question, one which no serious students of Chinese poetry can disregard.

According to the modern historian Ch'en Yin-k'o, the innovation of four tones during the Yung-ming period was directly inspired by a method of chanting the Chinese scriptures that became increasingly popular within Buddhist circles in the capital district at the time.[13] The chanting device called *hsin-sheng* (new sounds) was formulated by the local monks, and was said to be grounded on a system of their theoretical understanding of "three tones" modeled after the original Indian concept of "svara" (pitch-accent) as applied to the Sanskrit or Pali scriptures.[14] Although linguists have since proved that the poets' "four-tone" innovation was based on the tonal phonemic distinctions present in spoken Chinese itself,[15] Ch'en Yin-k'o's original theory gives us a new insight into the cultural milieu of the Yung-ming era.

What deserves most attention is the fact that the same Prince Ching-ling who sponsored the literary activities in his salon was also the one who showed the greatest support for the conception of the Buddhist "new sounds" (*hsin-sheng*). His enthusiastic involvement in the chanting of scriptures is recorded clearly in some extant Buddhist sources.[16] Most importantly, beginning with 487 his West Residence also served as the headquarter of such activities, as *The History of Southern Ch'i* (*Nan-Ch'i shu*) records:[17]

> In 487 ... he moved into his residence on Chi-lung Mountain, where he invited famous monks to expound Buddhist doctrines and

---

[12] From Knechtges, "Introduction," *Wen xuan*, p. 13.

[13] Ch'en Yin-k'o, "Ssu-sheng san-wen," *Ch'en Yin-k'o hsien-sheng wen-shih lun-chi*, I, 205–218.

[14] Ch'en Yin-k'o, "Ssu-sheng san-wen," p. 205.

[15] It is said by some historical linguists that Chinese may not have had tones before the Han Dynasty or later, and that Shen Yüeh's discovery was in fact the observation of a new phenomenon in Chinese language as it formed tones to compensate for the loss of some other phonemically distinctive features. I am indebted to F. W. Mote for a reminder of this point. See also Lo Ch'ang-p'ei, *Han-yü yin yün hsüeh tao-lun* (Hong Kong: T'ai-p'ing shu-chü, 1970), pp. 54–57.

[16] See sources cited in Ch'en Yin-k'o, "Ssu-sheng san-wen," pp. 208–210.

[17] See Hsiao Tzu-hsien, *Nan-Ch'i shu*, *chüan* 40 (Peking: Chung-hua shu-chü, 1972), III, 689.

invent new ways of chanting sutras. Buddhism had never been so popular in the south of the Yangtze before. (*Chüan* 40, III, 689)
〔永明〕五年...移居雞籠山邸，招致名僧，講語佛法，造經唄新聲，道俗之盛，江左未有也。

The climax of such collective experiments and innovations came two years later in an unprecedented grand performance of scripture-chanting in the capital, which Prince Ching-ling convened by gathering together notable Buddhist monks with linguistic skills.[18] The purpose of the event was obviously to demonstrate to the public the melodious nature of the "new sounds."

Did Shen Yüeh and his fellow poets know the tonal system of these "new sounds" constructed by contemporary monks? We lack sufficient evidence to prove this point. But it is possible that their literary patron Prince Ching-ling was well versed in it, and it would be unlikely that they were not in some way inspired by it. In any case, the theory of "four tones, eight prohibitions" was also constructed during this period, growing out of the same cultural milieu in the capital.

What the Yung-ming poets did was to make a system of prosodic rules out of what earlier poets might have known intuitively, in the same manner that the Buddhist monks established their "three-tone" chanting scheme based on the original "svara" of another language. The four tones that form the nucleus of Shen Yüeh's *Ssu-sheng p'u* are thought by many to have come from ordinary Chinese speech,[19] but still it was these innovative poets who provided names for the tones and made conscious efforts to create a self-regulating scheme for composing poetry. It seems that what these poets intended to do was to make the poetic prosody in *shih* poetry independent of the "five-tone" (*wu-yin*) musical scale, to which earlier poets had turned invariably, if not very precisely, for achieving melodious effects in their work.[20] This desire for separation from music was an expression of generic sophistication which was bound to bring about a new classification of tones and rhymes. Chung Jung, not knowing the rationale behind this transformation and still confined by his music-oriented poetics, was impelled to raise a simple-minded question:

---

[18] The performance was held in Chien-k'ang on the nineteenth day of the second month in the seventh year of Yung-ming (489). See biography of Shih Seng-pien, as cited in Ch'en Yin-k'o, "Ssu-sheng san-wen," p. 208.

[19] For this view, see sources cited in Kūkai, *Bunkyō hifuron* (Peking: Jen-min wen-hsüeh ch'u-pan-she, 1975), pp. 33–34. Chung Jung, who disapproved of the new "four-tone" scheme, also adopted this view: "... Regarding 'wasp waist' and 'crane's knee,' the country folk have already mastered them." (See Knechtges, *Wen xuan*, p. 13.)

[20] Kuo Shao-yü, *Chung-kuo wen-hsüeh p'i-p'ing shih*, pp. 73–74. Of course, the "four-tone" scheme might have been influenced by the "five-tone" scale in music (as Kūkai's many citations indicate), but it was still a newly refined system.

Hsieh T'iao
THE INWARD TURN OF LANDSCAPE

> Now that we no longer set our poems to music, what have we to benefit from tonal prosody? (*SPC*, 5)
> 今既不披管絃，亦何取於聲律耶？

Yet this was precisely the *raison d'être* of the new tonal system: to invent an artificial prosody that would be, in both theory and practice, self-sufficient.[21]

Although Shen Yüeh was the acknowledged spokesman for the tonal revolution, it was the talented Hsieh T'iao who exhibited the true merits of this new prosodic scheme in his poems, so that even hundreds of years later the T'ang poets, totally committed to their highly developed system of tonal correlation in prosody, looked back to Hsieh T'iao as an ideal model in poetry.[22] In his time Hsieh T'iao's formalism represented a definitive break from traditional verse, though he was unable to foretell that he was working toward a poetics of the greatest importance. As for Shen Yüeh, he was most gratified to see a young poet of Hsieh T'iao's stature so marvelously testing out his theories and breaking other new ground. It seems that the two became such close friends that their mere closeness gave a stimulating impact to contemporary poetic endeavors. Together their enthusiasm for the new poetics engendered a great variety of experiments, some of which were to evolve into important rules to be incorporated into the "Recent Style Poetry" (*chin-t'i shih*) of the T'ang.

Their experiments in the formal aspects of poetry are rather complex in nature, and I shall single out for brief discussion only the one area that serves as the backbone of their tonal innovations.

Let us begin with the tonal correlation within an individual line. As has been mentioned earlier, the true significance of the "four-tone" prosody lies in the correlation, and hence the opposition, of the "level" (○) and the "oblique" (×) tones. Through a systematic alternation of tones the Yung-ming poets were attempting to bring out the best rhythmic quality in the tonal system of the Chinese language. What follows are some of the patterns often encountered in Hsieh T'iao's five-character lines:[23]

(1) ○ ○ ○ × ×
(2) ○ ○ × × ○
(3) × × × ○ ○

---

[21] This should not be understood as applicable also to the writing of *yüeh-fu* poetry, which is primarily a song form. *Yüeh-fu* songs continued to be written until the High T'ang, but were considered apart from the new tonal prosody.

[22] In their poems Li Po and Tu Fu especially praised Hsieh T'iao for his ability to produce melodious verse. See *Li T'ai-po ch'üan-chi*, I, 450; and *Tu shih hsiang-chu*, commentary by Ch'iu Chao-ao (Peking: Chung-hua shu-chü, 1979), III, 1,262.

[23] See also Hung Shun-lung, "Hsieh T'iao sheng-p'ing chi ch'i tso- p'in yen-chiu," in *HHCC*, 20–25.

Hsieh T'iao
THE INWARD TURN OF LANDSCAPE

(4) × × ○ ○ ×
(5) ○ ○ × × ×
(6) × × ○ ○ ○

The first four patterns eventually became the four prescribed patterns in T'ang Regulated Verse (*lü-shih*).[24]

The tonal correlation between the two lines of a couplet is arguably more difficult to carry out, and it is easy enough to find in Hsieh T'iao's poetry violations against the rules which the Yung-ming poets had set for themselves. For example, Rule #1 of the "Eight Prohibitions" says: "the first two characters in the second line should not repeat the tones of the first two characters in the first line." Yet one of Hsieh T'iao's most famous couplets is a perfect illustration of such violation:

○ ○ ○ × ×
<u>○</u> <u>○</u> × ○ ○
江南佳麗地
金陵帝王州
   (*HHCS*, 6)

Undoubtedly Hsieh T'iao's poetry represents only an early experimental stage in the long evolution of the Regulated Verse.[25] And some of the "Eight Prohibitions" were later dropped from T'ang poetics. But to the T'ang poets Yung-ming poetry, which was later called "new style poetry" (*hsin-t'i shih*),[26] remained the product of a golden age in which experiment was the goal and form was its own expression.

Another formal development, or aesthetic choice, that was to exercise a definitive impact on T'ang poetry was the increasing compactness in these "new style" poems. Among the extant one hundred and thirty odd *shih* poems by Hsieh T'iao, about one third of them are eight-line poems, which bear a striking resemblance to the regulated octave verse of the T'ang. There is every reason to assume that this structural compactness made Hsieh T'iao's poetry particularly appealing to young contemporary readers. Hsiao Yen (later Emperor Wu of the Liang) singled out Hsieh T'iao and Ho Hsün (?–ca. 535), a younger poet who specialized in the "new style" poetry, as the two

---

[24] See François Cheng, *Chinese Poetic Writing*, trans., Donald A. Riggs and Jerome P. Seaton (Bloomington: Indiana Univ. Press, 1982), p. 48.

[25] Even regulated poems by Early T'ang poets are often found faulty in terms of tonal correlations.

[26] The term was first adopted by Wang K'ai-yün in his *Pa-tai shih-hsüan*. It has since become the standard term to refer to Yung-ming poetry. (See Liu Ta-chieh, *Chung-kuo wen-hsüeh fa-chan shih* [Shanghai: Chung-hua shu-chü, 1957–1958], I, 287; Lu K'an-ju and Feng Yüan-chün, *Chung-kuo shih-shih* [Peking: Tso-chia ch'u-pan-she, 1957], II, 382.)

Hsieh T'iao
THE INWARD TURN OF LANDSCAPE

ablest poets, whose works were distinguished by quality, not by length.²⁷ Hsiao Kang, the son of Hsiao Yen, criticized the verbosity (*jung-ch'ang*) of Hsieh Ling-yün's poetry, but regarded Hsieh T'iao's and Shen Yüeh's works as "the crowning glory of literature and models for writing" (*CKLT*, I, 328). Though disapproving the new tonality, Chung Jung had to admit that Hsieh T'iao's poetry was an object of envy to the younger generation (*SPC*, 48). All this only reaffirms our general belief that when poetry acquires a new structural basis, readers will also develop a new set of critical criteria. As in the case of the Ch'i and Liang poetry, the readers' aesthetic preference was clearly for the shorter verse.

That this eight-line verse should arise from the salon environment is something that needs further attention. I have observed that most of the extant poems produced in the poetry meetings during this period are in eight lines. In addition, the poems are more often than not *yung-wu* poems (i.e., odes on objects), composed during certain literary games at banquets, with each person writing on a certain object according to a set topic.²⁸ Some of the poetry meetings that Hsieh T'iao attended focused on topics such as the following (*HHCC*, 447–462):

(1) "Together We Write Odes on Certain Musical Instruments"
同詠樂器

(2) "Together We Write Odes on Certain Household Utensils Seen at the Banquet"
同詠坐上器玩

(3) "Together We Write Odes on a Certain Object Seen at the Banquet"
同詠坐上所見一物

There could be no doubt that this kind of poetic exercise was primarily designed for social purposes. But such was the original goal of the literary salon. The more social the occasion, the more it achieves a "total" communication.

The most important aspect of *yung-wu* poetry concerns the symbolic correspondence between its form and content. The very compactness of the

---

²⁷ See Yao Ssu-lien, *Liang shu*, chüan 49, III, 693.
²⁸ It should be noted that two hundred years later the poetic circle of Prince Nagaya (684–729) in Japan began to develop a mode of composition similar to that of "odes on objects." According to Konishi Jin'ichi, Prince Nagaya seemed to know about the "eight friends" of Prince Ching-ling and "deliberately emulated" the Chinese prince. See Chapter 9, "The Composition of Poetry and Prose in Chinese," in Konishi Jin'ichi, *A History of Japanese Literature, Vol. I, The Archaic and Ancient Ages*, trans. Aileen Gattan and Nicholas Teele, ed. Earl Miner (Princeton: Princeton Univ. Press, 1984), pp. 377–392.

Hsieh T'iao
THE INWARD TURN OF LANDSCAPE

eight-line structure seems to mirror an equally compressed world of the self-contained. It is unlikely that these poets consciously worked out a new form to reflect the idea of their privileged life-style. Nevertheless, the brief eight-line form seemed to find its proper setting in the salon environment and gradually to acquire a formal distinction that set it apart from traditional poetry. There was in this poetry an odd combination of trivial content and serious form. But, the more formal it became, the more it gained a distinct identity not unlike that of an independent genre.

The following poem by Hsieh T'iao composed in one of those social evenings bears witness to the nature of this poetry:

> THE ZITHER
> This is a tree trunk that endured the storms of Lake Tung-t'ing.
> This is a branch which grew and died on Mt. Lung-men.[29]
> A piece of wood is carved with intricate designs,
> Its sound reverberates, pure and sharp.   4
> When spring breezes stir the fragrant grass,
> The autumn moon fills the luxuriant pond,
> At this time someone plays the "Departing Crane,"
> And the guests' tears fall down like rain.
> (*HHCS*, 159)

琴
洞庭風雨幹
龍門生死枝
雕刻紛布濩
沖響鬱清危
春風搖蕙草
秋月滿華池
是時操別鶴
淫淫客淚垂

This poem on the zither (i.e., *ch'in*) was written as a response to the topic given in the banquet: "Together We Write Odes on Certain Musical Instruments." The piece has the descriptive style typical of this kind of poetry: it begins with a description of the raw material out of which the instrument is made, and then moves on to depict its shape and sound, and finally its effect on the audience. The poet's attempt to provide details of the objects in view seems to bring back Pao Chao's closeup technique. In particular, this poem reminds us of Pao Chao's *yung-wu* poem on the *t'ung* tree, where the poet focuses on a

---

[29] Lake Tung-t'ing and Mt. Lung-men are both known for the *t'ung* tree, the ideal material for making zithers.

Hsieh T'iao
THE INWARD TURN OF LANDSCAPE

description of the tree's location, its shape, its sound, and its potential to touch the human heart.[30] What is most interesting is that Pao Chao's *t'ung* tree is just the kind of raw material out of which Hsieh T'iao's zither is made. Even more striking, the lonely *t'ung* tree in Pao Chao's poem cries out to be made into a useful zither.

> I wish to be carved and hewn,
> To become a zither in your hall.
>   (*PTCC*, 410)
> 幸願見雕斲
> 爲君堂上琴

It seems that Hsieh T'iao's poem is in some way influenced by Pao Chao's piece. At least the two poems can be studied as a pair exemplifying the descriptive mode of poetry. However, it is their differences, rather than their similarities, that would lead us to further understanding of the newly developed salon style. Several new tendencies are noticeable in Hsieh T'iao's poem. First, the object for description is much reduced in size; it is no longer a tall tree but a small zither to be played with one's hands—perhaps those of a female performer. Second, the object at issue has shifted from the wild mountain site to the lavishly prepared banquet. Just in case readers will at this point wonder whether this particular poem of Hsieh T'iao's is in any sense exceptional, let us see some of the other titles of poems by the salon members:

> "On a Bamboo Flute" (Shen Yüeh)
> "On a P'i-p'a Lute" (Wang Jung)
> "On a Leather Cushion" (Hsieh T'iao)
> "On a Bamboo Plate" (Hsieh T'iao)
> "On a Curtain" (Wang Jung)
> "On a Hanging Screen" (Yü Yen)
> "On a Mat" (Hsieh T'iao)
> "On a Mat" (Liu Yün)
> "On a Brazier" (Hsieh T'iao)
> "On a Brazier" (Shen Yüeh)
> "On a Mirror Stand" (Hsieh T'iao)
> "On a Lamp" (Hsieh T'iao)
> "On a Candle" (Hsieh T'iao)

These poems are also more formalized than Pao Chao's sixteen-line poem, as they are uniformly written in the eight-line pattern (*HHCC*, 449–461).

---

[30] I refer to Pao Chao's poem entitled "I Met a Lonely *T'ung* Tree on My Journey to the Mountain," which has already been discussed in Section I of Chapter Three. It should be mentioned that a similar emphasis on the tree as raw material can be found in earlier *fu* literature, such as "*Fu* on the Lute" by Hsi K'ang (223–262).

Hsieh T'iao
THE INWARD TURN OF LANDSCAPE

Yet the octave structure, however popular it had become in the salon circle, could not claim substantial literary value for itself until it finally transcended its rather trivial content. More exactly, this new poetic medium became truly important only after these poets began to develop their individual lyrical voice in it. This is indeed a great irony: without the social atmosphere in the salon, the new poetic form would not have found its formalized status. And yet one must eventually detach oneself from the surroundings of imitation in order to create a self-reflective poetry. This is what happened to Hsieh T'iao: he discontinued his *yung-wu* poetry composition after leaving Prince Ching-ling's salon at the age of twenty-six, and moved gradually toward the cultivation of a lyrical voice in poetry.

II. The Structure of Feelings

To Hsieh T'iao it all came as a surprise. In 490 he was offered a prestigious position as Prince Sui's *wen-hsüeh* (literary scholar) and was to follow Prince Sui far west to Ching-chou in modern Hupei, then a growing city as flourishing as Chien-k'ang. The joy of promotion was great, but the thought of leaving behind his literary friends in Chien-k'ang seemed to him unbearable. During the farewell banquet the usual exuberant spirits surrounding the salon were replaced by gloomy thoughts of separation. In response to the numerous farewell poems given by his friends at the banquet, Hsieh T'iao presented the following verse:

> On this spring night, we take leave, pure wine in our goblets,
> I shall become a wanderer by the river's banks and marsh's
>   edge.³¹
> I can only sigh at the river flowing east,
> Imagine how fields have grown in my homeland—   4
> Crowded trees flourish day by day,
> Fragrant islets multiply in heaps.
> When I look down from the pavilion in Ching-chou,
> I dream at night about returning home.   8
>   (*HHCS*, 107)
> 春夜別清樽
> 江潭復爲客
> 歎息東流水
> 如何故鄉陌

---

³¹ For the allusion of this line, see "The Fisherman," in *Ch'u Tz'u*, trans., Hawkes, p. 90: "When Ch'ü Yüan was banished,/He wandered along the river's banks, or walked at the marsh's edge...."

Hsieh T'iao
THE INWARD TURN OF LANDSCAPE

重樹日芬薀
芳洲轉如積
望望荆台下
歸夢相思夕

Understandably, all the farewell poems in the same poem-series are written in the usual salon style, the eight-line form. But the tone is lyrical, clearly different from that of the *yung-wu* poetry. There is no longer in these poems the object-oriented description and the concentrated focus on interior space. Of course, it is hardly correct to claim that these farewell poems were the first lyrical octave poems to be written by the Yung-ming poets, but the poem-series as a whole may be seen as a symbolic break from the *yung-wu* mode which they had cherished all along.

To Hsieh T'iao himself, this farewell poem represents only a beginning, the beginning of an awareness of a new lyrical structure. Already in this poem we witness a striking feature that was to become the norm of the lyrical structure in T'ang poetry: i.e., the orderly distribution of parallel and non-parallel lines. The foremost rule in the syntax of T'ang Regulated Verse was to be this: of the four couplets that constitute the eight-line verse, the second and the third should be made up of parallel lines, while the last couplet is always non-parallel and the first couplet usually non-parallel as well. This formal structure corresponds to the dynamic movement of a temporal-spatial-temporal sequence symbolic of the lyrical progression. For the lyrical self in a typical T'ang Regulated poem undertakes, so to speak, a symbolic two-stage journey: (1) from the non-parallel, and time-charged, world of imperfection (couplet one) to the parallel and time-free state of perfection (couplets two and three); (2) from the world of parallelism and fullness back to that of non-parallelism and imperfection (couplet four). Through such a formalized structure of cyclical movement, the T'ang poets perhaps felt that their poetry captured the essential quality of a self-contained universe in both form and content.

Indeed we notice that Hsieh T'iao's farewell poem has a structure like the tripartite form of the T'ang verse:[32]

Couplet one (non-parallel)
Couplets two and three (parallel)
Couplet four (non-parallel)

Part of the novelty of this kind of lyrical poetry lies in the orderly balance of personal emotions and external scenes, which directly corresponds to that of non-parallelism and parallelism. The fact that Hsieh's Ching-chou trip in 490

---

[32] It should be noted that the tendency to have parallel or semi-parallel couplets cluster in the center of poem goes back at least as far as Western Chin. Such a poetic structure did not emerge suddenly at the time of Hsieh T'iao.

Hsieh T'iao
THE INWARD TURN OF LANDSCAPE

should suddenly awaken in him what seemed to be self-reflectiveness of the most intense kind is something difficult to explain. Yet for some reason his departure from Chien-k'ang did signify a complete break—a break from innocent frivolity and carefree luxury. Life in the capital had been simple, though in its own way intense. But life in Ching-chou would be unpredictable; he had yet to learn to cope with other officials in Prince Sui's court. On the eve of his westward trip Hsieh T'iao climbed a tower in Chien-k'ang and wrote a most poignant confession of his fears and sorrow:

CLIMBING THE BEACON FIRE TOWER BEFORE SETTING
OUT FROM STONE CITY

Lingering, I long for the capital,
Faltering, I walk along the layered mountain slope.
The hill is high, the palace seems near,
I look out afar, winds and clouds are numerous.   4
Ching-chou and Wu are separated by mountain peaks,
Rivers and seas are filled with billows and waves.
I have no wings to fly back,
This parting—what can be done?   8
　　(*HHCS*, 33)

將發石頭上烽火樓

徘徊戀京邑
躑躅躘曾阿
陵高堞闕近
眺迥風雲多
荊吳阻山岫
江海含瀾波
歸飛無羽翼
其如離別何

The significance of the poem lies in the fact that its method of organizing feelings and natural scenes was to become a distinct style of Hsieh T'iao's octave verse in the years to come—i.e., couplet one introduces an emotional attitude, couplets two and three center on natural description, and couplet four returns to the emotional concern, with a projection into the unknown future. Once again we observe the striking similarity between Hsieh T'iao's poetics and that of the T'ang Regulated Verse. In retrospect we can say that there is nothing more ingenious than this extremely complex yet seemingly simple structuring of feeling and form. The octave verse is a perfect form which simultaneously unfolds a lyrical vision and its natural correlations. When the lyric eye passes over the various scenes in nature, it discovers itself at

Hsieh T'iao
THE INWARD TURN OF LANDSCAPE

the center of an all-inclusive landscape, indeed vast and overpowering. There is always a sense of the enormous spectacle, be it enchanting or formidable, about this lyric experience. But the "I" eventually has to withdraw, to situate itself once again in the human world. All this is done in eight lines, in a most economic manner.

Of course, with Hsieh T'iao the octave verse was not yet a sanctioned genre, and its name *lü-shih* (Regulated Verse) would not be coined until the T'ang. However, Hsieh T'iao was the first poet to be so concerned with creating a miniature totality in poetry. It is reasonable to assume that Hsiao T'iao continued to experiment with every possible form in order to express most economically his self-contained poetic world. His was a significant step toward finding a satisfactory method of correlating content and form, and of molding them into a minimal structure. Hsieh T'iao expressed his notion of ideal poetry to his contemporaries by means of a simile:

> Good poetry should be round and beautiful;
> it should roll and turn like a ball.[33]
> 好詩圓美，流轉如彈丸

The image of a ball gives the impression of a self-sufficient roundness. Its roundness refers to tonal harmony and structural perfection—indeed to everything flawless. But, most important, it suggests that good poetry must embody its own infinity in a small ball of something mobile, such that it needs no exterior force.

When Hsieh T'iao arrived in Ching-chou, he discovered that he was at the center of the attention of Prince Sui, a gifted poet himself. The atmosphere of Prince Sui's garden had the same scenic charm and cultivated vivacity as Prince Ching-ling's, and there was also a literary group of sorts surrounding the prince. Yet there was something new in Prince Sui's fascination for nature's wondrous sights. He gave his scenic tours the double significance of private fulfillment and public participation. Hsieh T'iao's poem best describes the garden's picturesque scenery amidst the grand spectacle of a spring outing:

> The square pond is filled with water,
> Its clear flow as bright as a mirror.
> Round lily pads receive the sunlit dew,
> Colorful fish swim with the currents of the wind. 4
> Water, the highest good, harmonizes with our innermost
>   heart,[34]

[33] Li Yen-shou, *Nan shih, chüan* 22, II, 609.

[34] This line alludes to an important concept of Lao Tzu: "Highest good is like water. Because water excels in benefiting the myriad creatures without contending with them and settles where none would like to be, it comes close to the way." (See D. C. Lau, trans., Chapter 8, p. 64.)

128

Hsieh T'iao
THE INWARD TURN OF LANDSCAPE

> The still river gives fair warning to our easily aroused nature.[35]
> Luckily fragrant spring has arrived,
> So I can accompany my lord in the grand stroll along the Hao River.[36]   8
> (*HHCS*, 146)

方池含積水
明流皎如鏡
規荷承日泛
影鱗與風泳
上善叶淵心
止川測動性
幸是芳春來
側點游濠盛

The poem is from a series of sixteen poems that Hsieh T'iao wrote in response to Prince Sui's poems (*HHCC*, 409–412). Hsieh's sixteen poems are a witness to the kind of life he led in Ching-chou. They contain not only colorful depictions of the prince's garden during different seasons, but also expressions of Hsieh T'iao's secret thoughts that preoccupied him in that period.

Ten out of these sixteen poems are in octave form; and, among those which are not, three are made up of ten lines. Compared to other groups of poems by Hsieh T'iao, this series of poems has the highest percentage of eight-line verse, which gives them the unmistakable impression of a new style. This fact, I believe, has significant bearing upon the nature of Hsieh T'iao's poetic practice during his Ching-chou years. His position as a *wen-hsüeh* must have provided him with a special opportunity to exert influence on Prince Sui's poetic style and on the styles of other members in the literary circle. We can guess from the usual practice that the original sixteen poems by Prince Sui to which Hsieh T'iao responded might have been written in exactly the same length and rhyme as Hsieh T'iao's. If so, we can then assume that under Hsieh's influence Prince Sui also came to prefer the octave form. Moreover, the one extant poem that we have by Prince Sui (*CHSK*, II, 754) bears a striking similarity to Hsieh's new style poetry, except for its having ten rather than eight lines.

It was during his Ching-chou years that Hsieh T'iao began to refine his technique of combining feelings and landscape in his octave verse. He found Prince Sui's life-style particularly congenial to his poetic discipline and tem-

---

[35] Confucius is said by Chuang Tzu to have made the following statement: "Men do not mirror themselves in running water—they mirror themselves in still water. Only what is still can still the stillness of other things...." (See Chapter Five of *Chuang Tzu*, in Watson, trans., *The Complete Works of Chuang Tzu*, p. 69.)

[36] The Hao River is the site where Chuang Tzu and Hui Shih carried on their famous debate about the happiness of fish swimming in the water. (See Watson, trans., *The Complete Works of Chuang Tzu*, Chapter 17, pp. 188–189).

Hsieh T'iao
THE INWARD TURN OF LANDSCAPE

perament at this time. Unlike Prince Ching-ling, who was less a poet than an advocate, Prince Sui was a talented and hard-working poet who spent much of his time practicing poetry. It was inevitable that under these circumstances Hsieh T'iao quickly became the prince's best friend, and day and night the two were found exchanging messages in verse.[37] The feeling that Hsieh T'iao expressed for the prince was calm and earnest, in contrast to the innocent joviality which characterized his earlier friendships. Moreover, the prince's love for natural scenery seemed to have quickened Hsieh T'iao's descriptive sensitivity and consequently enriched his general poetic techniques. Indeed, we find that Hsieh's poetry at this time exhibits a quality of visual refinement that blends spontaneously with feeling:

> The gaiety of youthful years is washed away and gone,
> The night is long, I am enjoying this nocturnal scene.
> Young duckweeds often flow with water,
> The fragile grass cannot stand in the wind.   4
> The chamber is secluded—the zither's sound echoes easily,
> The terrace is remote—the moon finds it hard to focus on it.
> All things in the spring are illuminated by the moonlight,
> I shall wear orchids and day-lilies forever.   8
>   (HHCS, 151)

年華豫已滌
夜艾賞方融
新萍時合水
弱草未勝風
閨幽瑟易響
台迥月難中
春物廣餘照
蘭萱佩未窮

There is a subtle tone of self-reflection beneath the description of the tranquil moonlit scene in the above poem. The feeling, whatever it is, is conveyed implicitly through natural images, not by direct statement. We feel that the poetic voice has turned somewhat inward.

What exactly are the feelings that the poet wishes to express? From the biography of Hsieh T'iao in the *History of Southern Ch'i* we know that the poet's intimate friendship with Prince Sui eventually incurred the jealousy of some officials in Ching-chou. For the first time in his life Hsieh understood the price one must pay for getting involved in political circles. His poetic skill and charming presence, which had seemed so much in his favor, suddenly became suspect in the eyes of his envious colleagues. Poetry was his only comfort,

---

[37] See biography of Hsieh T'iao, in Hsiao Tzu-hsien, *Nan-Ch'i shu*, chüan 47, III, 825.

Hsieh T'iao
THE INWARD TURN OF LANDSCAPE

and he apparently felt the compulsion to express through this medium his melancholy feelings. Yet the result is an imagistic poem, with the principal effect of presenting a radiant moonlight scene. Perhaps only a second reading of the poem will reveal a possible connection between the natural images and the poet's troubled thoughts—that he is the helpless wind-blown grass by the riverbank (lines 3–4), and that, despite all the slander, he remains silent like the moon and as pure as the fragrant orchid (lines 5–8). We have no way of proving that this is what the poet wishes to convey. But the beauty of the poem lies precisely in this quality of ambiguity. Such imagistic play permits Hsieh T'iao to endow his poetry with both a vividness of natural description and a quality of endless overtones. This imagistic suggestiveness was to become a most important quality of Hsieh T'iao's poetry.

The disquieting tension in the political circle of Ching-chou was brought to a climax in 493 when Emperor Wu suddenly summoned Hsieh T'iao back to Chien-k'ang. The truth was that Wang Hsiu-chih, a subordinate of Prince Sui, had secretly reported to the Emperor about Hsieh's exerting a more than usual influence upon the prince.[38] The Emperor was greatly alarmed by the news, and decided to separate the two youths. This all came as a great blow to Hsieh T'iao. He had no choice but to leave Ching-chou immediately.

Hsieh T'iao's true greatness as a lyric poet began to swell following this sudden mishap. On his way back to the capital he wrote what was to be his most celebrated poem, beginning with the powerful couplet:

> The great river runs day and night,
> The traveler's heart is sorrowful without end....
>   (*HHCS*, 40)
> 大江流日夜
> 客心悲未央....

What is notable here is the unobstructed lyric flow, whose surging energy pours forth like the unending river. As a lonely traveler who grieves over his misfortune, the poet strives to make all natural phenomena immediately meaningful to him: why is there such a contradiction between the joy of nature and human misery? Is there a way to possess oneself, to enlarge oneself, to live like nature itself, free of all threats and uncertainties? These questions must be answered. But, far from being a comfort, nature at this time only joins in to intensify the despairing human reality. The Yangtze river flows on silently in its vast power, as if to confirm the enduring quality of the poet's suffering. The night is dark, and darkness lies upon darkness, as he approaches the capital:

---

[38] Hsiao Tzu-hsien, *Nan-Ch'i shu*, *chüan* 47, III, 825.

Hsieh T'iao
THE INWARD TURN OF LANDSCAPE

> The Milky Way at dawn glimmers,
> The cold islets at night are dark,
> I stretch my neck to get a glimpse of the capital—
> Its palace walls face each other.
> The moon's golden waves brighten Magpie Tower,
> The Jade Cord stars sink below Chien-chang Hall.
> 秋河曙耿耿
> 寒渚夜蒼蒼
> 引領見京室
> 宮雉正相望
> 金波麗鳷鵲
> 玉繩低建章

Facing the familar palaces, he knows that it will no longer be possible to go back to where Prince Sui is. The separation is complete, in both time and space:

> My carriage hastens to the Southern Gate,
> As I long to see the sunlit tomb of King Chao.[39]
> I cannot see the galloping sunlight,
> Let alone those separated from me by the barriers of two regions.
> In the wind-tossed clouds there are paths for the birds,
> Yet men are barred by the Yangtze and Han—no bridge to get across.
> 驅車鼎門外
> 思見昭丘陽
> 馳暉不可接
> 何況隔兩鄉
> 風雲有鳥路
> 江漢限無梁

Finally there comes the moment of realization, and the hope of independence is made clear to him. The past is nothing but the past, but the future is still his. So he concludes his poem with something like a declaration of freedom:

> I send this message to those who set nets:
> "I have flown away into the depths of the sky."
> 寄言蔚羅者
> 寥廓已高翔

Freedom it was not to be. For very soon a reign of terror was to begin in Chien-k'ang, throwing everyone into a panic. It happened that, soon after Hsieh T'iao arrived in the capital, Emperor Wu died, and the court was plagued by a series of succession problems, betrayals, and murders. During less

---

[39] The tomb of King Chao of Ch'u is located in Ching-chou.

Hsieh T'iao
THE INWARD TURN OF LANDSCAPE

than a two-year period, the throne changed hands three times. The literary salon that used to provide artistic cultivation for the capital collapsed without a trace—first Wang Jung was executed, and then Prince Ching-ling died of worry and indignation. In 494, another climax followed: Prince Sui was murdered in Ching-chou. With this, Hsieh T'iao's despair was complete.

As an observer of the relentless political scene, the poet gained in wisdom. If he could not be a real recluse, he could at least live in semi-retirement somewhere. But where, and how?

The chance came in 495 when he was appointed Magistrate of Hsüan-ch'eng by the new Emperor, Ch'i Ming-ti (reigned 495–498). Hsüan-ch'eng was a county in Anhwei Province, known for its beautiful mountains and rivers. It was there that Hsieh's grand-uncle Fan Yeh—then Magistrate of Hsüan-ch'eng—produced his masterpiece, *The History of the Latter Han*. Hsüan-ch'eng would be an ideal place for him to both serve and retire at the same time, a perfect compromise:

> I can enjoy both official salary
> And delightful walks along the rustic waterside.
> Noise and dust are blocked out from now on,
> My heart's content will here be fulfilled.
> Though I lack the beauty of a panther,
> At last I can retire into the South Mountain mist.[40]
>   (*HHCS*, 53)

既歡懷祿情
復協滄洲趣
囂塵自茲隔
賞心於此遇
雖無玄豹姿
終隱南山霧

Hsieh T'iao was soon to discover that indeed he had finally found a land of paradise. He called Hsüan-ch'eng "the town of mountains and waters" (*shan-shui tu*), and here he was to produce memorable *shan-shui* poems that eventually captured the imagination of many T'ang poets, particularly Li Po.

III. Landscape as Artistic Experience

It is hardly surprising that in writing his *shan-shui* poems Hsieh T'iao would look up to his kinsman Hsieh Ling-yün—the renowned poet of "mountains

---

[40] A panther in the South Mountain was said to have soaked in heavy mist for seven long days with complete abstinence from food in order to refine the quality of its hair and patterned skin. (See Note 6 in *HHCS*, 54.) The allusion is especially appropriate here, since Hsieh T'iao wishes to devote himself to moral growth in semi-retirement.

Hsieh T'iao
THE INWARD TURN OF LANDSCAPE

and rivers"—as his precursor. For one thing, his life-style reminds one of Hsieh Ling-yün's. During his one-and-a-half-year residence in Hsüan-ch'eng, Hsieh T'iao seems to have spent a great deal of his time touring around the scenic area in that county. All this is clearly shown by some of the titles of his poems:

Mountain-Climbing and Sight-Seeing in the Prefecture of Hsüan-ch'eng
宣城郡內登望

Overlooking the Three Lakes
望三湖

Wandering in the Mountains
遊山

Touring Mt. Ching-t'ing
遊敬亭山

Touring the Eastern Field
遊東田

His enthusiastic search for dramatic scenes of craggy peaks and winding streams also brings us back to the world of Hsieh Ling-yün. He says in his poem "Making an Excursion to the Mountains":

Luckily I've come to this town of mountains and rivers,
And come at the time of clear winter.
I labor up crags, never less than eight thousand feet high,
I follow streams with ten thousand turns.
Solid cliffs are towering and craggy,
Meandering currents curve and twist.
　　(*HHCS*, 64)
幸蒞山水都
復值清冬緬
淩崖必千仞
尋溪將萬轉
堅崿既崚嶒
迴流復宛澶

What is new in Hsieh T'iao is a different attitude toward "semi-eremitism in office"—what the Chinese call "*ch'ao-yin*."[41] To Hsieh T'iao, holding an office in this "town of mountains and waters" was a wonderful way to

[41] Wang Yao, *Chung-ku wen-jen sheng-huo* (1951; rpt. Hong Kong: Chung-liu ch'u-pan-she, 1973), p. 107.

Hsieh T'iao
THE INWARD TURN OF LANDSCAPE

withdraw from active participation in public life. On the one hand, he was able to enjoy all the leisure-time pursuits of a recluse; and yet at the same time he did not need to openly denounce the values of officialdom. Indeed he was self-congratulatory about the attainment of such a way of life, as he confessed to his good friend Shen Yüeh in a poem:

> And now that I reside in this coign of the South Mountain,
> Is this different from leading a recluse's life?
> (*HHCC*, 363)
> 況復南山曲
> 何異幽棲時

In response, Shen Yüeh also expressed his firm conviction in this shared credo:

> To serve, yet not befriend authorities,
> To withdraw from the world, but not from worldly noise.
> (*WH*, Chüan 30, I, 672)
> 從宦非宦侶
> 避世不避喧

To have such an easy conscience about semi-eremitism in office is a long step beyond the dilemma of choice between service and retirement that infected Hsieh Ling-yün. As has been discussed in Chapter Two, Hsieh Ling-yün's life was plagued by this conflict—a reflection of the general intellectual climate of his time. By temperament Hsieh Ling-yün aspired to the leisured life of a recluse, but he could never forget the commitments or the lures of public life. Thus, in office he tended to long for retirement, but once living in his family estate he yearned for public service. As a result, he often swerved back and forth between the two. More than once he tried to live like a recluse in office, but he would irrevocably feel guilty and unsatisfied in doing so. On his way to voluntary retirement from Yung-chia, Hsieh Ling-yün admitted his failure to bring about a reconciliation between withdrawal and service:

> Looking back, I see I was committed to withdrawal
> But unable to act according to my wish.
> (*HLYS*, 62)
> 顧己雖自許
> 心迹猶未并

To Hsieh T'iao, however, living in seclusion has become more of a state of mind than a physical withdrawal. Although occasionally he expresses in his poetry a desire to retire, it is rather the quality of freedom that he aspires to.[42] Indeed, life in Hsüan-ch'eng seems to demonstrate a relaxed atmosphere

[42] Wang Yao, *Chung-ku wen-jen sheng-huo*, pp. 108–109.

Hsieh T'iao
THE INWARD TURN OF LANDSCAPE

reminiscent of the ideal recluse's life. In the following poem Hsieh T'iao describes the joyous experience of viewing scenery from his lofty study:

LOOKING OUT LEISURELY FROM THE LOFTY STUDY
IN MY COMMANDERY—A POEM IN REPLY TO
THE OFFICER OF JUSTICE, LÜ

How secluded and lofty is this building,
I gaze into the distance, and see heights and abysses.
My window frames remote peaks,
Tall trees bow their heads around the courtyard.   4
When the sun rises, flocks of birds disperse,
When the mountains darken, lonely apes cry.
I have drunk some wine by the pond,
And now I play the zither in the wind.   8
If not for you, most virtuous man,
For whom would I tax my soul?
Out of gracious affection for me,
You have sent me a poem, melodious as the sound of jade— 12
It is as though you had come out from your Golden Gate,
And visited me at this mountain peak.
    (*HHCS*, 100)

郡內高齋閑望答呂法曹

結構何迢遰
曠望極高深
窗中列遠岫
庭際俯喬林
日出衆鳥散
山暝孤猿吟
已有池上酌
復此風中琴
非君美無度
孰爲勞寸心
惠而能好我
問以瑤華音
若遺金門步
見就此山岑

The word "leisurely" (*hsien*) in the title reveals the central meaning of the poem. It is the unhurried leisure that gives a recluse a sense of fullness beyond temporal limits. The fullness is also spatial: when the poet gazes far into the

Hsieh T'iao
THE INWARD TURN OF LANDSCAPE

high mountains and deep valleys, distance seems to disappear (lines 1–2). For at this moment all sensory impressions are compressed into art, crystallized into the moment—all framed by the window (line 3). Quietude, true quietude, governs this world of self-containment: birds are easily frightened away by the silent sun rising; one hears nothing but the lonely monkey's cry (lines 5–6). All is constant and full—perfect scenery, wine, music, and now the pleasure of writing poetry (lines 7–10).

Thus Hsieh T'iao, by an extraordinary internalization of the *shan-shui* landscape, creates a spirit of withdrawal, a consciousness that is solitary but not deficient. Such a feeling of perfect equilibrium must have inspired the T'ang poet Li Po to place Hsieh T'iao alongside T'ao Ch'ien as his model poet *par excellence*:

> My house is near the blue mountain, like Hsieh T'iao's,
> At my door green willow branches hang down, like T'ao Ch'ien's.[43]
> 宅近青山同謝朓
> 門垂碧柳似陶潛

Yet Hsieh T'iao is different from T'ao Ch'ien in that his scenery is "framed," "enclosed" by a window. There is an inward direction and withdrawal in Hsieh T'iao which makes artificiality the equivalent of nature. Explicitly or implicitly, consciously or unconsciously, almost everything he creates represents the desire to structure and refine.

His *shan-shui* poems in the octave form may be born out of this desire to enclose the landscape in a structural frame. As has been mentioned, the two middle couplets in his octave verse are usually made of parallel lines that are descriptive in principle. Now, the middle couplets are not just descriptions of nature, but more specifically those of "mountains and waters," as in the following poem:

> From the mountain rises the fragrant moon,
> Old friend, you've come with a jug of pure wine.
> By the distant ridges, a hundred layers of green,
> In the winding streams, ten thousand feet of reflections.   4
> Blossoming branches pile up like snow,
> Wild weeds scatter like webs.
> How I will think of you after we part!
> How sad that we serve in different parts of the country!   8
>   (*HHCS*, 73)
> 山中上芳月
> 故人清樽賞

---

[43] See Li Po, *Li T'ai-po ch'üan-chi, chüan* 25, II, 1,156.

Hsieh T'iao
THE INWARD TURN OF LANDSCAPE

遠山翠百重
迴流映千丈
花枝聚如雪
蕉絲散猶網
別後能相思
何嗟異封壤

Line 3 is about a mountain scene, and line 4 a river scene. Couplet two describes a far-off scene, and couplet three a nearby sight. This method of alternation recalls the basic technique of Hsieh Ling-yün's *shan-shui* poetry. Yet, instead of borrowing Hsieh Ling-yün's enumerative description, Hsieh T'iao frames his mosaic-like images in a minimum number of lines. As a result, the poem seems to achieve a different kind of existence—a self-contained world comparable to the scenes framed by the window. There is a new restraint, a sense of economy, an aesthetic retreat toward formalism.

But I do not mean to suggest that all the *shan-shui* poems that Hsieh T'iao wrote during his Hsüan-ch'eng days are in the compact octave form. In fact, more than half of them are in the "ancient style."[44] What stands out as distinctively new about Hsieh T'iao's *shan-shui* poetry—new in the sense of expressing the formalistic attitude of the Southern Ch'i era—is its tendency to compress images of landscape. This tendency was to blossom into the basic style of nature poetry in the T'ang.

IV. Aesthetics of the Miniature Form

Another important contribution that Hsieh T'iao made to Chinese poetry during this period was in his creative experiments with yet another miniature form—this time the quatrain. Once again this form found its proper setting first in a certain social situation.

From the beginning Hsieh T'iao was not alone as a sightseer in his "town of mountains and waters." The feeling of loneliness so characteristic of Hsieh Ling-yün's landscape poetry is thus absent in Hsieh T'iao's *shan-shui* poetry. Instead, we find in Hsieh T'iao a wealth of descriptions of traveling joyously with friends, accompanied by drinking and childlike games. As magistrate of the town, Hsieh T'iao managed to gather around himself a privileged literary group not unlike the earlier salon to which he had belonged in his younger days. What is new here is that the participants in Hsieh T'iao's group not only practice writing poetry but explore the beautiful landscape together.

---

[44] I am using the term anachronistically here. "Ancient Style poetry" (*ku-shih*) as a term did not emerge until the T'ang, when it became necessary for poets to distinguish the Regulated Style Poetry from poems written in the old style.

Hsieh T'iao
THE INWARD TURN OF LANDSCAPE

Hsieh T'iao and his friends did not employ the octave form to describe their collective sightseeing experience, as Prince Ching-ling's salon members did for their *yung-wu* poetry. Rather, they chose the quatrain sequence called *lien-chü*, in which poets took turns composing four-line verse, the whole linked as in a circle. The practice was somewhat similar to the Japanese *renga* developed later, though not as complicated.[45] In China the practice of writing *lien-chü* did not start with Hsieh T'iao; it can be traced back to as early as the Chin Dynasty.[46] Poets like T'ao Ch'ien and Pao Chao had occasionally produced poem sequences with their friends. However, it was with Hsieh T'iao that the *lien-chü* began to be formalized into a consistent quatrain sequence pattern. Prior to this time, the *lien-chü* often was comprised of poems of varying length. More important, Hsieh T'iao and his friends managed to create a distinctly descriptive mode in this social genre, making the *shan-shui* landscape its main content. The following quatrain sequence entitled "On Our Way to Ching-t'ing Road" (*HHCS*, 171) is one such example:

1. Hsieh T'iao:

> In the mountain fragrant pollia are green,
> South of the Yangtze lotus leaves are purple.
> If we don't make merry together in our sweet years,
> We'll be left stranded, and feel so empty.
> 山中芳杜綠
> 江南蓮葉紫
> 芳年不共遊
> 淹留空若是

2. Assistant Gentleman (*ts'ung-shih*) Ho:

> The green water is rich in ripples,
> The blue mountain abounds with ornamental patterns.
> New branches are growing everyday,
> Fallen flowers have withered one by one.
> 綠水豐漣漪
> 青山多繡綺
> 新條日向抽
> 落花紛已委

---

[45] For the Japanese renga, see Earl Miner, *Japanese Linked Poetry: An Account with Translations of Renga and Haikai Sequences* (Princeton: Princeton Univ. Press, 1979).

[46] Lo Ken-tse, "Chüeh-chü san-yüan," in *Chung-kuo ku-tien wen-hsüeh lun-ts'ung* (Peking: Wu-shih nien-tai ch'u-pan-she, 1955), pp. 28–53. For a discussion of *lien-chü* poetry in the T'ang, see Stephen Owen, *The Poetry of Meng Chiao and Han Yü* (New Haven: Yale Univ. Press, 1975), pp. 116–136.

Hsieh T'iao
THE INWARD TURN OF LANDSCAPE

3. Assistant (*chü-lang*) Ch'i:

   Young trees are bluish green,
   Light grasses are just becoming lush.
   The gulls have departed to wander,
   Small deer sport and rest.
   弱鬖既青翠
   輕莎方靃靡
   鷖鷗沒而遊
   麚麂騰復倚

4. Gentleman (*lang*) Ch'en:

   I gaze at the the spring bank—it extends endlessly,
   I see the clear river overflow.
   Luckily, because of you, I have come for this outing,
   Strolling and lingering, I am too happy to move on.
   春岸望沈沈
   清流見瀰瀰
   幸藉人外遊
   盤桓未能徙

5. Hsieh T'iao:

   Boating swiftly down the river, we grasp fragrant flowers,
   Following the mountain, we visit spiritual beings.
   The beautiful railing is surrounded by many rugged hills,
   In the forest, so many jagged rocks.
   鷁枻把瓊芳
   隨山訪靈詭
   榮楯每嶙峋
   林堂多碕磯

These poems are joined in chain-link succession to make a long descriptive verse on mountains and waters. The above sequence may be summed up as follows:

   Poem 1: Mountains and waters (couplet one)
           Prelude to the excursion (couplet two)
   Poem 2: Mountains and waters (couplet one)
           Trees and flowers (couplet two)
   Poem 3: Trees and flowers (couplet one)
           Birds and animals (couplet two)
   Poem 4: Water scene (couplet one)
           Comment on the excursion (couplet two)

Hsieh T'iao
THE INWARD TURN OF LANDSCAPE

>   Poem 5: Comment on the excursion (couplet one)
>   Mountain scene (couplet two)

All the couplets in the sequence, with the two minor exceptions in Poems 1 and 4, are made up of parallel lines. One may say that parallelism is the characteristic feature of this kind of quatrain sequence. Since all such extant sequences except one were produced during Hsieh's term of office in Hsüan-ch'eng, we assume that the form became popular only after Hsieh T'iao began to assemble his literary group there. Judging from the social nature of this genre, we have reason to believe that Hsieh T'iao and other members of the group were using the quatrain sequence mainly as a practice game to improve their skill in parallel construction. And the parallel structure perceived within the natural mountain-water coordinates must have appeared to them as a good model to emulate.

There were times when the individual quatrains were written by poets at different places, and were later strung together to make one sequence (e.g., HHCC, 469). When individual poets were unable to link their verses together with poems of their friends, they called their independent quatrains *chüeh*, meaning "something cut-off."[47] This practice gave rise to the term *chüeh-chü* ("cut-off verse") in the Liang Dynasty, which later became a standard term for all types of quatrains.

Yet the quatrain as a form, long before it was baptized by name, had existed in the *yüeh-fu* tradition all along. During the Six Dynasties the quatrain grew vigorously into a major form of popular songs; its popularity and success among the common people were a known fact. Nevertheless, the form was long ignored by the elite poets until Pao Chao, a versatile poet with a fascination for generic innovation, began to produce a few delightful quatrains in imitation of the popular style. For example, we have the following *yüeh-fu* by Pao Chao:

>   Plum blossoms dazzle just one season,
>   Bamboo leaves are beautiful for a thousand years.
>   I hope your heart is like the pine and cypress,
>   Shining forever without end.
>   (*PTCC*, 216)
>   梅花一時艷
>   竹葉千年色
>   願君松柏心
>   采照無窮極

The contribution of Hsieh T'iao lies in his giving this rather precarious form of the quatrain a sophisticated structure—he readily applied the formal

---

[47] Lo Ken-tse, "Chüeh-chü san-yüan," p. 43.

rules of the octave form to this essentially popular genre. The result was a new poetic form, a crystallization of the poet's creation. To Hsieh T'iao a quatrain was a "minor versification" (*hsiao-shih*) whose essential compactness was most suited for realizing his self-contained lyricism.

In sharp contrast to his contributions to the collective quatrain sequence which are characteristically descriptive, his own *hsiao-shih* are eminently lyrical. It is in this poetry that his arresting power as a master of the minimum form is best revealed. Just one example suffices to demonstrate his philosophy that less is more:

THE SORROW OF BRONZE BIRD TOWER

The setting sun above the lofty city wall,
Its dim light penetrates the curtain.
Quiet and lonely stand the pine trees deep at night,
How can they know the lament on the zither [*ch'in se*]?[48]
    (*HHCS*, 28)

銅爵悲

落日高城上
餘光入綖帷
寂寂深松晚
寧知琴瑟悲

This poem opens with a vivid image of a sunset, and ends with a rhetorical question conveying a sense of sadness. At first glance the quatrain appears to be no more than a simple statement of a momentary perception, and indeed it could be quite appropriately appreciated on that level. But, in truth, the sunset scene is no ordinary view. It is sunset on a graveyard.

Nor is the graveyard an ordinary graveyard: it is one full of historical significance and human implications. It belongs to Ts'ao Ts'ao (155–220), a hero whose ruthless pursuit of power made him a famous figure in Chinese history and popular fiction. Ts'ao Ts'ao first succeeded in unifying North China during the final days of the Eastern Han, but he had an ambition to conquer the whole of China and to establish his own dynasty. Then in 208 he suffered a severe defeat at the Red Cliffs of Hupei which prevented him from taking over the Yangtze valley. According to popular legend, it was this Battle of the Red Cliffs that was eventually to bring about the division of

---

[48] *Ch'in se*, literally "a seven-stringed zither and a twenty-five-stringed zither," also suggests a conjugal couple. The sorrow of Ts'ao Ts'ao's widow and concubines is implied in this line.

Hsieh T'iao
THE INWARD TURN OF LANDSCAPE

China into three kingdoms: Wei under the Ts'ao family (220–265), Shu-Han under Liu Pei (221–263), and Wu under Sun Ch'üan (222–280). For the first time, Ts'ao Ts'ao realized the limits of his strength; it was a feeling of loneliness resulting from his failure to realize his greatest ambitions. He wanted to create his own image of immensity and eternity through other means. So in 210 he built a sky-high tower in the western suburb of the city of Yeh (in modern Honan), with a gigantic bronze bird standing on top of the tower. The idea was that the bird, a permanent symbol of his high-reaching ambitions, was always ready to soar into the sky. He willed that upon his death his body should be buried on the nearby hill, with his tomb facing the Bronze Bird Tower. The numerous women that he left behind—his widow and concubines—were to reside in this one-hundred-and-twenty roomed tower, overlooking his resting place. On the fifteenth day of each month singing girls were to be summoned to perform in the tower, while his sons were to climb the tower to view his burial mound.[49]

Hsieh T'iao's quatrain, a *yüeh-fu*, is entitled "The Sorrow of Bronze Bird Tower," and by this title it directs its readers explicitly to the tragedy of Ts'ao Ts'ao. The hero's artificial monument of personal glory is itself a symbol of emptiness and imperfection. Great as he was, Ts'ao Ts'ao was unable to overcome death. Out of this arose his wish to go beyond the present, to leave himself an illusion of immortality. The power of Hsieh's poem lies in its ability to focus on one moment in time that is by nature most transitory: the sunset will disappear and darkness will soon reign over the tower and the graveyard. At this moment we see faint remnants of sunlight creep through the curtain screen, while sad music is played in the tower. Ts'ao Ts'ao's women are still mourning his death, and yet the lonely hero in the tomb, accompanied by the silent pines, is dead forever. He is no longer aware of human emotions, let alone of his own greatness.

All these meanings are embodied in the imagistic suggestiveness of the poem, which contains but four lines.[50] There is a feeling of endless overtones established by the rhetorical question at the end of the poem. By this question the poet seems to project his view into something beyond—beyond the immediate confines of the poem, beyond the personal history of Ts'ao Ts'ao. We are being led to contemplate the universal tragedy of life and its many implications. The impression created is that the poem does not end with its ending.

There is another type of quatrain by Hsieh T'iao which concludes with a negative statement, and yet achieves a similar effect of endless overtones:

---

[49] This story is recorded in *Yeh-tu ku-shih*, as cited in *YFSC*, *chüan* 31, II, 454.

[50] Shuen-fu Lin calls such poetic effect "the aesthetics of subtlety." See his "The Nature of the Quatrain," in *ESP*.

Hsieh T'iao
THE INWARD TURN OF LANDSCAPE

A PRINCE WENT WANDERING

The green grass is dense like silk,
All kinds of trees put forth their crimson blossoms.
Don't bother to tell me you won't return—
Even if you return, the flowers will have withered.
   (*HHCS*, 27)

王孫遊

綠草蔓如絲
雜樹紅英發
無論君不歸
君歸芳已歇

By the strong ending the poem seems to engender a feeling of continuing anxiety; it is rather like a bridge to a new state of mind.

Hsieh T'iao's general poetic device is this: to begin a quatrain with an evocative natural image, and end it with an expression of strong feeling, either by a rhetorical question or a negative statement. This stylistic feature of Hsieh's was to become an important conventional device in the later *chüeh-chü*.[51] The aesthetics of the endless overtones remains one of the supreme expressions of the Chinese sense of "meaning beyond words."

Hsieh T'iao might have been able to bring about more poetic innovations, but he had no opportunity to do so because of his early death. His life was brought to an abrupt end at the age of thirty-five, when a friend's secret plot, and unfounded implications drawn from it, led directly to his execution. Like the quatrain, Hsieh T'iao's life stops at a point of incompletion, leaving a pang of sorrow for future poets. Although China seems to value its poetry highly, it treats its poets lightly.

Only three years after Hsieh's death, Hsiao Yen, one of the "eight friends of Prince Ching-ling," proceeded to the capital to usurp the throne from his own cousin. A new dynasty, the Liang, was founded in 502, and literature again sustained itself—this time more vigorously—in the struggle over dynastic change.

---

[51] Yu-kung Kao and Tsu-lin Mei, "Ending Lines in Wang Shih-chen's Ch'i-chüeh: Convention and Creativity in the Ch'ing," in *Artists and Traditions*, ed. Christian F. Murck (Princeton: Princeton Univ. Press, 1976), p. 134.

8. A picture of Emperor Wu of the Liang by an unidentified artist. Color and ink on silk.

V
Yü Hsin

THE POET'S POET

I. Literature Inside and Outside the Palace

With Hsiao Yen, Emperor Wu of the Liang, Southern Dynasties literature burst into full bloom. The Emperor's unusually long life—which began the same year as Hsieh T'iao's, but lasted fifty years longer—provided China with a sense of peace and stability crucial for the flowering of literature. As a practicing poet himself, Emperor Wu was particularly interested in creating a literary environment in the palace. He set up two new offices in the government, the Departments of Literary Virtues (*Wen-te*) and Everlasting Light (*Shou-kuang*), exclusively for the recruitment of young talent and the promotion of poetic activities. Morever, his old friends from Prince Ching-ling's salon circle—with the exception of Hsieh T'iao and Wang Jung—were still alive and active. Shen Yüeh in particular exchanged poems regularly with the Emperor in banquets held frequently in the literary quarters of the palace. Such activities were not limited to the central court, however. The generous Emperor even encouraged his many brothers, who were lords of provincial districts, to develop similar literary groups. And in barely a generation his sons were to establish their own salons which eventually became the centers of the major literary schools of the Liang.[1] For the first time in China salon culture was brought to a peak of success.

Unlike Prince Ching-ling, who was primarily interested in the formal aspects of literature, Emperor Wu had a special fascination for the romantic popular *yüeh-fu* songs currently in vogue in the south. The straightforward expression of sensual love in the songs sung by singing girls set them apart from the more orthodox *yüeh-fu* of the Han and the Wei. The two most

---

[1] See John Marney, *Liang Chien-wen Ti* (Boston: Twayne Publications, 1976), pp. 60–75.

Yü Hsin
THE POET'S POET

popular styles of the newly emerging *yüeh-fu*—namely, the Wu songs (*Wu-ko*) and Western melodies (*hsi-ch'ü*), both in the quatrain form—were developed in the capital area and the Ching-chou region respectively. Emperor Wu happened to be particularly familiar with the social customs of these two cities, thanks to his earlier provincial days in Ching-chou and his longstanding association with the capital at Chien-k'ang.

The popularity of the new *yüeh-fu* songs—what the Liang people called "modern" (*chin-tai*) songs—resulted directly from the growing prosperity of cities since the Yung-ming era of the Ch'i.[2] *The Southern History* (*Nan shih*) explains convincingly the correlation between urban development and the common pursuits for new forms of entertainment:

> The Yung-ming reign continued to thrive, and [Emperor Wu] devoted himself to affairs of government.... For more than ten years the people were never startled by a dog barking at a thief. The cities were prosperous, and men and women lived in abundance and leisure. Everywhere one could hear singing voices and rhythms of dancing steps, and see dazzling costumes and elaborate make-ups. Along the peach-blossom bank, by the green water, in the autumn wind, under the spring moon—there was no place where one could not have one's desire fulfilled. (*Chüan* 70, VI, 1696–1697)
> 永明繼運，垂心政術。...十許年間，百姓無犬吠之驚，都邑之盛，士女昌逸，歌聲舞節，炫服華妝，桃花淥水之間，秋風春月之下，無往非適。

It is not at all surprising that the love songs that became popular in the cities reflected the life of the singing girls. These women, parading in heavy make-up and elaborate costumes, became the objects of frivolous affection. They entertained their guests with songs like the following:

> Green lily pads overspread the azure water,
> Lotus in full bloom, pink and fresh.
> Seeing me, that man desires to pluck me,
> My heart longs to embrace the lotus [*lien*].
>   (*YFSC*, II, 646)
> 青荷蓋淥水
> 芙蓉葩紅鮮
> 郎見欲採我
> 我心欲懷蓮

[2] For the term "modern," see *chüan* 10 of *Yü-t'ai hsin-yung* (*New Songs from a Jade Terrace*) edited by Hsü Ling (507–583). For the relationship between the emergence of these songs and the social phenomena of the time, see Liao Wei-ch'ing, "Nan-ch'ao *yüeh-fu* yü tang-shih she-hui te kuan-hsi," in *CKWH*, 569–589.

Yü Hsin
THE POET'S POET

Emperor Wu was so delighted by these short *yüeh-fu* that he set out to compose quatrain songs in his imperial palace in imitation of the popular song style:

> Lotus [*lien*] flowers bloom in the South of Yangtze,
> Their pink radiance spreads over cerulean water.
> Their colors are one as their hearts are one,
> Though their roots are apart, their hearts are together.
>   (*YFSC*, 649)
> 江南蓮花開
> 紅光復碧水
> 色同心復同
> 藕異心無異

In terms of diction and theme—and especially in its use of the popular pun *lien* (lotus) to mean *lien* (love)—the Emperor's poem could easily pass for a singing girl's song. The Emperor's imitation of popular songs is evidence of the new literary tendencies at the time.

Certainly the so-called "Wu songs" and "Western melodies" had already caught the fancy of some emperors in the south prior to the Liang. For example, Emperor Hsiao-wu of the Liu-Sung (Sung Hsiao-wu ti) wrote this verse in imitation of Wu songs:

A Song to Chief Commandant Ting

> The Chief Commandant is on a northern expedition,
> I bid him farewell at the ruins of Fallen Star Tower.[3]
> His ship's mast is like a large weeping willow,
> Chief Commandant, where are you headed today?
>   (*CHSK*, II, 580)

> 丁督護歌
>
> 督護北征去
> 相送落星墟
> 帆檣如芒穊
> 督護今何渠

And Emperor Wu of the Ch'i (Ch'i Wu-ti), the father of Prince Ching-ling, wrote a quatrain set to a Western melody:

---

[3] The Fallen Star Tower, located near modern Nanking, was built by the Wu in the third century.

Yü Hsin
THE POET'S POET

TRAVELER'S SONG

Long ago, campaigning through Fan and Teng,[4]
We were stopped by the turbulent tide at the Mei-ken sandbar.[5]
Now, full of emotion, recalling the past events,
My heart overflows with feelings no words can express.
   (*YFSC*, III, 699)

估客樂

昔經樊鄧役
阻潮梅根渚
感憶追往事
意滿辭不叙

Such sporadic literary endeavors were no doubt important experiments that paved the way for Hsiao Yen's extensive involvement with the popular song culture. Yet Hsiao Yen's attitude was significantly new: whereas his royal predecessors focused their songs on the description of battlefields, a subject that matched well their imperial status, Hsiao Yen chose to write about the world of beautiful women. No other era in prior Chinese history saw an emperor so comfortably display in his poetry frivolity over women.

Yet Emperor Wu's songs on women are different from the contemporary popular songs in one particular aspect: the emotional content to typical of the Wu songs and Western melodies is generally absent in his *yüeh-fu* quatrains. In his poetry there is little personal feeling expressed; instead, there is objective contemplation of female beauty. Moreover, it is the man's view—not the woman's view of herself—that is at issue. His song "*Tzu-yeh ko*" is a typical example:

The morning sun shines upon the open-worked window,
A light breeze caresses her fine silk garment.
A captivating smile brightens her temples,
Her pretty eyes heighten her delicate eyebrows.
   (*CHSK*, II, 853)

朝日照綺窗
光風動紈羅
巧笑蒨兩犀
美目揚雙蛾

Emperor Wu's poetic style was without doubt influenced by that of Pao Chao. As has been observed in Chapter Three, Pao Chao was the only

---
[4] Both places are located in modern Hupeh.
[5] Mei-ken River, in An-hui Province, has been known for its rapid and dangerous currents.

Yü Hsin
THE POET'S POET

literatus poet in his time to write so extensively in the *yüeh-fu* form. Most of his songs, it is true, were written in the longer form typical of the orthodox *yüeh-fu*, with subjects ranging from social criticism to personal complaints. Yet he also produced several (as many as thirteen still extant) quatrains to contemporary popular tunes.[6] The following song by Pao Chao reminds one of the typical descriptive style of Emperor Wu's quatrains:

TO THE TUNE, "NATIONAL REVIVAL"

The bright sun shines on the front window,
Charming in her fine silk dress,
A beauty covers her face with a light fan,
Full of longing, she sings in the spring wind.
    (*PTCC*, 214)

中興歌

白日照前窗
玲瓏綺羅中
美人掩輕扇
含思歌春風

It is no coincidence that the basic notion of description coveyed in these songs resembles that of the *yung-wu* poetry popular since the Southern Ch'i Dynasty. As discussed in the previous chapter, one of the most important products of Prince Ching-ling's salon, of which Hsiao Yen was a member, was the collective composition of octave poems that sing of various objects present at the literary gatherings. Now, as Emperor Wu of the Liang, Hsiao Yen continued this practice of poetry writing in his own palace salon, except that for his *yung-wu* poetry he preferred the four-line verse to the octave form—proof of the growing popularity of the quatrain. See, for example, his "Ode on the Bamboo Flute":

Near K'o Pavilion, there is a rare bamboo,
Full of feeling, its sounds are rich in melody.[7]
Sweet music now comes from her jade fingers,
Dragon melodies echo the songs of phoenixes.
    (*CHSK*, II, 869)

---

[6] See his Wu songs and *yüeh-fu* series entitled "The Songs of Chung-hsing," in *PTCC*, 206–207, 213–216.

[7] K'o Pavilion was located in what is modern Shao-hsing in Chekiang Province. The poet Ts'ai Yung (133–192) once spent a night there while traveling. Recognizing the unusual quality of the bamboo growing around the pavilion, he made a flute out of it, which became one of his dearest treasures.

Yü Hsin
THE POET'S POET

柯亭有奇竹
含情復抑揚
妙聲發玉指
龍音响鳳凰

This poem calls attention not only to the flute itself, but more importantly to the jade-like fingers of the female performer.[8] This is a crucial point, for it shows that women had become indispensable components of salon life. As a result, women came to be treated as favorite "objects" of description. Gradually, poems on women—and their attributes and movements—came to be considered a major type of descriptive poetry.

Yet in this kind of poetry women often seem more lively than other "objects." This is because when a female "object" springs into action, a scene of performance is naturally presented. A case in point is Emperor Wu's poem on a female dancer:

ODE ON DANCING

Delicate arms flutter up and down,
Her body light, turning freely round and round.
Truly she lets herself go,
Only then does she fulfill her heart's desire.
    (*CHSK*, II, 868)

詠舞

腕弱復低舉
身輕由迴縱
可謂寫自歡
方與心期共

At this point it becomes clear to us that such courtly verse, despite its distinctly descriptive style, has the same concern with feminine sensuality as the romantic *yüeh-fu* songs in vogue in the capital and the Ching-chou areas. An active convergence of the salon poetry and popular songs in the early sixth century is thus clearly revealed.

When Hsiao Yen ascended the throne, he was thirty-eight years old. It is believed that soon after he turned fifty he became almost a new person—a devout Buddhist and ascetic, denying himself the enjoyment of women, wine, and music.[9] His dramatic change in life-style was reflected in the many Bud-

---

[8] Emperor Wu might have borrowed this image from one of Shen Yüeh's early octave poems composed in the Ching-ling circle (*HHCC*, 450). In any case, this only corroborates the view that the emergence of a predominant literary trend is never sudden or without a reason.

[9] Yao Ssu-lien, *Liang shu*, chüan 3, I, 97.

Yü Hsin
THE POET'S POET

dhist poems he produced, supposedly during his old age. We assume that by this time his literary salon, which at first had staged for Chinese literature a new poetic sensualism, had already changed its emphasis. The Emperor's palace now displayed a wise old man shunning the relaxed frivolity of his good "old" days.

The heir apparent, Prince Chao-ming, named Hsiao T'ung (501–531), was slowly reaching maturity as his father Emperor Wu became a devout Buddhist. By nature Hsiao T'ung preferred the more orthodox literature and classics to the ornate and sensuous poetry in vogue. And the reformed views of his father were most congenial to his individual literary taste. At the age of fifteen, he had already assembled many scholars and poets in his eastern court, and engaged in all kinds of literary activities with an enthusiasm unprecedented at the imperial court. He built a grand hall for editorial and other literary enterprises, and had the portraits of his distinguished poet-friends displayed in the hall.[10] Years later Hsiao T'ung, together with his friends, compiled the famous anthology *Wen-hsüan*, selecting and organizing according to genres the literary works by past authors from the Han down to the Liang.[11] This anthology, the first of its kind in Chinese literature, may be seen as a reaction against the many new and frivolous tendencies in the contemporary poetry. It is striking that Hsiao T'ung excludes from the collection all sensuous *yüeh-fu* of the south and the descriptive *shih* on "objects," although he himself also produced two or three *yung-wu* poems (*CHSK*, II, 878). But, at the same time, the anthology contains many *yung-wu* pieces in the *fu* form—e.g., "The *Fu* on Snow," by Hsieh Hui-lien, and "The *Fu* on the Moon," by Hsieh Chuang. Why such inconsistency? Perhaps Hsiao T'ung felt that *yung-wu* as a mode should be limited to the *fu* genre, while *shih* must always be kept within the limits of lyricism—a conservative view which his liberal contemporaries would not endorse.

Then we face the most interesting case of what may be called literary revisionism. Among all the previous literary figures, Hsiao T'ung singled out T'ao Ch'ien—a poet who had been neglected and forgotten for a century—as a model of perfection. He set out to edit the collected works of T'ao Ch'ien, and wrote a preface that revealed his unqualified respect for the poet:

> His literary works are never common, and his verbal embellishments are refined and distinguished. Unrestrained and splendid, his writings are unique and supreme in all genres.... Moreover, he always held on to his moral integrity, and was at ease with hardships.... I have a special fondness for his writings; when reading

---

[10] See biography of Liu Hsiao-ch'o, in Yao Ssu-lien, *Liang shu, chüan* 33, II, 480.

[11] See Knechtges' *Wen xuan*, vol. 1, the first of a projected eight-volume translation of the entire anthology.

Yü Hsin
THE POET'S POET

> them I can never put them down. I think of his virtue with admiration, and regret that I did not live in his time.... (*TYMC*, 10)
> 其文章不羣，詞采精拔，跌宕昭彰，獨超衆類。...加以貞志不休，安道苦節。...余愛嗜其文，不能釋手，尚想其德，恨不同時。...

This was to become the declaration of literary independence for Hsiao T'ung: just as T'ao Ch'ien, who produced poetry that was set apart from contemporary trends by virtue of its plain diction and "respectable" content, so would he rise above the general crowd in realizing his individual taste. Indeed the sober Hsiao T'ung went so far as to regard all expressions of love between men and women as improper. He commented with considerable regret that T'ao Ch'ien's "*Fu* on Calming the Passions" was like a "minor flaw in a white jade" (*TYMC*, 10), even though the message of the *fu* is precisely the denial of untrammeled emotion.

Hsiao T'ung's unprecedented collection of T'ao Ch'ien's work no doubt generated a revived interest in T'ao Ch'ien among contemporary poets and readers. However, readers at this time were obviously more impressed with T'ao Ch'ien's exemplary virtues than with his poetic style. They hoped to learn from him his tranquil attitude toward life, but not his "less than refined" poetry. A case in point was Hsiao T'ung's younger brother Hsiao Kang (503–551), who greatly admired T'ao Ch'ien's works, but whose own poetry was imbued with ornate sensualism.[12] Hsiao Kang's letter to the Lord of Tang-yang explains this peculiar combination of ethical self-cultivation in life and sensual indulgence in literature:

> The way of cultivating the self is different from the process of writing. To cultivate oneself one must first of all be prudent and sober. But in writing one should be wanton and untrammeled.[13]
> 立身之道，與文章異。立身先須謹重，文章且須放蕩。

The two brothers Hsiao T'ung and Hsiao Kang could not be more different in their poetic tastes. As heir apparent, Hsiao T'ung grew up in the court under the influence of his old father's reformed views. In contrast, from the tender age of six Hsiao Kang was continually moving from one provincial appointment to another, and thus had the opportunity to become familiar with the local popular song milieu. He possessed almost from the beginning an innate sensitivity toward Wu songs and Western melodies, and he had a particular gift for rich verbal formulations. His literary activities seemed to recall the youthful adventures of his father. But fate endowed him with yet more pri-

---

[12] See Chapter 9 of Yen Chih-t'ui's (531–591) *Yen-shih chia-hsün*, in Teng Ssu-yü, trans., *Family Instructions for the Clan* (Leiden: Brill, 1968), p. 107.
[13] Ou-yang Hsün, *I-wen lei-chü*, *chüan* 23 (Shanghai: Ku-chi ch'u-pan-she, 1982), I, 424.

Yü Hsin
THE POET'S POET

vileges: as the Emperor's son, he had the good fortune to receive constant guidance from excellent tutors from early childhood on. His two tutors, Yü Chien-wu (ca. 487–551) and Hsü Ch'ih (472–551), were poets of the highest caliber, and they accompanied him on all his official appointments. As Hsiao Kang gradually reached maturity, he became the leader of a salon, with the two tutors serving as his literary advisers. He eventually served in Yung-chou, a city not far from Ching-chou, where Western melodies originated. It was during the seven years in Yung-chou that Hsiao Kang came to learn from the popular songs the definitive style of sensory realism, and consequently his salon grew dramatically in size and influence.[14]

The climax came in 531, when suddenly the heir apparent, Hsiao T'ung, died in an accident. Hsiao Kang was immediately summoned back to the capital and became the crown prince at the age of twenty-seven. It is hardly surprising that with the appearance of the new heir apparent court literature again changed its direction, this time into what was to be known as the somewhat notorious Palace Style Poetry (*kung-t'i shih*).

The Palace Style Poetry was to a large extent similar to Emperor Wu's early poetry. But when this poetry first achieved a sensationally widespread popularity in the court, it met with the old Emperor's disapproval. In no time the angry Emperor Wu summoned Hsiao Kang's tutor Hsü Ch'ih to reprimand him for misconduct in teaching.[15] The Emperor then examined him on all branches of learning, including that of Buddhism, but was surprised to find that Hsü Ch'ih had all the correct answers. Thereupon Emperor Wu received the tutor with unusual respect and affection, and never again questioned the quality of the crown prince's education.

Hsiao Kang and his literary friends described their Palace Style Poetry as a kind of "innovation" (*hsin-pien*), perhaps with the implication that theirs was a movement equal in importance to the tonal innovation a few decades before. Indeed the term "innovation" became almost a trademark of their poetry. Soon after arriving in the Eastern Palace, Hsiao Kang wrote to his younger brother Hsiao I (then Prince of Hsiang-tung and later Emperor Yüan) to complain about the banality and sluggishness of the capital literature.[16] The talented Hsiao I (508–554) soon joined in his elder brother's literary cause, and eventually produced an important essay on criticism, "To Leave Worthy Writings to Posterity" (*Li-yen*), which is included in his well-known collection of works, *Chin-lou tzu* (*Master of the Golden Tower*). With an eye to promoting the new notion of literature, Hsiao I argued in his essay that their age demanded a more sophisticated way to distinguish *wen* (belles-lettres)

---

[14] See the biography of Yü Chien-wu, in Li Yen-shou, *Nan shih*, *chüan* 30, IV, 1246.

[15] See the biography of Hsu Ch'ih, in Yao Ssu-lien, *Liang shu*, *chüan* 30, II, 447.

[16] See Hsiao Kang's letter to Prince of Hsiang-tung, in *CKLT*, I, 327. Also in Marney, *Liang Chien-wen Ti*, p. 80.

from *pi* (plain writing). The current method of treating rhyme as the sole criterion of *wen* already seemed insufficient and out of date. To him *wen* should possess the following three qualities: emotion (*ch'ing*), ornate color (*ts'ai*), and rhyme (*yün*).[17] In other words, to rhyme, the Palace Style poets now added emotion and ornate diction as the criteria of belles-lettres. What is most interesting is that their definition of emotion (*ch'ing*) was anything but conventional: it referred primarily to the erotic feeling between men and women. For this reason, the so-called *ch'ing* (feeling) in traditional literature, such as that in Hsieh Ling-yün's poetry, was bound to seem rather cold to them.[18]

However, to twentieth-century readers it is the the Palace Style Poetry that appears to be cool, if not cold, in its approach. Despite its sensual suggestiveness, the Palace Style Poetry is essentially a form of objective description: it gives details about the palace women's heavy make-up, their embroidered clothes, their slender waistlines, and in general their radiant beauty. Of course, the alluring assemblages of details in such poetry cannot be said to be totally dissociated from *ch'ing* (feeling). However, since the feeling is not individualized, the impression created is one of objective representation—even in those poems where sexual activities are described.[19]

The Palace Style poets insist on the autonomy of their object—in most cases a beautiful woman. A brief survey of Hsiao Kang's extant poems reveals that many of them bear titles containing the expression "the beautiful woman" (*mei-jen*, or *li-jen*).[20] That beauty itself is the concern of poetry implies a primarily aesthetic attitude. By "aesthetic" I mean that which is free from the stimulus of emotion, since emotional involvement is never in its pure sense aesthetic. What Western aestheticians say about the aesthetics of disinterested contemplation may very well describe the poetic act involved in the Palace Style Poetry.

Poetry to Hsiao Kang is art about art, not just about life. He believes that the function of poetry is to portray beauty as an aesthetic quality that embodies its own reality and *raison d'être*. This attitude is most clearly revealed in poems that deal with paintings. For example, in Hsiao Kang's "Ode on the Beauty Viewing a Painting":

> In the hall a portrait of a divine woman,
> From the palace a splendid woman emerges.

---

[17] For a more detailed discussion of this point, see Lo Ken-tse, *Chung-kuo wen-hsüeh p'i-p'ing shih.* (rpt. Hong Kong: Tien-wen ch'u-pan-she, 1961), p. 143.

[18] See Hsiao Tzu-hsien, "Nan-Ch'i shu chuan lun," in *CKLT*, I, 264–165.

[19] See, for example, Hsiao Kang's poem on a seductive sleeping beauty (*CHSK*, II, 910), and his rather detailed account of a catamite engaged in a homosexual act (*CHSK*, II, 911).

[20] See *CHSK*, II, 908, 910, 919, 920, 932.

Yü Hsin
THE POET'S POET

> So lovely, both are painted beauties,
> Who can separate reality from art?
> Each has sharply defined eyes and brows,
> Their slender waistlines are one and the same.
> The only difference between them:
> One forever has that lively spirit.
>   (*CHSK*, II, 920)

殿上圖神女
宮裡出佳人
可憐俱是畫
誰能辨僞眞
分明淨眉眼
一種細腰身
所可持爲異
長有好精神

The poet's careful comparison of the palace woman and the goddess in the painting is interesting: it is like scrutinizing two art objects. Everything in the poem concerns the exact description of the beauty's appearances, creating an artificial detachment from the outside world. And the meaning implied in the concluding couplet is most pertinent to Hsiao Kang's belief in the permanent value of art—that the beauty in the painting will live forever, while the real woman's existence is only ephemeral.

But what literary value can such poetry have? In answering this challenge from his contemporaries, Hsiao Kang asked Hsü Ling (507–583), son of Hsü Ch'ih, to compile an anthology of poetry on women ranging from antiquity to the current Liang Dynasty—in order to demonstrate that there were classical models for their Palace Style Poetry. The result was the ambitious *Yü-t'ai hsin-yung* (*New Songs from a Jade Terrace*) in ten *chüan*, with the seventh and eighth *chüan* reserved exclusively for the courtly poetry by Hsiao Kang, his families and salon members.[21]

In every way this anthology is the direct opposite of Hsiao T'ung's *Wen-hsüan*. Unlike *Wen-hsüan*, which is limited to works of authors already dead, and consequently excludes from the collection all the contemporary *yung-wu* poems and sensual songs, Hsiao Kang's new anthology focuses on the taboo subjects and their antecedents. *Yü-t'ai hsin-yung* is not nearly as comprehensive as *Wen-hsüan* in terms of coverage of genres, but it has the advantage of reflecting contemporary tastes.

---

[21] For an English translation of this anthology, see Anne Birrell, *New Songs from a Jade Terrace* (London: Allen & Unwin, 1982).

Yü Hsin
THE POET'S POET

When Hsiao Kang first became heir apparent in 531 he of course could not have predicted that he was to remain in that position for another eighteen years. But Emperor Wu was to rule China until 549, and the two decades of carefree life that Hsiao Kang led as crown prince were no ordinary decades. Those years bore witness to the success of Palace Style poetry—both its superficial glow and its rich potentialities. And that period has stimulated new concepts in Chinese literature, despite certain derogatory terms which critics have used to describe its literary achievements.

II. Conformity and Innovations

The greatest poet of this period, Yü Hsin (513–581), was in every sense the supreme product of the time. As the son of Yü Chien-wu, one of Hsiao Kang's tutors, Yü Hsin was allowed to enjoy all kinds of privileges—educational, social, political—at court. By the age of fourteen he was already enrolled in the same class as the then Crown Prince Hsiao T'ung, who was twelve years his senior. It is hardly surprising that when Hsiao Kang entered the Eastern Palace in 531, he was immediately impressed with the learned and talented Yü Hsin. For the next twenty years, Yü Hsin and his father—along with Hsü Ch'ih and his son Hsü Ling—lived at the center of courtly literature and imperial favor. As the youngest member of the group, Yü Hsin received widespread public adulation, and his literary fame reached as far as the northern courts. Few poets in Chinese history enjoyed such favorable treatment and respect from the ruling class at large. And fate seemed to provide him with many fortunes and misfortunes that together would bring out the best of his poetic genius.

Yü Hsin's early works were obviously influenced by Hsiao Kang's poetic style, and by that of his own father. This was also the era in which singing and dancing performances reigned supreme in the imperial court. Brought up in leisure and aristocratic pursuits, Yü Hsin came to develop an unusual sensitivity toward the entertainment arts in general. It is the "theatrical" aspect of palace life that often gives his Palace Style poetry a particularly energetic flavor. In his lively description, the imperial palace looks like a theatrical stage where high-quality performance gives every musical note and every dancing step an artistic significance:

> In a cloistered chamber floral candles are radiant,
> Two dancers perform the light steps of Fei-yen.[22]

[22] Chao Fei-yen, the imperial consort of Emperor Ch'eng of Han, was known for her slender beauty and her light dancing movements.

Yü Hsin
THE POET'S POET

> They stamp their heels in time with the slow beat of music,
> Lower their coiffures, and keep pace with the high notes.   4
> Making a rapid turn, they begin to dance in rows,
> Their sleeves flutter as the music goes on.
> When the phoenixes turn, their profiles fill the mirror,
> When the crane looks back, the whole town will surely follow
>   and fall.²³   8
> Truly their dancing was learned from Heaven,
> Who would think that they are born of this world?
>   (*YTSC*, I, 261)

洞房花燭明
燕餘雙舞輕
頓履隨疏節
低鬟逐上聲
步轉行初進
衫飄曲未成
鸞迴鏡欲滿
鶴顧市應傾
已曾天上學
詎是世中生

Yü Hsin's poetry, extending Hsiao Kang's conviction that literature is autonomous, insists on the self-contained nature of all the arts. To him art must transcend the principle of verisimilitude to create its own reality, its own identity. It is the function of a poet to transform life into art. In his famous poem series "Twenty-four Odes on Paintings on a Screen," Yü Hsin does precisely that. Through intense observation and keen imagination, the poet recreates in his poems twenty-four paintings, each having a "frame" and a world of its own. Neither "description" nor "realism" suffices to define such a self-contained artistic world. One is tempted to compare it with John Keats's "Ode on a Grecian Urn," where life and energy are contained in the time-frozen objects depicted on the urn.²⁴

Most of the paintings described in Yü Hsin's series are scenes from the imperial palace.²⁵ The following poem, the sixth of the series, is typical:

---

²³ This is an allusion to an ancient legend. When a King of Wu of the Spring and Autumn Period was about to bury his daughter at Mt. Hu-ch'iu, he had a white crane dance around the city. So enchanted were thousands of people by the bird's dancing that they followed the crane into the tomb, and were buried with the princess. (See *Yü Hsin shih fu hsüan*, ed. T'an Cheng-pi and Chi Fu-hua [Shanghai: Ku-tien wen-hsüeh ch'u-pan-she, 1958], p. 134, Note 8.)

²⁴ See *John Keats: Selected Poetry and Letters*, ed. Richard Harter Fogle (San Francisco: Rinehart Press, 1969), pp. 249–250.

²⁵ Some are on such varying subjects as knight-errantry. See James J. Y. Liu, *The Chinese Knight-Errant*, p. 60.

Yü Hsin
THE POET'S POET

> Towering pavilions rise ten thousand feet high,
> Long corridors are joined on all sides.
> Singing voices soar up toward the fan-shaped moon,
> Dancers' shadows blend into the zither's melody.
> Valley streams are just outside the window,
> Mountain flowers are before my very eyes,
> I wish happiness to us always,
> From now until the limit of our mortal span.
>   (*YTSC*, I, 354)
> 高閣千尋起
> 長廊四注連
> 歌聲上扇月
> 舞影入琴弦
> 澗水纔窗外
> 山花即眼前
> 但願長歡樂
> 從今盡百年

It is through the poet's imagination that the boundary between painting and reality is transcended. Despite its miniature size, the painting described above strives to create a self-contained world of plenitude: in this world there are high pavilions and long corridors (lines 1–2), music and dance (lines 3–4), and mountain and water scenes (lines 5–6). Indeed, the infinite space in the poetic imagination prompts the poet to wish for a prolonged state of happiness (lines 7–8), one which is possible only in art.

Yü Hsin's poem series reflects a very important cultural phenomenon of the time, namely, the art of landscape painting in aristocratic circles. Two men stood out as the best landscape painters at the time. One was Hsiao I, brother of Hsiao Kang and author of *Chin lou tzu* (who later became Emperor of the Liang in 552). The other was Hsiao Pen (fl. 530), a grandson of Prince Ching-ling of the Ch'i, who was known for his miniature landscape on moon-shaped fans in vogue among the palace ladies. The aesthetics of the small-size painting is covincingly expounded by later art critics:

> Within a foot measure, one can view the scenery as far as three thousand miles. Within an inch square, one is able to discern eight-thousand-foot cliffs.[26]
> 咫尺之內，而瞻萬里之遙，
> 方寸之中，乃辨千尋之峻。

---

[26] See *Hsü hua-p'in*, by Yao Tsui, as cited in T'ung Shu-yeh, "Chung-kuo shan-shui hua ch'i-yüan k'ao," in *Shan-shui hua shih chih yen-chiu*, vol. I of *Chung-kuo hua lun-ts'ung*, ed. Ts'un-ts'ui hsüeh-she (Hong Kong: Ta-tung t'u-shu kung-ssu, 1978), I, 30.

Yü Hsin
THE POET'S POET

This comment is equally applicable to Yü Hsin's poem series. The relation of landscape painting to the new trends of sixth-century poetry is extremely pertinent.

In Yü Hsin there is something beyond the so-called Palace Style Poetry. The description of the palace lady is of course important in his poetry, as in the poem quoted above, but what is more important is the fact that she is merely part of the picture. Reading Yü Hsin's poem series, we discover that it is the creation of a Utopia that is at issue, for each of the twenty-four paintings contains in itself a carefree world of seclusion. The impression is that the poet strives to make a new artistic version of T'ao Ch'ien's ideal land, the Peach Blossom Spring:

> I roam freely to the cassia park,
> To the quiet and secluded Peach Blossom garden.
> (*YTSC*, I, 354)

逍遙遊桂苑
寂絕到桃源

The crucial point is that Yü Hsin's Utopia is condensed into a painting, and that it has dwindled much in size.

Much of Yü Hsin's work has the feel of meticulous structure and rhythmic balance. His poetry represents a step closer than that of Hsieh T'iao's to the T'ang Regulated Verse aesthetics. Over half of his extant poems are in the octave form, and the poem series on "Paintings on the Screen" are, with the exception of Poems 23 and 24, all in eight lines. Moreover, in terms of tonal alternation and verbal juxtaposition his poetry can sometimes pass for T'ang Regulated Verse.[27] Such considerations are of course anachronistic; it would be better for us to examine how Yü Hsin's successful experiments in form and tonality came to influence the poetics of the T'ang.

By sheer coincidence Yü Hsin was born the same year that Shen Yüeh died. With the death of Shen Yüeh, all the tonal innovators of that generation were gone. Symbolically Yü Hsin may be viewed as the successor to the past promoters of tonality. And in reality it was Yü Hsin and Hsü Ling, the two younger poets in the court circle, who actively revived the tonal movement by following the rules meticulously. Emperor Wu, though belonging to the Ching-ling circle during his youthful days, nonetheless refused to subscribe to the four-tone prosody.[28] Hsiao Kang as a poet was more sensitive than his

---

[27] For example, his "Looking at the Moon from My Boat" (*YTSC*, I, 347) could be considered a perfect Regulated Verse. Poems 11 and 15 of his series on "Paintings on the Screen" fall short of being Regulated Verse only because of violations of a rule called *nien*, according to which the second syllable in each of lines 3, 5, and 7 should repeat the tone of the second syllable in the previous line.

[28] Yao Ssu-lien, *Liang shu*, *chüan* 13, I, 243. See also note 8 in the previous chapter of the present study.

Yü Hsin
THE POET'S POET

father to tonality, but he criticized the blind adherence to rules on the part of some contemporary authors.[29] At last in Yü Hsin we find a new unity of tonal refinement and sensualism in Palace Style Poetry.

Yü Hsin's creative endeavor took yet another form that was to bring about a new phenomenon in the Chinese literary tradition—in his hands, the *fu* genre suddenly turned into something like a subgenre of *shih*. As discussed in Chapter Two, *shih* poetry in the fifth century was beginning to show signs of influence by the *fu* in its new focus on verisimilitude. But now, a century later, it was *shih* that returned the favor by giving the *fu* genre a new formalistic outlook. In Yü Hsin's case, the new cross-generic phenomenon may reflect only the tendencies of personal taste, for his disposition was inclined toward formal innovations. But eventually his works served as the firm basis for later literary interplay in China.

Rhythm plays an important part in a genre. From the beginning the *fu* was largely made up of even-number character lines which tended to create a more or less prosaic impression despite its use of rhymes. By Yü Hsin's time, the *fu* had acquired a somewhat fixed four-and-six character rhythm, obviously under the overwhelming influence of *p'ien-wen* (parallel prose) or what was later called "Four-Six Prose." These Six Dynasties *fu*, known as *p'ien-fu*, are thus directly opposed to *shih* poetry in terms of rhythm. The adoption of the four-six character lines in *p'ien-fu* is in sharp contrast to the standardization of the five- or seven-character lines in *shih* poetry. To the *shih* poets the five-character line is especially powerful, for it is the model form of poetic economy. In as few as five characters the poet is able to create in a single line an opposition between the even-number and the odd-number character rhythm, a poetic effect which perhaps reflects the aesthetic principle of dissimilarity within similarity. The T'ang Regulated Verse is grounded precisely in this system of rhythmic variation.

Undoubtedly the difference of rhythm between *fu* and *shih*—the one more prosaic and the other more poetic—was always present in Yü Hsin's mind. But, out of a mere imaginative compulsion, the poet seems to have decided to impart a more "poetic" spirit to the *fu* rhythm by mixing in it odd-number character lines. For example, his "*Fu* on the Spring" begins with the seven-character rhythm:

> In the I-ch'un Garden spring has returned,
> In the P'i-hsiang Palace spring garments are made.[30]
> The new-year birds chirp in a thousand variations,
> The second-month poplar blossoms drift all over the road.

---

[29] For a discussion of this point, see Marney, *Liang Chien-wen Ti*, pp. 82–83.
[30] The I-ch'un Garden, attached to I-ch'un Palace in Ch'ang-an, was a temporary abode for the Ch'in Emperor on tour. P'i-hsiang Palace was built in the Han to house palace ladies.

Yü Hsin
THE POET'S POET

> Throughout Ho-yang County there are flowers,
> As always, Chin-ku Park is full of trees.³¹
> One thicket of fragrant grass does get in the way,
> Gossamer, a few feet long, blocks the road.
>   (*YTSC*, I, 74)

宜春苑中春已歸	(7)
披香殿裡作春衣	(7)
新年鳥聲千種囀	(7)
二月揚花滿路飛	(7)
河陽一縣併是花	(7)
金谷從來滿園樹	(7)
一叢香草足礙人	(7)
數尺遊絲即橫路	(7)

And it concludes with a mixture of seven-character and five-character lines:

> On the third day they go to the ferry for the "winding water" ceremony,³²
> In the evening, by the riverbank, with many offerings to the gods.
> Under the trees some float wine cups,
> By the sandbank others are waiting to cross.
> Sleeves are decorated with colorful patterns,
> Collars are adorned with strung pearls.
> Behind the ten-thousand-foot mountaintop, the sun sets,
> Unless you are drunk at dusk, do not go home!
> Reflections in the pond shimmer more than in a mirror,
> Garments indoors are not as fragrant as the flowers.
>   (*YTSC*, I, 78)

三日曲水向河津	(7)
日晚河邊多解神	(7)
樹下流杯客	(5)
沙頭渡水人	(5)
鏤薄窄衫袖	(5)
穿珠帖領巾	(5)
百丈山頭日欲斜	(7)
三晡未醉莫還家	(7)

---

³¹ Ho-yang County, known for its peach blossoms, is located in modern Honan. The Chin-ku Park belonged to the rich merchant Shih Ch'ung (249–300), known for his devoted affection for the singing girl Lü-chu.

³² The "winding water" ceremony traditionally took place on the third day of the third month. It was a spring purification ritual in which the participants set wine cups afloat in the upper part of the winding river, and were then supposed to pick up their cups and drink the water at the lower part of the river.

Yü Hsin
THE POET'S POET

池中水影懸勝鏡 (7)
屋裡衣香不如花 (7)

Similar examples can be found in all his other early *fu* that are extant today: "*Fu* on the Lamp," "*Fu* on Facing the Candle," "*Fu* on the Mirror," "*Fu* on Mandarin Ducks," "*Fu* on the Roaming Traveler." It is said that Yü Hsin's innovation led to a widespread fashion in the palace circles to produce *fu* with the *shih* rhythm.[33]

Yü Hsin's experiment with rhythmic patterns represents an attempt to impose a new "formal realism" on *fu* in keeping with the general poetic style at the time. His *fu* are either in the mode of *yung-wu* or of Palace Style Poetry. In other words, they share with the contemporary *shih* poetry a basic emphasis on the sensual object. Now, with a more poetic rhythm added to them, these *fu* have gained a new metrical sophistication, a quality especially valued by the Six Dynasties poets. Thus, beneath the formal innovations, it is the particular expression of the spirit of the time that sustains the transformation.

Yü Hsin was a nearly perfect embodiment of his era. But his personal circumstances were so exceptional that he often had to rise above them. The time came when he could no longer be confined to the decorated walls of the palace. In 545 he was chosen by Emperor Wu as a diplomatic envoy to the Eastern Wei in the north. At that time North China was troubled by a political division. Following a long civil war, the Northern Wei was replaced by two separate empires in 534: the Eastern Wei in the Yeh area (southern Hopei) and the Western Wei in the Ch'ang-an region. The two non-Chinese northern states viewed each other as antagonists, as they each did the Southern Chinese government. But as time went on they began to have something in common: they both were eager to learn the Chinese cultural heritage, and often requested that distinguished literary men from South China such as Yü Hsin be sent as cultural envoys.[34] By temperament and necessity, Emperor Wu was most interested in such cultural exchanges, as he himself also invited Buddhist monks from the north to his imperial court.[35]

Yü Hsin's diplomatic mission to the Eastern Wei was a timely one. At age thirty-two, Yü Hsin was already known to the northerners as China's best poet. As soon as he arrived in the capital of the Eastern Wei, he became the center of national attention. People in the north were greatly impressed with

---

[33] It is of course not possible to prove that it was Yü Hsin who first initiated this prosodic practice of rhythmic intermingling. But most critics, basing their views on the commentary by Ni Fan (the Ch'ing editor of Yü Hsin's Collected Works), believe that Yü Hsin was the innovator of the style (see *YTSC*, I, 74). In any case, Yü Hsin was the most productive poet in this form among the palace circles.

[34] Peter Bear, "The Poetry of Yü Hsin" (diss. Yale Univ., 1969), p. 11.

[35] Arthur F. Wright, *Buddhism in Chinese History* (Stanford: Stanford Univ. Press, 1959), pp. 50–51.

Yü Hsin
THE POET'S POET

his poetic eloquence and cultivated poise, and the court entertained him with the most elaborate banquets and social activities. Indeed, no other equally foreign court could have prized so highly a poet-envoy from another state. Soon afterward a peace treaty was signed, and, upon leaving, Yü Hsin composed a farewell poem charged with appreciation:

> ... Happily I made your acquaintance, dear sirs,
> I met all these princes in your grand reception.
> How can I praise the fine tree of your graciousness?[36]
> Only by reciting joyfully the Song of Herbs.[37]
> With choice dishes of fine meat, you feasted me,[38]
> Three times you filled my goblet and drank to me.
> No common official can tread on a foreign land.
> How could I ever have this happy gathering with you?
> Our customs are set apart,
> Let alone the mountains and rivers.
> No reason to stay in the Southern Lodge again
> Or to expect offerings at your Western Gate.[39]
> With loving thoughts, I bid you farewell,
> Best wishes to you all!
> (YTSC, I, 198)
> ...交歡值公子
> 展禮覯王孫
> 何以譽嘉樹
> 徒欣賦采蘩
> 四牢欣折俎
> 三獻滿罍樽
> 人臣無境外
> 何由欣此言
> 風俗既殊阻

---

[36] The original line reads literally: "How can I praise the beautiful tree?" It alludes to a famous story in *Tso Chuan*: in order to express his gratitude for his host's hospitality, Han Hsüan-tzu praised the beauty of a tree at the banquet. The beautiful tree clearly stands for the gracious host in this context. (See note 5, in *YTSC*, I, 199.)

[37] "The Herbs" is a poem from the *Shih-ching* in which a lady plucks the *fan* plants and uses them as an offering in the temple of the prince. (See Poem 13, in Bernhard Karlgren, trans., *The Book of Odes* [Stockholm: The Museum of Far Eastern Antiquities, 1974], p. 8.)

[38] There were different grades of courtesy in ancient China, due to differences in rank. Various kinds of meat were selected for different guests. The one chosen here is called *Ssu-lao* (fourth grade), applicable to dukes and marquesses.

[39] This is an allusion to the story of Ch'ien Fu in the Warring States period. The people of Chao respected Ch'ien Fu so much that they made offerings to him at the Western Gate, as they would to the gods.

Yü Hsin
THE POET'S POET

山河不復論
無因旅南館
空欲祭西門
眷然惟此別
夙期幸共存

From this poem it becomes clear that Yü Hsin's poetry was not so exclusively confined to the Palace Style as was that of his contemporary poets. Indeed, his forceful lyricism and plain diction are strongly reminiscent of T'ao Ch'ien's poetry. This is not surprising, since style is always intimately associated with subject matter. The more cosmopolitan Yü Hsin had become, the broader was his poetic scope. If he had a tendency toward ornate diction and sensualism, that was true only in his representation of life in the Liang Palace. What is interesting is that whenever he had a need to present a more expressive voice in poetry, he was invariably more conscious of the classical rhetorical devices. The abundant use of allusions in the above poem, for example, immediately sets it apart from the typical Palace Style Poetry, where allusion is generally avoided.

III. Lyricism Regained

Yü Hsin's, or rather the entire era's, lighthearted gaiety was not to last long. Only three years after returning from his successful trip to the Eastern Wei domain, Yü Hsin found his own country stricken by a disaster of the most severe kind. In 548 a military general named Hou Ching, a defector from Eastern Wei to Liang, suddenly took up arms against Emperor Wu's government. The entire city of Chien-k'ang, where Yü Hsin served as Assistant Magistrate, soon fell to the rebel forces. For the next three years the capital was continuously haunted by murders and deaths. First, Emperor Wu died, and the heir apparent, Hsiao Kang, ascended as Hou Ching's puppet emperor (Emperor Chien-wen, reigned 550–551). Then, Hsiao Kang, who had been blessed with leisure and good fortune all his life, suddenly met with a violent death. He was murdered by Hou Ching's men, and replaced by his own relative. In the midst of all this political turmoil, Yü Hsin suffered from a series of family tragedies, chief among them the death of his three children. But he somehow managed to escape to Chiang-ling (in today's Hupei), where Hsiao I, the brother of Hsiao Kang, established a rival court. Finally in 552 Hou Ching's forces were exterminated, and Hsiao I proclaimed himself Emperor, known posthumously as Emperor Yüan. The Imperial Library was then moved from Chien-k'ang to Chiang-ling, and the Emperor had Yü Hsin oversee the Literature Department in the court. So for the first time since the

Yü Hsin
THE POET'S POET

outbreak of the Hou Ching rebellion, Yü Hsin was able to involve himself in court literature again.

In May 554 Yü Hsin was once again chosen as a cultural envoy to North China, but this time to a different state, the Western Wei. No one could foresee that with this trip Yü Hsin would never again see his homeland, for he was to be retained in the north for the rest of his life.

As it happened, shortly after Yü Hsin's arrival in the north, the army of the Western Wei moved south to invade Chiang-ling, the new capital of the Liang. The Chinese court was again beset with endless murders and betrayals within the royal family. Emperor Yüan was killed by his own nephew Hsiao Ch'a, by that time a defector to the enemy. Finally, after a sequence of political upheavals, a former commander of Emperor Yüan, Ch'en Pa-hsien, usurped the throne in 557 and established a new dynasty called Ch'en. Thus the ill-fated Liang Dynasty vanished from sight only three years after Yü Hsin's departure.

Meanwhile Yü Hsin, for all his grief over the tragic fate of his country, was not permitted to return south. Earlier, when Western Wei first sacked Chiang-ling in 554, it brought back in semi-captivity a large number of the Liang nobles and officials, and Yü Hsin was fortunate enough to find his own family members among them. In fact, the northern court could not have been more generous to Yü Hsin. He was honored with many important titles, and was consistently treated with respect. In 557 when a leader of the cultural elite, Yü-wen Chüeh, seized imperial power in Ch'ang-an and established his new empire, the Northern Chou, Yü Hsin began to occupy even higher positions with real official power to match. The Yü-wens were known admirers of Chinese culture, and they were of course overjoyed to have at their disposal the best poet from the southern court. Gradually, as time went on, they won the friendship of Yü Hsin, and their common interest in literature seemed to provide some consolation to the grief-stricken poet.

Yet Yü Hsin could never forget the catastrophe that had caused the fall of the Liang Dynasty. As one of the many subjugated Chinese living under foreign rule, he was haunted by the persistent feeling of shame and helplessness. We begin to see in his poetry a new focus on what may be called "expanded lyricism," in which the two main systems of order—namely, the personal and the political-historical—appear as a single entity.

It was perhaps during the first years of his exile in the north that Yü Hsin composed his famous poem-series, "The Imitation of *Yung-huai*."[40] By this title he clearly identified himself with Juan Chi (210–263), the poet who wrote the celebrated lyric cycle "*Yung-huai*" ("Expressing My Innermost Feelings").

---

[40] For a translation of this poem-series, see William T. Graham, Jr., and James R. Hightower, "Yü Hsin's 'Songs of Sorrow,'" in *Harvard Journal of Asiatic Studies*, 43, No. 1 (1983), 5–55.

Yü Hsin
THE POET'S POET

Like Juan Chi, Yü Hsin attempts to express in his own *yung-huai* poems his feelings—feelings of the inner self that cry out for free expression. But in both poets the feeling in question can only be defined as one of the interplay of the self and its political world.[41] Reading Yü Hsin's *Yung-huai* series, and indeed most of his works in exile, one has the impression that through the use of rich allusions his poetry seems to describe the same kind of complex phenomena as would cultural or political history. Yet there is always an inner unity of self in lyric poetry that coordinates the manifold reality into a totally private voice. For the poet reveals only as much of history and politics as can be revealed through his private thoughts on them. It is the role of subjective feeling that is most important in this historical mode of lyricism.

For a long time Yü Hsin lived in an intense recollection of past—of the past history of his own country, the Liang. It is obvious that there was nothing at all he could have done to save Emperor Yüan and his compatriots. But the fact that it was during Yü Hsin's peace negotiations in Ch'ang-an that the forces of the Western Wei came to sack the city of Chiang-ling greatly saddened him. It is quite understandable that one of the main topics of the *yung-huai* series is the poet's lament over this unfortunate incident. Yü Hsin writes in Poem 23:

> The fighting unicorns could eclipse the sun,
> The naval battle was sure to startle the dragons.
> War drums raised the alarm for the Seven Regiments,
> Wind-blown dust troubled the ninefold imperial gate.[42]   4
> From Tripod Lake Palace he had departed, never to return,
> At Ts'ang-wu they grieved they could not follow him.[43]
> In vain they had asked the singers of Bronze Bird Tower
> To look out at the pines on Western Mound.   8
>   (*YTSC*, I, 246)

鬭麟能食日
戰水定驚龍
鼓鞞喧七萃
風塵亂九重
鼎湖去無返
蒼梧悲不從
徒勞銅爵妓
遙望西陵松

---

[41] For this particular quality in Juan Chi's poetry, see Holzman, *Poetry and Politics*.

[42] The nine-fold imperial gate stands for the Emperor himself. The line alludes to the fact that the Liang Emperor suffered shame and insult (literally, "to be covered with wind-blown dust") when forced to flee the palace.

[43] Tripod Lake Palace was built by Emperor Wu of the Han at the supposed site where the Yellow Emperor ascended to Heaven. According to tradition, Emperor Shun was buried at Ts'ang-wu, and his two grieving wives were unable to follow him in death.

Yü Hsin
THE POET'S POET

The description of the fateful battle that took place in Chiang-ling (lines 1–4) is of course imaginary. What is noteworthy is the emotion and drama that accompany the graphic vividness invented by the poet. There is always in Yü Hsin a predominant tendency to describe the visual aspects of things, no matter how general the description seems to be. And this descriptive vigor makes possible a truly penetrating yet concrete expression. For this reason, Yü Hsin's style often appears to be more direct than is the somewhat ambiguous poetry of Juan Chi.[44]

Thus, despite its abundant display of allusions, this poem smacks of the precise nature of the political climate at issue. The poet attempts to narrate the tragic outcome of the war: Emperor Yüan's violent end, with no one left to stand vigil at his grave mound. Compared with Ts'ao Ts'ao, who could at least ask his concubines and singing girls to mourn for him in a grand display of ceremonies, how much more pathetic and lonely was Emperor Yüan? It breaks Yü Hsin's heart to think that he, as a loyal subject of the Emperor, could not even carry out the mourning observances as he should. After all, it was the Liang court that had bred him and enabled him to live his life to the full. He laments the unpredictable turn of events that makes it impossible for him to pay back his heavy debt of gratitude to his country. In another poem of the same series Yü Hsin speaks most explicitly about this disquieting agony:

> Some time ago I was honored as the nation's most distinguished man,
> I always treasured the true friendship of my lord.
> It was thought I would spit out pearls in return,
> Who would have known I would swallow lye for him?[45]   4
> One glance was worth more than a foot-wide piece of jade,
> A thousand in gold less than a single word.[46]
> I grieve for the heir of the Liu Clan,
> And bemoan the Emperor's grandson Shih,[47]   8

---

[44] Holzman, *Poetry and Politics*, pp. 1–33.

[45] A certain Marquis of Sui saved the life of an injured snake, and the snake came back at night with a pearl to repay his kindness. Yü Jang was once treated with special favor by the Lord of Chih, and later Yü Jang swallowed lye to change his voice and made himself unrecognizable in order to avenge the death of the lord. (See *Yü-hsin shih-fu hsüan*, ed. T'an Cheng-pi and Chi Fu-hua, p. 48, Note 5; p. 122, Note 2.)

[46] My interpretation of this couplet is based on William T. Graham, Jr. and James R. Hightower, "Yü Hsin's 'Song of Sorrow,'" *Harvard Journal of Asiatic Studies*, 43, No. 1 (1983), 21–22.

[47] The Heir of the Liu Clan refers to Liu Ying of the Han, who was first set up as a puppet emperor (reigned A.D. 6–8) by Wang Mang and was later killed. Shih, the grandson of the Han Emperor Wu, was put to death along with his parents. Yü Hsin is drawing an analogy between the political situation in the Han and that of the Liang.

Yü Hsin
THE POET'S POET

> Yet I cannot be like the Cavalry Guard,
> To go back and care for the Pa-ling Park.[48]
>   (Poem 6, *YTSC*, I, 232)

疇昔國士遇
生平知己恩
直言珠可吐
寧知炭欲吞
一顧重尺璧
千金輕一言
悲傷劉孺子
悽愴史皇孫
無因同武騎
歸守灞陵園

The poet finally expresses his deepest sorrow of all: an utter sense of loneliness. His is an unredeemed feeling that no one understands his inner thoughts. Perhaps no one but his precursor Juan Chi could understand the quality of this sorrow:

> Only Juan, wailing at the end of his road,
> Can know the hardship of my traveling.
>   (*YTSC*, I, 231)

惟彼窮途慟
知余行路難

Yet nothing hurts him more than the realization that his life in exile is like a form of paralysis, a sort of living death. He describes this feeling by means of the image of a dying locust tree:

> Afflicted with sorrow, the tree begins to decay,
> In its heart, it seems anguished and reluctant.
> What a pity, the will to live is gone,
> No wonder, the locust tree is dying.
>   (*YTSC*, I, 244)

懷愁正搖落
中心愴有違
獨憐生意盡
空驚槐樹衰

The image is based on an allusion to a story of Yin Chung-wen, a famous man in the Eastern Chin, who once remarked: "The locust tree is declining; it no

---

[48] This couplet alludes to the famous Han poet Ssu-ma Hsiang-ju, who once served as a Cavalry Guard and was later appointed Supervisor of the Pa-ling Park, where Emperor Wen was buried.

longer has the will to live."[49] However casual Yin Chung-wen's original remark might seem to be, it has nevertheless become the most predominant symbol in Yü Hsin's work. Forced to become an exile in mid-life, the poet must have felt himself caught in the midst of advancing nowhere. The real force, the energy that used to sustain his inner being, is now gone. Thus, the symbol of a withering tree has become almost an obsession for Yü Hsin: he even goes so far as to compare a broken mountain ridge to an old tree (*YTSC*, I, 324). All this preoccupation with the tree image eventually culminates in his well-known "*Fu* on the Barren Tree," which later became a "parent text" for similar allegorical works by poets in the T'ang.[50]

The disillusioned Yü Hsin resolved to live his own life with integrity in the face of adverse circumstances. He learned to play his public roles while maintaining his ultimate values within himself as an individual. His choice was something like Hsieh T'iao's during the Hsüan-ch'eng years—i.e., the practice of semi-eremitism. Though always holding official positions, Yü Hsin began to live, at least in his own mind, like a recluse. All this is reflected in his frequent allusions to historical recluses such as Chang Heng, Shu Kuang, Shu Shou, and above all T'ao Ch'ien.[51] Yü Hsin pretends, not without justification, that the simple life he now has is comparable to T'ao Ch'ien's:

> Old farmers visit me at times,
> Monks from the mountain call on me now and then.
> I have chrysanthemums, but lack wine,[52]
> Strings are missing, yet it is still a zither.[53]
>   (*YTSC*, I, 283)
> 野老時相訪
> 山僧或見尋
> 有菊翻無酒
> 無絃則有琴

[49] See Richard Mather, trans., *Shih-shuo hsin-yü, A New Account of Tales of the World* (Minneapolis: Univ. of Minnesota Press, 1976), p. 453. For the original passage, see Liu I-ch'ing, *Shih-shuo hsin-yü* [*chiao-chien*], ed. Yang Yung, Section 28, Item 8, p. 650.

[50] Stephen Owen, "Deadwood: The Barren Tree from Yü Hsin to Han Yü," *Chinese Literature: Essays, Articles, Reviews*, 1 (1979), 157–179.

[51] See, for example, *YTSC*, I, 305, 279, 280, 283, 306, 362.

[52] The Chinese used to drink chrysanthemum wine to ward off evil influences on the Double Nine Festival (i.e., on the ninth of the ninth month). Legend has it that on a Double Nine Festival T'ao Ch'ien went out to pluck chrysanthemums. There was no more wine left in his house, so he sat down by the flower bushes for a long time with chrysanthemums in his hands. Suddenly a servant of Wang Hung (Provincial Governor of Chiang-chou) came with a good supply of wine, and T'ao Ch'ien ended up getting drunk that day.

[53] T'ao Ch'ien did not know music, but he owned a stringless zither which he often "played" after drinking.

Yü Hsin
THE POET'S POET

And in his "*Fu* on a Small Garden" ("*Hsiao-yüan fu*"), he describes his "shabby" house in words that remind one unmistakably of T'ao Ch'ien's small hut:

> I have a few acres, a shabby hut,
> Lonely and still, beyond the world of men,
> Enough to fend off the worst of summer and winter,
> Enough to shelter me from wind and frost.[54]
> 余有數畝敝廬
> 寂寞人外
> 聊以擬伏臘
> 聊以避風霜....

Yü Hsin's retreat to the small garden is not to be taken literally, however. At most it serves the poet as a symbol of self-sufficient individuality. By temperament he is rather a realist with a natural tendency toward moderation, and this innate quality provides him with a sense of security necessary for self-preservation. Despite his dissatisfaction with worldly affairs, his inner equilibrium enables him to maintain an unswerving aspiration toward poetic imagination. In any event, nature—both its superficial beauty and its fathomless meaning—is all his. He has enough of freedom within himself to create a poetic world that transcends his personal sorrow.

Thus in Yü Hsin's poetry we begin to see a new sensitivity toward nature, especially nature's changing phases. The poet is like a self-possessed painter who, with his particular gift of sensory touch, endeavors to grasp the phenomena of every passing season. He has a genuine fascination for the sharp contrast between the northern climate and that of the south.[55] The example of the plum blossom is particularly pertinent. The plum tree in the south always blooms in the winter, never waiting long enough for poets to sing of its alluring charm. But it is already spring in the north, and the plum tree, still blanketed by snow, refuses to let its flowers blossom:

> In those days, in the middle of the twelfth month,
> The plum blossoms already seemed to be withering.
> Hard to believe the flowers bloom so late this year,
> All of us come out in the snow to look for them.
> The trees stir, and icicles fall down,
> The branches are high, our reaching hands feel cold.
> I wish I knew these blossoms are nowhere to be found!
> Truly I regret I am not dressed warm enough.
>   (*YTSC*, I, 364)

[54] Translation taken from Watson, *Chinese Rhyme-Prose*, p. 203.
[55] Uchida Michio, "Kōnan no shi to sakuhoku no shi," *Shūkan Tōyōgaku*, no. 16 (1966), 1–8.

Yü Hsin
THE POET'S POET

當年臘月半
已覺梅花闌
不信今春晚
俱來雪裡看
樹動懸冰落
枝高出手寒
早知覓不見
真悔著衣單

The snow scene indeed gives an entirely new picture to Yü Hsin's poetry. The poet seems to be particularly fascinated, or saddened, by the blustery snowstorm, with the wind crying in the cold. Perhaps, through such visual realism, he attempts to convey the feeling of a lonely individual forever separated from the warm south.

Yü Hsin seems to strive to make every image directly relevant to his recollection of the past. By mere association, he is able to present with amazing vividness an enduring scene that lives in his memory. His dramatic encounter with a tropical fruit is a classic example of such poetic achievement. The poet, unexpectedly seeing betel-nuts imported from the south, is immediately reminded of the lush appearance of the trees that grow such fruits:

SUDDENLY I SAW THE BETEL-NUTS

In green pods, a thousand nuts are ripe,
A hundred purple flowers burst into bloom.
Don't tell me you have come thousands of miles away,
We have met before.
    (*YTSC*, I, 381)

忽見檳榔

綠房千子熟
紫穗百花開
莫言行萬里
曾經相識來

Yü Hsin's descriptive style at this time gives us the strong impression that it is sharply different from the luxurious sensualism typical of his early poetry. However, any absolute separation of an earlier style and a later style, as the traditional scholarship on Yü Hsin has confidently assumed, would be a mistake. To be sure, Yü Hsin's later development in poetry goes far beyond the realm of what is generally called the Palace Style Poetry, but in effect he has depended, for much of his descriptive technique, upon his earlier mastery of sensory similitude. In some cases—though not overwhelmingly so—his later

Yü Hsin
THE POET'S POET

poetry reads exactly like his earlier Palace Style Verse. This is particularly true with the several poems he wrote in reply to his good friend Yü-wen Chao, the talented Prince of Chao.[56] The following poem is a case in point:

TO MATCH PRINCE CHAO'S "LOOKING AT THE COURTESANS"

Lü-chu sings, her fan is delicate,
Fei-yen dances, her gown is long.
The zither melody follows the flowing water,
The flute music soars to pursue the phoenixes.   4
Bells are strung up with fine threads,
Drums decorated with round and flowery pins.
I believe this music is flawless,
No need to be afraid of Chou Yü.[57]   8
   (*YTSC*, I, 341)

和趙王看伎

綠珠歌扇薄
飛燕舞衫長
琴曲隨流水
簫聲逐鳳凰
細縷纏鐘格
圓花釘鼓牀
懸知曲不誤
無事畏周郎

In fact, it was Yü Hsin's Palace Style Poetry that first impressed the Northern Chou royal families. The Prince of Chao and his several brothers, chief among them Emperor Ming (Yü-wen Yü) and the Prince of T'eng (Yü-wen Yu), were all devout imitators of the southern Palace Style. *The History of the Chou* (*Chou shu*) describes Prince of Chao as one who "loved to write poetry in imitation of Yü Hsin's style, and whose poems were mostly frivolous and ornate."[58]

"Frivolous and ornate" (*ch'ing-yen*) was not at all regarded as an unfavorable quality by the Northern Chou court; instead, it represented the cultural ornaments of China to which the northerners constantly paid homage. It is thus very unlikely that this poet in exile would purposely abandon the craft that had already won him such widespread popularity. But the important

---

[56] See poems in *YTSC*, I, 259–260, 374.

[57] Chou Yü (175–210) was known for his ability to detect the slightest flaw in music. (See Note 4, in *YTSC*, I, 342.)

[58] Ling-hu Te-fen, et al., *Chou shu*, chüan 13 (Peking: Chung-hua shu-chü, 1971), I, 202.

Yü Hsin
THE POET'S POET

point is that Yü Hsin's new emphasis on individual values gives rise to a new style, or rather a mixed style, in which broader realism and verbal embellishment, direct lyricism and sensual description, are combined.

In order to see how Yü Hsin turns his sensory realism into a new style, let us read a poem which deals with a subject that is far removed from any frivolous concerns:

WRITTEN WHILE I WAS A HYDRAULIC GRANDEE
IN CHARGE OF THE WEI BRIDGE

The Hydraulic Grandee holds a low position,
I perform my job on the south of Wei River.
Metal parts were shipped from Fu-p'ing,
Stones and beams are from Kan-ch'üan.   4
Like a rainbow, the bridge joins the isolated banks,
Like a floating tortoise, it links the divided shore.
Spring islets the color of parrots,
Flowing waters fragrant as peach blossoms.   8
Once the Star-goddess presented herself to the Han Emperor
   here,
And the old fisherman met with the Duke of Chou.[59]
By the level dike the stone bank is sheer,
Along the high levee the shadows of the willows are long.   12
How I envy Tu Yüan-k'ai—
At the Bridge, the emperor drank a toast to him alone.[60]
   (YTSC, I, 269)

忝在司水看治渭橋

大夫參下位
司職渭之陽
富平移鐵鎖
甘泉運石梁
跨虹連絕岸
浮黿續斷航

---

[59] Legend has it that Emperor Wu of Han on his way to Kan-ch'üan saw the Star-Goddess swimming in the Wei River. The old fisherman in line 10 alludes to Lü Shang, whom the Duke of Chou met on the south of Wei River during his hunting trip. Lü Shang later became one of the duke's important advisers.

[60] This refers to Tu Yü in the Chin Dynasty, who supervised the construction of a new bridge near Meng-chin. After the bridge was completed, the Emperor drank a toast to Tu Yü as a token of his appreciation.

Yü Hsin
THE POET'S POET

春洲鸚鵡色
流水桃花香
星精逢漢帝
釣叟值周王
平堤石岸直
高堰柳陰長
羨言杜元凱
河橋獨舉觴

This poem was written in 557, when Yü Hsin, appointed Grandee in the Ministry of Water Control, was inspecting the renovation of a bridge east of the Wei River. There is a predominant tendency in the poem, especially in the second half, to combine scenic description and personal feelings, whether implicit or explicit. Devices such as this are absent in Yü Hsin's earlier description-oriented poems, where emotions are generally suspended. One clearly recognizes here the poet's effort to balance the two modes—the descriptive and the expressive—so that each makes its way into the total effect of the poem.

Yet the manner of description in the poem is grounded, both in diction and syntax, upon the Palace Style aesthetics, though the overall effect is different in the new context. First, the sensual delight in color and smell, as is demonstrated in lines 7–8, strikes one as rather familiar:

> Spring islets the color of parrots,
> Flowing waters fragrant as peach blossoms.
> 春洲鸚鵡色
> 流水桃花香

The scene, of course, is a typical spring scene. The lush green which characterizes the small islands does not seem unusual. Spring after spring all those living near the river must have experienced the lovely peach-blossom fragrance coming from the water. But in poetry, at least in literati poetry, such beautiful scenes did not become important until the Liang Dynasty, when the courtly poets began to develop a taste for ornately sensory experience. The young Yü Hsin was especially skilled at describing the charm of such peach-blossom scenes. The following lines are from one of his earlier poems, "Odes on Paintings on a Screen":

> Flowing waters the color of peach blossoms,
> Spring islets fragrant as sweet pollia.
>   (*YTSC*, I, 355)
> 流水桃花色
> 春洲杜若香

Yü Hsin
THE POET'S POET

Any reader can identify this couplet as the model for Yü Hsin's scenic description of the Wei River Bridge. The words are repeated almost verbatim, and the descriptive style is the same. Yet how very different are the circumstances of the two poems: the "Ode" is on a palace garden scene in which beautiful ladies linger at dusk; the later poem is written from the perspective of a hydraulic grandee who is gratified with the splendid view of the newly repaired bridge spanning the river.

If we look further, we shall see that the scenic description of the willow-shaded riverbanks by the Wei River (lines 11–12) is also a direct borrowing from his earlier poetry. Compare the following couplets:

(1)
In the Shang-lin Park the spring trails are dense,
By the floating bridge the willow-paths are long.
   (*YTSC*, I, 358)
上林春逕密
浮橋柳路長

(2)
By the level dike the stone bank is sheer,
Along the high levee the shadows of the willows are long.
平堤石岸直
高堰柳陰長

Example (1) is from Poem 16 of the "Odes on Paintings on a Screen"; example (2) comes from the poem discussed above. Again, the themes of the two poems are completely different, and yet when the lines are recited in isolation, they recall very similar scenes. There are many other such examples, and one is tempted to conclude that the only thing new about Yü Hsin's descriptive technique in his later years is the extraordinary way in which he mingles the already acquired imagistic sensitivity with a more sophisticated expression.

It is his *chüeh-chü* quatrain which captures in the truest sense the dynamism of his lyricism. Through the four-line verse, Yü Hsin manages to achieve a lyric voice that is both personal and direct. The poet also knows how to bring out the best in this miniature form: he often treats his quatrains something like personal letters. We have already mentioned the quatrain's special power of creating lingering overtones, and it seems that there is nothing more appropriate than to use this poetry as a means of communicating private feelings with subtle implications. Forced to become an exile in the north, Yü Hsin often felt a strong compulsion to correspond with his old friends in the south. He must have found in the quatrain form the kind of lyrical potentiality that was most suitable to his purpose. What follows are two such letters, one to Wang

Yü Hsin
THE POET'S POET

Lin and another to Hsü Ling:

(1) TO WANG LIN

Beyond the Jade Pass, the road is far,
Few couriers come from Chin-ling.
Alone, I shed a thousand lines of tears,
When I opened your letter from thousands of miles away.
  (*YTSC*, I, 368)

寄王琳

玉關道路遠
金陵信使疏
獨下千行淚
開君萬里書

(2) TO HSÜ LING

Old friend, if you think of me,
Do so while I am still alive.
Don't wait until you pass the Shan-yang road,
Listening in vain to the sad flute melody.
  (*YTSC*, I, 367)

寄徐陵

故人倘思我
及此平生時
莫待山陽路
空聞吹笛悲

The first quatrain was obviously a reply to Wang Lin's letter. From historical sources we know that Wang Lin eventually died as a Liang loyalist in combat against the Ch'en in 557. His correspondence with Yü Hsin must have taken place sometime between 554 and 557, the last years of the Liang Dynasty, during which the court was directly threatened with political chaos. One can well imagine the degree of emotional anguish that Yü Hsin experienced upon receiving a letter from a dear friend who was left to fight for his own country back home. The poet must have felt a strong need to articulate his feelings, but what he has finally produced in poetry is something else—a short quatrain that tells only of the dramatic moment of opening Wang Lin's letter. All else is implied by the power of silence.

  Yü Hsin's quatrain to Hsü Ling, his close friend since the old days at court,

Yü Hsin
THE POET'S POET

creates a similar tone of suggestiveness through a very different device—that of an urgent command. Behind the command itself there is an allusion which has far-reaching historical implications: soon after Hsi K'ang's untimely death by execution in 262, his good friend Hsiang Hsiu wrote a *fu* in memory of him (*WH*, I, 330–332). The *fu* is one of those lyrical pieces produced out of sheer uncontrollable grief. But it might be dangerous to openly acknowledge one's affection for a political offender, even if he was already dead. So, Hsiang Hsiu explains in his Preface the reason for writing the *fu*: when he passed by his old residence in Shan-yang he happened to hear a neighbor playing the flute, and he was so stirred by the music that he could not help thinking of the joy of his friendship with Hsi K'ang in days gone by and commemorating the moment in a *fu* composition. Here Yü Hsin twists the meaning of this allusion to accord with his own lyrical voice. What he says is more direct and pressing: "Don't wait until I die to think of me, as in the case of Hsiang Hsiu and Hsi K'ang." The whole poem consists of this simple message, and nothing else. But it is a message which breeds more pain than it wishes to dispel. The poet's imperative tone conveys his unmistakable feeling of insecurity and uncertainty.

Such lyrical forcefulness can hardly be found, if at all, in the object-oriented *yung-wu* quatrains that previously had prevailed in the court salons. In Yü Hsin's later poetry there is a great deal of self-expression and self-realization that seems quite unique. Compared with Hsieh T'iao's *yüeh-fu* quatrains, his *chüeh-chü* are far more personal, since they no longer speak in the voice of an omnipresent observer, as often happens in Hsieh T'iao's case. Historically, this personal turn of lyricism on the part of Yü Hsin was crucial to the development of *chüeh-chü* as the predominant lyric genre.

Yet Yü Hsin's ultimate achievement in lyricism lies in integrating what is intimately personal with a larger concern with history—a concern which would eventually transcend his narrow self. His "Lament for the South" ("*Ai chiang-nan fu*"), a very long piece in the *fu* form written during his old age, best demonstrates in substance and feeling the profundity of this lyrical experience. The subject of the *fu* is the tragic fall of the Liang Dynasty, but the narrative opens with a summary of the rise and fall of the southern governments from the Eastern Chin down to the Liang. The poet's dominant mode of perceiving this period in history is in the fullest sense of the word a lament, a lament so profound and real that he wishes to convey it to posterity:

> So looking back I wrote this *fu*
> That it might serve as a record;
> Not without words of fear and suffering,
> It is still, at the core, a lament.[61]

---

[61] Translation taken from William T. Graham, trans., *The Lament for the South: Yü Hsin's "Ai Chiang-Nan Fu"* (Cambridge: Cambridge Univ. Press, 1980), p. 53.

Yü Hsin
THE POET'S POET

追爲此賦
聊以記言
不無危苦之辭
惟以悲哀爲主

Already in his twilight years, when most of his friends had died, Yü Hsin felt a particular urgency to write this historical poem which he had conceived long before:

> The sun is setting, my road is long;
> How long have I left among men? . . .
> The rest have almost all withered and fallen,
> And, another Ling-kuang, I alone remain . . .[62]

日暮途遠
人間何世 . . . .
零落將盡
靈光歸然 . . . .

To grasp the full impact of this work as both poetry and history, we must understand its relation to the culturally important concept of "immortality through words" (*li-yen*). Like all the traditional Chinese intellectuals who were thwarted in their worldly careers, Yü Hsin attempted to fill the gap by leaving a literary masterpiece to future generations. It is the sense of self-identification that a literary man is striving for—the feeling that he is to be understood fully and correctly through a more permanent medium than that of the political roads. Two hundred years later Yü Hsin was to find in the T'ang poet Tu Fu, as T'ao Ch'ien eventually found in the Sung poet Su Shih, a true friend whose depth of understanding transcends the bounds of history. Modeling himself after the mature Yü Hsin, Tu Fu was to produce in his old age the famous ode to Yü Hsin, an immortal testament to the greatness of the Six Dynasties poet:

THOUGHTS ON HISTORICAL SITES

> He wandered in the northeast in windblown dust,
> Drifted in the southwest between heaven and earth.
> By the Three Gorges, he roamed in towers and terraces for days and months,
> At Five Streams he shared clouds and mountains with the brightly dressed natives.[63]   4

---

[62] William Graham, pp. 53, 101.

[63] The Five Streams are at the boundary of Kuei-chou and Hunan—i.e., in southwest China, where the so-called "Five-Stream savages" (Wu-hsi *man*) reside. These people are particularly fond of colorful clothing. To share "clouds and mountains" with them means to live with them.

Yü Hsin
THE POET'S POET

> That barbarian, serving the ruler, after all was a rascal,[64]
> The poet, lamenting the times, has not yet returned.
> All his life Yü Hsin was most forlorn,
> In his old age his poetry touched rivers and passes.[65] 8

詠懷古跡

支離東北風塵際
漂泊西南天地間
三峽樓台淹日月
五溪衣服共雲山
羯胡事主終無賴
詞客哀時且未還
庾信平生最蕭瑟
暮年詩賦動江關

As for Yü Hsin, he chose to identify himself with the grand historian of the Han, Ssu-ma Ch'ien who, despite great suffering in life, produced an immortal masterpiece, the *Shih chi* (*Records of the Grand Historian*). As an exile he seemed to experience the same feeling of alienation that Ssu-ma Ch'ien had under the humiliation of castration. Indeed, he believed that their lives so paralleled each other that it became imperative for him to write a similar work of history, as he acknowledged in the "Lament for the South":

> My life is similar to that of the man of Lung-men,
> My parting with my father was the same as that in Lo-yang:
> We both attended to our fathers' death-bed wish to gain achievement,
> And were entrusted with the task of completing their works.
>   (*YTSC*, I, 141)

生世等於龍門
辭親同於河洛
奉立身之遺訓
受成書之顧託

"The Lament for the South" is believed to have been written in 578, three years before Yü Hsin's death.[66] The dating of the work in this particular year

---

[64] The "barbarian" refers to Hou Ching, who took up arms against the Liang in 548. Scholars generally agree that this line also alludes to the rebel An Lu-shan of Tu Fu's time. For a detailed discussion of this point, see Ch'en Yin-k'o, *CYK*, I, 201–203. See also Hans Frankel, *The Flowering Plum and the Palace Lady*, p. 120.

[65] Tu Fu, *Tu shih [hsiang-chu]*, commentary by Ch'iu Chao-ao (Peking: Chung-hua shu-chü, 1979), *chüan* 17, IV, 1,499.

[66] Ch'en Yin-k'o, "Tu *Ai chiang-nan fu*," in *CYK*, II, 340. (See also discussion in Graham, pp. 173–174.)

Yü Hsin
THE POET'S POET

is important; for it was in 578 that Yü Hsin returned to Ch'ang-an after serving one year in Lo-yang, the city where Ssu-ma Ch'ien had received his father's deathbed command centuries before. Lo-yang originally belonged to the Eastern Wei (435–557), the court to which the young Yü Hsin was once sent as an envoy from the Liang. But for twenty years it had become the territory of Northern Ch'i, the conqueror of Eastern Wei. In 577, when the Northern Chou unified North China by overthrowing the Northern Ch'i government, Yü Hsin was honored with the important position of Military Governor of Lo-yang. By now the aging poet had already seen the same pattern of dynastic rise and fall repeated many times over—in the south his own country Liang was replaced by the Ch'en; in the north the Northern Ch'i and the Northern Chou took over the Eastern Wei and the Western Wei respectively, only to find each other at war again before long. Yü Hsin always reacted to such political vicissitudes with strong sentiment, and he was most eager to share that feeling with other individuals equally affected. When he was asked to entertain the Northern Ch'i envoys in 569, for instance, he could not help thinking of his old acquaintances in Lo-yang who, like him, were subjects of a conquered dynasty:

> If my old friends call on you,
> They will know I have already become a Chou official.
>   (*YTSC*, I, 318)
> 故人儻相訪
> 知余已執珪

It is indeed one of life's greatest ironies that Yü Hsin finally became the Military Governor of Lo-yang. For the Lo-yang area had been his ancestors' native place until the fall of the Western Chin, at which time the Yü family had moved south to serve in the Eastern Chin government. Now back in his ancestral homeland, the poet was more than ever stirred by a feeling of incompletion—that already in old age he had not yet accomplished the kind of work that his father wished for him. And it was at this time, I believe, that Yü Hsin made up his mind to write his definitive masterpiece, the "Lament for the South." This hypothesis may be supported by the fact that in a poem written during his Lo-yang days, the poet clearly declares his resolution to emulate the Grand Historian Ssu-ma Ch'ien:

> I would stay at Mt. Chung-nan,
> Just to be a historian.
>   (*YTSC*, I, 183)
> 留滯終南下
> 惟當一史臣

Yü Hsin
THE POET'S POET

The lyrical innovation of history in the "Lament for the South" seems to recall that of Pao Chao's "*Fu* on the Desolate City," despite their differences in length and subject matter. There is the same feeling of helplessness in the two poets—the same disillusionment in the face of political catastrophe. But Yü Hsin's *fu* is far more personal than Pao Chao's, as it combines political history with autobiography—treating his own life, and even that of his ancestors, as an integral part of the dynastic movement. This was because Yü Hsin's direct involvement in court circles and his numerous personal tragedies caused by the political unrest were of the most intense kind, so intense that few other poets, before or after, could match his.

Like Pao Chao, Yü Hsin often uses the invocation of heaven as a powerful rhetorical device. But, whereas Pao Chao is always implicit in his criticism, Yü Hsin is inclined to judge with a clearly reproachful tone. As an exile from a fallen dynasty, Yü Hsin seems to have gained freedom of speech. As a result, he is able to analyze in ruthless detail the causes of the dynastic fall. And sometimes he expresses his personal grief with a directness which is unabashedly emotional:

> An unhappy man will express himself in words,
> As the weary must sing of their toil.
> If Lu Chi laughs on hearing it,
> I shall be content;
> If Chang Heng looks on it with disdain,
> That is only right.[67]
> 窮者欲達其言
> 勞者須歌其事
> 陸士衡聞而撫掌
> 是所甘心
> 張平子見而陋之
> 固其宜也

The result is a most lyrical and detailed account of the history of the period. The poet narrates the tragic circumstances surrounding the Hou Ching rebellion, and mourns the human errors that made the rebel's quick success inevitable: Emperor Wu's failure, due to his own preoccupation with religious and cultural pursuits, to see the unruly Hou Ching as a potential problem and the unpreparedness of the officials at large for the coming combat. All these fatal situations weigh like a nightmare in the heart:

> Alas!
> When mountains crumbled,
> I passed through danger and destruction,

[67] William Graham, p. 57.

Yü Hsin
THE POET'S POET

> And now, as the seasons pass,
> I always grieve for what is gone.
> Whether it was heaven's will or man's doing,
> It breaks my heart.[68]

嗚呼
山嶽崩頹
既履危亡之運
春秋迭代
必有去故之悲
天意人事
可以悽愴傷心者矣

But the most heartbreaking truth for Yü Hsin is this: the eventual fall of the Liang was not caused by the rebel Hou Ching, but rather by conflicts, internal to the royal family, which exceeded all possible means of control. First, it was the treacherous Hsiao Cheng-te, Emperor Wu's adopted son and nephew, who called in the "barbarians" to launch a sudden attack upon the capital at Chien-k'ang.[69] Then, during the rebellion, the princes were busy fighting one another for the throne, rather than uniting against the common enemy. When Emperor Yüan finally put down the rebellion, there seemed to be a glimmer of hope for the restoration of the dynasty. But the Emperor's continuing wars with his relatives eventually led to a tragic end—as his nephew Hsiao Ch'a, a son of Hsiao T'ung, formed the secret alliance with the Western Wei which brought about the fall of the capital, Chiang-ling.[70] Narrating this final death blow to his country, Yü Hsin's fury and sorrow reaches its peak:

> What a pity that a unified empire
> Should have met with an uprising in the southeast,
> And to have given the Quail Head land to Ch'in!
> What is Heaven doing, acting so drunk?[71]
>   (*YTSC*, I, 165)

惜天下之一家
遭東南之反氣

---

[68] William Graham, p. 57.

[69] Considering himself entitled by contract of adoption to the heir-apparency, Hsiao Cheng-te had a grudge against Emperor Wu's choice of Hsiao T'ung as crown prince. See Marney, *Liang Chien-wen Ti*, p. 43.

[70] Again, Hsiao Ch'a's grievance was closely related to the problems of succession. A son of Crown Prince Chao-ming, Hsiao Ch'a felt that one of his brothers, rather than his uncle Hsiao Kang, should have been chosen as heir apparent upon his father's sudden death in 531. See Marney, *Liang Chien-wen Ti*, p. 47.

[71] Quail Head is the name of a constellation which is said to have governed the territory of Ch'in. A story has it that once Duke Mu of Ch'in feasted with the King of Heaven. The latter became so drunk that he gave the Quail Head region to the Ch'in.

Yü Hsin
THE POET'S POET

以鶉首而賜秦
天何爲而此醉

Thus, forever gone is the southern kingdom, the kingdom whose soul the poet desperately wishes to call back.[72]

"The Lament for the South" closes with a powerfully ironic note on the cyclical movement of human life, a conclusion which predicts the return of the north as China's political center:

> The heavens move in circles
> And man joins in them.
> My illustrious ancestor in the Western Chin
> First was driven away to the Eastern River.
> Now with me, in the seventh generation,
> The time had come to return to the north....[73]

且夫天道迴旋
生民預焉
余烈祖於西晉
始流播於東川
洎余身而七葉
又遭時而北遷....

In every sense the poet Yü Hsin sustains himself as the living expression of the spirit of Six Dynasties. He lived until the symbolic closure of the era in 581, at which time the Sui Dynasty founder, Yang Chien, usurped the imperial power in Ch'ang-an, hastening the end of the long political division that had separated the north and the south since 317. In literature the Six Dynasties period survives as an age of great poetic innovation, one which, in spite of—or perhaps because of—political disunity, explored China's poetic lyricism to the utmost.

---

[72] The title "Lament for the South" is taken from a poem attributed to the ancient Ch'u poet Sung Yü, "The Summons of the Soul" ("*Chao hun*"), where a crucial line reads: "Come back your soul! Ah, my lament for the South." It is obvious that Yü Hsin attempts to identify himself with the Ch'u poet, especially because it was in Chiang-ling, the native place of Sung Yü and the ancient region of the Ch'u state, that his southward-migrating ancestors finally had settled.

[73] William Graham, p. 101.

A Glossary of Chinese Characters

"*Ai chiang-nan fu*"　哀江南賦
An Lu-shan　安祿山
Ch'ai-sang　柴桑
Chang　張
Ch'ang-an　長安
Ch'ang-ch'eng kung-chu　長城公主
Chang Heng　張衡
Chang Hsieh　張協
Chang Hua　張華
Chao　趙
Chao Fei-yen　趙飛燕
"*Chao-hun*"　招魂
ch'ao-yin　朝隱
Chekiang　浙江
Ch'en　陳
chen-chün ts'an-chün　鎮軍參軍
Ch'en Pa-hsien　陳霸先
chi　記
ch'i　齊
"*Ch'i fa*"　七發
Ch'i Li-chi　綺里季
Ch'i-Liang　齊梁
Chi-lung　鷄籠
Ch'i Ming-ti　齊明帝
Ch'i Wu-ti　齊武帝
Chi Yün　紀昀
"*Chiang chin chiu*"　將進酒
Chiang-chou　江州
Chiang-ling　江陵
Chiang Yen　江淹
ch'iao　巧
ch'iao-ssu　巧似
Chien-an　建安
Ch'ien Fu　黔夫

Glossary

Chien-k'ang　建康
chih　志
chih-chih　質直
chih-kuai　志怪
Chih Po (Lord of Chih)　智伯
chih-yin　知音
Chin　晉
Ch'in　秦
Chin An-ti　晉安帝
Chin-lou tzu　金樓子
Ch'in Mu-kung (Duke Mu of Ch'in)　秦穆公
chin-tai　近代
chin-t'i shih　近體詩
ch'ing　情
ching-ch'iao　精巧
ch'ing-ching chiao-jung　情景交融
Ching-chou　荊州
Ching K'o　荊軻
Ching-ling pa-yu　竟陵八友
ch'ing-po chih t'u　輕薄之徒
ch'ing-t'an　清談
ch'ing-ya　清雅
ch'ing-yen　輕艷
chiu-chai　舊宅
Chou　周
chou chi-chiu　州祭酒
Chu　朱
Ch'u　楚
Ch'u Chao-wang (King Chao of Ch'u)　楚昭王
Chü-lang　舉郎
Ch'u-tz'u　楚辭
Ch'ü Yüan　屈原
chuan　傳
ch'uan-shen　傳神
Chuang Tzu　莊子
chüeh-chü　絕句
Chung Jung (Chung Hung)　鍾嶸
chung-p'in　中品
Chung Tzu-ch'i　鍾子期
Fan Yeh　范曄
feng-hua ch'ing-mi　風華清靡
feng-li　風力

Glossary

Feng T'ang　馮唐
fu　賦
Han Ch'eng-ti (Emperor Ch'eng of Han)　漢成帝
Han Hsien-ti　漢獻帝
Han Hsin　韓信
Han Hsüan-tzu　韓宣子
Han Wen-ti (Emperor Wen of Han)　漢文帝
Han Wu-ti (Emperor Wu of Han)　漢武帝
Heng-yang　衡陽
Ho　何
Ho Hsün　何遜
Honan　河南
Hopei　河北
Hou Ching　侯景
Hou-Han shu　後漢書
hsi-ch'ü　西曲
Hsi K'ang (Chi K'ang)　嵇康
hsi-ti　西邸
Hsia Huang Kung　夏黃公
Hsiang Hsiu　向秀
Hsiang-ming fu chi　香茗賦集
Hsiao Ch'a　蕭詧
Hsiao Cheng-te　蕭正德
Hsiao I (Prince of Hsiang Tung; later Emperor Yüan of the Liang)　蕭繹(湘東王, 梁元帝)
Hsiao Kang (Emperor Chien-wen of the Liang)　蕭綱(梁簡文帝)
Hsiao Pen　蕭賁
hsiao-shih　小詩
Hsiao T'ung (Prince Chao-ming)　蕭統(昭明太子)
Hsiao Tzu-liang (Prince Ching-ling)　蕭子良(竟陵王)
Hsiao Tzu-lung (Prince Sui)　蕭子龍(隋王)
Hsiao Yen (Emperor Wu of the Liang)　蕭衍(梁武帝)
"*Hsiao-yüan fu*"　小園賦
Hsieh An　謝安
Hsieh Chuang　謝莊
Hsieh Hui-lien　謝惠連
Hsieh Hun　謝混
Hsieh Hsüan　謝玄
Hsieh Ling-yün　謝靈運
Hsieh T'iao　謝朓
Hsieh Wan　謝萬
"*Hsien-ch'ing fu*"　閒情賦

Glossary

hsien-su 險俗
hsin-pien 新變
hsin-sheng 新聲
hsin-t'i shih 新體詩
"*Hsing-lu nan*" 行路難
hsing-ssu 形似
Hsü Ch'ih 徐摛
Hsü Hsien-chih 徐羡之
Hsü Hsün 許詢
hsü hua-p'in 續畫品
Hsü Ling 徐陵
Hsüan-ch'eng 宣城
hsüan-yen 玄言
Hsün Yang 潯陽
hua 化
Huan Hsüan 桓玄
Huang Chieh 黃節
Hui Shih 惠施
Hui Yüan 慧遠
Hunan 湖南
Hupeh 湖北
I-ching 易經
i-shao tsung-tuo 以少總多
Juan Chi 阮籍
jung-ch'ang 冗長
kan-wu 感物
"*Kao-t'ang fu*" 高唐賦
Ku 顧
ku-shih 古詩
Ku-shih yüan 古詩源
Kuang-ling 廣陵
Kuei-chi 會稽
"*Kuei-ch'ü-lai-hsi tz'u*" 歸去來兮辭
kung 功
kung-t'i shih 宮體詩
Kuo P'u 郭璞
"*Lan-t'ing*" 蘭亭
"*Lan-t'ing chi hsü*" 蘭亭集序
lang 郎
Lao Tzu 老子
li 理
li-jen 麗人

Glossary

Li Po　李白
"*Li sao*"　離騷
"*Li-tz'u*"　麗辭
li-yen　立言
Liang　梁
lien　憐
lien-chü　聯句
Lin-hai　臨海
Liu Hsiao-ch'o　劉孝綽
Liu Hsieh　劉勰
Liu I　劉毅
Liu I-chen (Prince Lu-ling)　劉義眞(廬陵王)
Liu I-ch'ing (Lord of Lin-ch'uan)　劉義慶(臨川王)
Liu I-min (Ch'eng-chih)　劉遺民(程之)
Liu Pang　劉邦
Liu Pei　劉備
Liu Shih-p'ei　劉師培
Liu-Sung　劉宋
Liu Tan (Lord Ching-ling)　劉誕(竟陵王)
Liu Ying　劉嬰
Liu Yü (Emperor Wu of the Liu-Sung)　劉裕(宋武帝)
Liu Yün　柳惲
"*Lo-shen fu*"　洛神賦
Lo-yang　洛陽
Lu　陸
Lu Chi　陸機
Lü Shang　呂尚
lü-shih　律詩
mei-jen　美人
Mei Sheng　枚乘
Meng-chin　孟津
Nanking　南京
Ni Fan　倪璠
"*Ni hsing-lu nan*"　擬行路難
nien　黏
P'an Yüeh　潘岳
Pao Chao　鮑照
Pao Ling-hui　鮑令暉
pen-chai　本宅
P'eng-tse　彭澤
pi　筆
p'ien-fu　駢賦

Glossary

p'ien-wen 駢文
Po Chü-i 白居易
Po-hun Wu-jen 伯昏無人
Po-i 伯夷
"*Shan-chü fu*" 山居賦
shan-shui 山水
shan-shui shih 山水詩
shan-shui tu 山水都
shan-shui wen 山水文
Shang 商
shang-p'in 上品
Shao-hsing 紹興
Shen Teh-ch'ien 沈德潛
Shen Yüeh 沈約
shih 詩
Shih-chi 史記
Shih-ching 詩經
Shih Ch'ung 石崇
Shih-hsing 始興
"*shih-hsü*" 時序
Shih-ning 始寧
Shih-p'in 詩品
Shih Seng-pien 釋僧辨
Shih-shuo hsin-yü 世說新語
shih-tsu 士族
Shou-kuang 壽光
Shou-yang 首陽
Shu Ch'i 叔齊
Shu Kuang 疏廣
Shu Shou 疏受
Shun 舜
Ssu-ma Chi-chu 司馬季主
Ssu-ma Ch'ien 司馬遷
Ssu-ma Hsiang-ju 司馬相如
ssu-sheng pa-ping 四聲八病
Ssu-sheng p'u 四聲譜
ssu-yu 四友
Su Shih 蘇軾
Sui 隋
sui 歲
Sui hou (Marquis of Sui) 隋侯
Sun Ch'o 孫綽

Glossary

Sun Ch'üan　孫權
Sun En　孫恩
Sung Hsiao-wu ti　宋孝武帝
Sung Shao-ti　宋少帝
Sung Yü　宋玉
"*Ta* Hsieh Chung-shu *shu*"　答謝中書書
Ta-lei　大雷
"*Ta tsung shih*"　大宗師
T'an Hsien　譚獻
T'ang Hui-hsiu　湯惠休
Tang Yang　當陽
T'ao Ch'ien (Yüan-ming)　陶潛（淵明）
T'ao Hung-ching　陶弘景（宏景）
T'ao K'an　陶侃
Tao-te ching　道德經
te　德
t'i-wu　體物
t'ien-chia yü　田家語
T'ien Ch'ou　田疇
T'o-pa　拓拔
tsa-shih　雜詩
ts'ai　采
Ts'ai Yung　蔡邕
Ts'ao Chih　曹植
Ts'ao P'i　曹丕
Ts'ao Ts'ao　曹操
Tso-chuan　左傳
Tso Ssu　左思
Tsung Ping　宗炳
ts'ung-shih　從事
Tu Fu　杜甫
Tu Yü　杜預
Tung Cho　董卓
tzu-jan　自然
"*Tzu-yeh ko*"　子夜歌
Wang Hsi-chih　王羲之
Wang Hsiu-chih　王秀之
Wang Hung　王弘
Wang Jung　王融
Wang Mang　王莽
Wang Ning-chih　王凝之
Wang Ts'an　王粲

Glossary

Wei 魏
Wei-Chin 魏晉
wen 文
wen-chang 文章
"Wen-fu" 文賦
Wen-hsin tiao-lung 文心雕龍
Wen-hsüan 文選
wen-hsüeh 文學
Wen-te 文德
Wu 吳
"Wu-ch'eng fu" 蕪城賦
Wu-hsi *man* 五溪蠻
Wu-ko 吳歌
wu-se 物色
Wu Shu-t'ang 伍叔儻
Wu wang (King of Wu) 吳王
wu-yen shih 五言詩
wu-yin 五音
Wu Yün 吳均
Yang Chien 楊堅
Yang Hsiu-chih 楊休之
Yangchow 揚州
Yao Tsui 姚最
Yeh 鄴
Yeh-tu ku-shih 鄴都故事
yen 言
"Yen-ko hsing" 燕歌行
Yen T'ai-tzu Tan 燕太子丹
Yen Yen-chih 顏延之
Yin Chung-wen 殷仲文
"Yin-hsiu" 隱秀
Ying Cheng 嬴政
yu-chi 遊記(游記)
Yü Chien-wu 庾肩吾
Yu-chou 幽州
"Yu hou-yüan fu" 遊後園賦
yu-hsien 遊仙
Yü Hsin 庾信
Yü Jang 豫讓
Yu ming-shan chih 遊名山志
"Yü Sung Yüan-ssu *shu*" 與宋元思書
Yü-t'ai hsin-yung 玉台新詠

Glossary

"*Yu T'ien-t'ai shan fu*"　　遊天台山賦
Yü-wen Chao (Prince of Chao)　　宇文招(趙王)
Yü-wen Chüeh　　宇文覺
Yü-wen Yü (Emperor Ming of Northern Chou)　　宇文毓(北周明帝)
Yü-wen Yu (Prince of T'eng)　　宇文逌(滕王)
yu-yen　　游衍
Yü Yen　　虞炎
Yüan　　袁
Yüan-chia　　元嘉
yüan ch'ing　　緣情
yüeh-fu　　樂府
yün　　韻
Yung-chia　　永嘉
Yung-chou　　雍州
yung-huai　　詠懷
Yung-ming　　永明
yung-shih　　詠史
yung-shih shih　　詠史詩
yung-wu　　詠物
yung-wu fu　　詠物賦

A Selected Bibliography

Ami Yūji 網祐次. *Chūgoku chūsei bungaku kenkyū: Nan Sei Eimei jidai o chūshin to shite* 中国中世文学研究—南齊永明時代を中心として. Tokyo: Shinjusha, 1960.
Bear, Peter. "The Lyric Poetry of Yü Hsin." Diss. Yale Univ. 1969.
Bielenstein, Hans. *The Bureaucracy of Han Times*. Cambridge: Cambridge Univ. Press, 1980.
Birch, Cyril, ed. *Studies in Chinese Literary Genres*. Berkeley: Univ. of California Press, 1974.
Birrell, Anne, trans. *New Songs from a Jade Terrace*. London: Allen & Unwin, 1982.
Bloom, Harold. *The Anxiety of Influence: A Theory of Poetry*. New York: Oxford Univ. Press, 1973.
———. *A Map of Misreading*. New York: Oxford Univ. Press, 1975.
———. *Poetry and Repression: Revisionism from Blake to Stevens*. New Haven: Yale Univ. Press, 1976.
Bodman, Richard W. "Poetics and Prosody in Early Medieval China: A Study and Translation of Kūkai's *Bunkyō Hifuron*." Diss. Cornell Univ. 1978.
Bush, Susan. "Tsung Ping's Essay on Painting Landscape and the 'Landscape Buddhism' of Mount Lu." In *Theories of the Arts in China*, ed. Susan Bush and Christian Murck. Princeton: Princeton Univ. Press, 1983, pp. 132–164.
Chan Ying 詹鍈. *Wen-hsin tiao-lung te feng-ke hsüeh* 文心雕龍的風格學. Peking: Jen-min wen-hsüeh ch'u-pan-she, 1982.
Chang, H. C. *Chinese Literature, Vol. 2: Nature Poetry*. New York: Columbia Univ. Press, 1977.
Chang, K. C. *Art, Myth and Ritual: The Path of Political Authority in Ancient China*. Cambridge: Harvard Univ. Press, 1983.
Chang, Kang-i Sun. "Chinese 'Lyric Criticism' in the Six Dynasties." In *Theories of the Arts in China*. Ed. Susan Bush and Christian Murck. Princeton: Princeton Univ. Press, 1983, pp. 215–224.
———. "Description of Landscape in Early Six Dynasties Poetry." In *ESP*.
———. "Su Shih and the Evolution of the *Tz'u* Genre." In her *The Evolution of Chinese Tz'u Poetry: From Late T'ang to Northern Sung*. Princeton: Princeton Univ. Press, 1980, pp. 158–206.
Chang P'u 張溥. *Han Wei Liu-ch'ao pai-san-chia chi t'i-tz'u* [chu] 漢魏六朝百

Selected Bibliography

三家集題辭[注]. Ed. Yin Meng-lun 殷孟倫. Peking: Jen-min wen-hsüeh ch'u-pan-she, 1981.

Chao I 趙翼. *Nien-erh shih cha-chi* 廿二史劄記. 2 vols. Rpt. Taipei: Shih-chieh shu-chü, 1973.

Chaves, Jonathan. *Mei Yao-ch'en and the Development of Early Sung Poetry.* New York: Columbia Univ. Press, 1976.

Chen, Shih-hsiang. "The Genesis of Poetic Time: The Greatness of Ch'ü Yuan, Studied with a New Critical Approach." *The Tsing Hua Journal of Chinese Studies*, New Series X, No. 1 (June 1973), 1–43.

———. "The *Shih-ching*: Its Generic Significance in Chinese Literary History and Poetics." In *Studies in Chinese Literary Genres*. Ed. Cyril Birch. Berkeley: Univ. of California Press, 1974, pp. 8–41.

Ch'en Yin-k'o 陳寅恪. "Ssu-sheng san-wen" 四聲三問. In his *CYK*, I, 205–218.

———. "T'ao-hua yüan chi p'ang cheng" 桃花源記旁證. In his *CYK*, I, 183–193.

———. "T'ao Yüan-ming chih ssu-hsiang yü ch'ing-t'an chih kuan-hsi" 陶淵明之思想與清談之關係. In his *CYK*, I, 381–407.

———. "Tu Ai chiang-nan *fu*" 讀哀江南賦. In his *CYK*, II, 339–345.

———. "Tung-Chin Nan-ch'ao chih Wu-yü" 東晉南朝之吳語. In his *CYK*, II, 143–148.

———. "Yü Hsin Ai chiang-nan fu yü Tu Fu Yung-huai ku-chi shih" 庾信哀江南賦與杜甫詠懷古跡詩. In his *CYK*, I, 201–203.

Ch'en Yüan 陳垣. *Erh-shih shih shuo-jun piao* 二十史朔閏表. 1925; rpt. Taipei: I-wen yin-shu-kuan, 1958.

Ch'en Yüan-lung 陳元龍, ed. [Yü ting] *li-tai fu hui* [御定]歷代賦彙. 140 *chüan*. Preface 1706.

Cheng, François. *Chinese Poetic Writing*. Trans. Donald A. Riggs and Jerome P. Seaton. Bloomington: Indiana Univ. Press, 1982.

Cherniack, Susan. "The Eulogy for Emperor Wen, and Its Generic and Biographical Contexts." Draft, 1984.

Chiang Liang-fu 姜亮夫. *Li-tai jen-wu nien-li pei-chuan tsung-piao* 歷代人物年里碑傳綜表. Rpt. Taipei: Hua-shih ch'u-pan-she, 1976.

Ch'ien Chung-lien 錢仲聯. "Pao Chao nien-piao" 鮑照年表. In his *PTCC*, pp. 431–442.

Ch'ien Chung-shu 錢鍾書. *Kuan-chui pien* 管錐編. 4 vols. Peking: Chung-hua shu-chü, 1979.

———. *T'an i lu* 談藝錄. 1948; rpt. Hong Kong: Lung-men shu-tien, 1965.

Ch'ien Mu 錢穆. *Chung-kuo hsüeh-shu ssu-hsiang shih lun-ts'ung* 中國學術思想史論叢. Vol. III. Taipei: Tung-ta t'u-shu yu-hsien kung-ssu, 1977.

———. *Chung-kuo t'ung-shih ts'an-k'ao tzu-liao* 中國通史參考資料. Introd.

Selected Bibliography

Yü Ying-shih 余英時. Taipei: Tung-sheng ch'u-pan shih-yeh kung-ssu, 1982.
Chou, Chao-ming. "The Beholder in *Shan-shui* Poetry." Unpublished paper, 1983.
Chou Chen-fu 周振甫. *Shih-tz'u li-hua* 詩詞例話. Rev. ed. Peking: Chung-kuo ch'ing-nien ch'u-pan-she, 1979.
Chou, Shan. "Beginning with Images in the Nature Poetry of Wang Wei." *Harvard Journal of Asiatic Studies*, 42, No. 1 (1982), 117–137.
Chou Shao-hsien 周紹賢. *Wei Chin ch'ing-t'an shu-lun* 魏晉清談述論. Rpt. Taipei: Commercial Press, 1966.
Chow, Tse-tsung. "Ancient Chinese Views of Literature, the Tao, and Their Relationship." *Chinese Literature: Essays, Articles, Reviews*, 1, No. 1 (1979), 3–29.
———. "The Early History of the Chinese Word *Shih* (Poetry)." In *Wen-lin, Studies in the Chinese Humanities*. Ed. Tse-tsung Chow. Madison: Univ. of Wisconsin Press, 1968, pp. 151–209.
Ch'ü T'ui-yüan 瞿蛻園, ed. *Han Wei Liu-ch'ao fu hsüan* 漢魏六朝賦選. Rev. ed. Shanghai: Ku-chi ch'u-pan-she, 1979.
Ch'ü Yüan 屈原, et al. *Ch'u tz'u* 楚辭. Commentary by Wang I 王逸. Rpt. Hong Kong: Kuang-chih shu-chü, n.d.
Chuang Tzu 莊子. *Chuang Tzu [chi-shih]* 莊子[集釋]. Ed. Kuo Ch'ing-fan 郭慶藩. Peking, 1961. Rpt. in one vol. Taipei: Ho-lo t'u-shu ch'u-pan-she, 1974.
Chung Ch'i 鍾祺. *Chung-ku shih-ko lun-ts'ung* 中古詩歌論叢. Hong Kong: Shanghai Book Co., 1965.
Chung Hsing 鍾惺 and T'an Yüan-ch'un 譚元春, eds. *Ku-shih kuei* 古詩歸. Preface 1617.
Chung Jung 鍾嶸. *Shih-p'in [chu]* 詩品[注]. Commentary by Ch'en Yen-chieh 陳延傑. Hong Kong: Commercial Press, 1959.
Chung-kuo mei-hsüeh shih tzu-liao hsüan-pien 中國美學史資料選編. Ed. Dept. of Philosophy, Peking University. Peking: Chung-hua shu-chü, 1980.
Chung Yu-min 鍾優民. *T'ao Yüan-ming lun-chi* 陶淵明論集. Hunan: Jen-ming ch'u-pan-she, 1981.
Davis, A. R. *T'ao Yüan-ming: His Works and Their Meaning*. 2 vols. Cambridge: Cambridge Univ. Press, 1983.
de Bary, William Theodore, et al., comp. *Sources of Chinese Tradition*. New York: Columbia Univ. Press, 1960. Vol. I.
De Woskin, Kenneth. "Early Chinese Music and the Origins of Aesthetic Terminology." In *Theories of the Arts in China*. Ed. Susan Bush and Christian Murck. Princeton: Princeton Univ. Press, 1983, pp. 187–214.
———. *A Song for One or Two: Music and the Concept of Art in Early China*.

Selected Bibliography

Michigan Papers in Chinese Studies, No. 42. Ann Arbor: Univ. of Michigan, 1982.

Eberhard, Wolfram. *The Local Cultures of South and East China*. Leiden: E. J. Brill, 1968.

Egan, Ronald C. "Poems on Paintings: Su Shih and Huang T'ing-chien." *Harvard Journal of Asiatic Studies*, 43, No. 2 (1983), 413–451.

Eliot, T. S. *On Poetry and Poets*. 1943; rpt. New York: The Noonday Press, 1961.

Elliott, Robert C. *The Shape of Utopia: Studies in a Literary Genre*. Chicago: Univ. of Chicago Press, 1970.

Eoyang, Eugene. "Moments in Chinese Poetry: Nature in the World and Nature in the Mind." In *Studies in Chinese Poetry and Poetics*. Ed. Ronald C. Miao. Vol. I. San Francisco: Chinese Materials Center, 1978, pp. 105–128.

———. "The Solitary Boat: Images of Self in Chinese Nature Poetry." *Journal of Asian Studies*. 32, No. 4 (1973), 593–621.

Fang, Achilles, trans. "Rhymeprose on Literature, the *Wen-fu* of Lu Chi (A.D. 261–303)." In John L. Bishop, ed. *Studies in Chinese Literature*. Cambridge: Harvard Univ. Press, 1966, pp. 3–42.

Fang Hsüan-ling 房玄齡, et al. *Chin shu* 晉書. 10 vols. Ed. Editorial Board of Chung-hua shu-chü. Peking: Chung-hua shu-chü, 1974.

Feng Ch'eng-chi 馮承基. "Lun Yung-ming sheng-lü—pa ping" 論永明聲律——八病. In *CKWH*, pp. 637–649.

Fichter, Andrew. *Poets Historical: Dynastic Epic in the Renaissance*. New Haven: Yale Univ. Press, 1982.

Fong, Wen C. "Images of the Mind." In *Images of the Mind*. By Wen C. Fong et. al. Princeton: Princeton Univ. Press, 1984, pp. 1–212.

Frankel, Hans. H. "Classical Chinese." In *Versification: Major Language Types*. Ed. W. K. Wimsatt. New York: New York Univ. Press, 1972, pp. 22–37.

———. "The Development of Han and Wei Yüeh-fu as a High Literary Genre." In *ESP*.

———. *The Flowering Plum and the Palace Lady: Interpretations of Chinese Poetry*. New Haven: Yale Univ. Press, 1976.

———. "Poetry and Painting: Chinese and Western Views of Their Convertibility." *Comparative Literature* 9 (1957), 289–307.

———. "Six Dynasties *Yüeh-fu* and Their Singers," *Journal of the Chinese Language Teachers Association*, 13 (1978), 189–196.

———. "*Yüeh-fu* Poetry." In Cyril Birch, ed. *Studies in Chinese Literary Genres*. Berkeley: Univ. of California Press, 1974.

Frodsham, J. D. *The Murmuring Stream: The Life and Works of the Chinese Nature Poet Hsieh Ling-yün (385–433), Duke of K'ang-lo*. 2 vols. Kuala Lumpur: Univ. of Malaya Press, 1967.

Selected Bibliography

———. "The Nature Poetry of Pao Chao." *Orient/West*, 8, No. 6 (1963), 85–93.

———. "The Origins of Chinese Nature Poetry." In *Asia Major* (n.s.), 8, No. 1 (1960), 68–104.

——— and Ch'eng Hsi, trans. *An Anthology of Chinese Verse: Han Wei Chin and the Northern and Southern Dynasties*. Oxford: Clarendon Press, 1967.

Fujiwara no Hamanari 藤原濱成. *Kakyō* hyōshiki 歌經標式. In *Nihon kagaku taikei* 日本歌学大系. Ed. Sasaki Nobutsuna 佐佐木信綱. Tokyo: Kazama shobō, 1956, I, 1–17.

Fung Yu-lan. *A History of Chinese Philosophy*. Trans. Derk Bodde. Vol. II. Princeton: Princeton Univ. Press, 1953.

Gernet, Jacques. *A History of Chinese Civilization*. Trans. J. R. Foster. Cambridge: Cambridge Univ. Press, 1982.

Giamatti, A. Bartlett. *The Earthly Paradise and the Renaissance Epic*. Princeton: Princeton Univ. Press, 1966.

Gibbs, Donald A. "Literary Theory in the *Wen-hsin tiao-lung*, Sixth Century Chinese Treatise on the Genesis of Literature and Conscious Artistry." Diss. Univ. of Washington 1970.

Graham, A. C., trans. *The Book of Lieh-tzu*. London: J. Murray, 1960.

———., trans. *Chuang-tzu: The Seven Inner Chapters and Other Writings from the Book Chuang-tzu*. London: Allen and Unwin, 1981.

Graham, William T., Jr., trans. *The Lament for the South: Yü Hsin's "Ai Chiang-Nan Fu."* Cambridge: Cambridge Univ. Press, 1980.

——— and James R. Hightower. "Yü Hsin's 'Songs of Sorrow.'" *Harvard Journal of Asiatic Studies*, 43, No. 1 (1983), 5–55.

Hawkes, David, trans. *Ch'u Tz'u: The Songs of the South, An Ancient Chinese Anthology*. London: Oxford Univ. Press, 1959.

———. "The Quest of the Goddess." In *Studies in Chinese Literary Genres*. Ed. Cyril Birch. Berkeley: Univ. of California Press, 1974, pp. 42–68.

Helsinger, Elizabeth K. *Ruskin and the Art of the Beholder*. Cambridge: Harvard Univ. Press, 1982.

Henricks, Robert G., trans. *Philosophy and Argumentation in Third-Century China: The Essays of Hsi K'ang*. Princeton: Princeton Univ. Press, 1983.

Hervouet, Yves. *Un Poète de cour sous les Han: Sseu-ma Siang-jou*. Paris, 1964.

Hightower, James R. "Allusion in the Poetry of T'ao Ch'ien." In *Studies in Chinese Literary Genres*. Ed. Cyril Birch. Berkeley: Univ. of California Press, 1974, pp. 108–132.

———. "The *Fu* of T'ao Ch'ien." In *Studies in Chinese Literature*. Ed. John L. Bishop. Cambridge: Harvard Univ. Press, 1966, pp. 45–106.

———. "Literary Criticism through the Six Dynasties." In his *Topics in Chinese Literature*. Rev. ed. Cambridge: Harvard Univ. Press, 1971, pp. 42–48.

Selected Bibliography

———. *The Poetry of T'ao Ch'ien*. Oxford: Clarendon Press, 1970.

———. *Topics in Chinese Literature: Outlines and Bibliographies*. Rev. ed. Cambridge: Harvard Univ. Press, 1971.

———. "The Wen Hsüan and Genre Theory." In *Studies in Chinese Literature*. Ed. John L. Bishop. Cambridge: Harvard Univ. Press, 1966, pp. 142–163.

Holman, C. Hugh. *A Handbook to Literature*. 4th ed. Indianapolis: Bobbs-Merill, 1980.

Holzman, Donald. "Confucius and Ancient Chinese Criticism." In *Chinese Approaches to Literature from Confucius to Liang Ch'i-ch'ao*. Ed. Adele Austin Rickett. Princeton: Princeton Univ. Press, 1978, pp. 21–41.

———. "La Poésie de Ji Kang." *Journal Asiatique*, 268 (1980), 107–177, 323–378.

———. *La Vie et la Pensée de Hi K'ang*. Leiden: Brill, 1957.

———. "Literary Criticism in China in the Early Third Century A.D." *Asiatische Studien*, 28, No. 2 (1974), 113–149.

———. *Poetry and Politics: The Life and Works of Juan Chi, A.D. 210–263*. Cambridge: Cambridge Univ. Press, 1976.

———. Rev. of *The Lament of the South: Yü Hsin's "Ai Chiang-nan fu,"* by William T. Graham, Jr. *Chinese Literature: Essays, Articles, Reviews*, 4, No. 2 (1982), 255–258.

Hsiao I 蕭繹. *Chin-lou tzu* 金樓子. In *Ssu-k'u ch'üan-shu chen-pen pieh-chi* 四庫全書珍本別輯. Taipei: Commercial Press, 1975.

Hsiao Ti-fei 蕭滌非. *Tu shih san cha-chi* 讀詩三札記. Peking: Tso-chia ch'u-pan-she, 1957.

Hsiao T'ung 蕭統. *[Chao ming] wen hsüan* [昭明]文選. Commentary by Li Shan 李善. 2 vols. Rpt. Taipei: Ho-lo t'u-shu ch'u-pan-she, 1975.

Hsiao Tzu-hsien 蕭子顯. *Nan-Ch'i shu* 南齊書. Ed. Editorial Board of Chung-hua shu-chü. 3 vols. Peking: Chung-hua shu-chü, 1972.

Hsieh Ling-yün 謝靈運. *Hsieh K'ang-lo shih [chu]* 謝康樂詩[注]. Ed. Huang Chieh 黃節. 1924; rpt. Taipei: I-wen yin-shu kuan, 1967.

———. *Hsieh Ling-yün shih hsüan* 謝靈運詩選. Ed. Yeh Hsiao-hsüeh 葉笑雪. Shanghai: Ku-tien wen-hsüeh ch'u-pan-she, 1957.

Hsieh T'iao 謝朓. *Hsieh Hsüan-ch'eng chi [chiao-chu]* 謝宣城集[校注]. Ed. Hung Shun-lung 洪順隆. Taipei: Chung-hua shu-chü, 1969.

———. *Hsieh Hsüan-ch'eng shih [chu]* 謝宣城詩[注]. Ed. Lee Chik-fong 李直方. Hong Kong: Universal Book Co., 1968.

Hsü Fu-kuan 徐復觀. *Chung-kuo wen-hsüeh lun-chi* 中國文學論集. 2nd ed. Taipei: Student Book Co., 1974.

Hsü Ling 徐陵, ed. *[Chien-chu] Yü-tai hsin-yung* [箋注]玉臺新詠. Commentary by Wu Chao-i 吳兆宜. Rpt. Taipei: Kuang-wen shu-chü, 1967.

Hsü Shih-tseng 徐師曾. *Wen-t'i ming-pien hsü-shuo* 文體明辨序說. Printed

Selected Bibliography

with *Wen-chang pien-t'i hsü-shuo* 文章辨體序說, by Wu Na 吳訥. Peking: Jen-min wen-hsüeh ch'u-pan-she, 1962.

Hu Kuo-jui 胡國瑞. *Wei-chin Nan-pei-ch'ao wen-hsüeh shih* 魏晉南北朝文學史. Shanghai: Wen-i ch'u-pan-she, 1980.

Hui Chiao 慧皎. *Kao seng chuan* 高僧傳. (ca. A.D. 519) Collected in the Taishō shinshū daizōkyō 大正新修大藏經. Tokyo: Society for the Publication of the Taishō Edition of Tripitaka, 1924–1932, vol. 50, pp. 322–423 (Text no. 2059).

Hung Shun-lung 洪順隆. "Hsieh T'iao sheng-p'ing chi ch'i tso-p'in yen-chiu" 謝朓生平及其作品研究. In *HHCC*, pp. 1–35.

———. *Liu-ch'ao shih-lun* 六朝詩論. Taipei: Wen-chin ch'u-pan-she, 1978.

Ikkai Tomoyoshi 一海知義, trans. *Tō En-mei* 陶淵明. *Chūgoku shijin senshū* 中国詩人選集, No. 5. Tokyo: Iwanami, 1965.

Kao, Yu-kung. "The Esthetic of the Lü-shih." In *ESP*.

——— and Tsu-lin Mei. "Ending Lines in Wang Shih-chen's Ch'i-chüeh: Convention and Creativity in the Ch'ing." In *Artists and Traditions*. Ed. Christian Murck. Princeton: Princeton Univ. Press, 1976, pp. 131–135.

——— and Tsu-lin Mei. "Syntax, Diction and Imagery in T'ang Poetry." *Harvard Journal of Asiatic Studies*, 31 (1970), 49–136.

Karlgren, Bernhard, trans. *The Book of Odes*. Stockholm: The Museum of Far Eastern Antiquities, 1974.

Keats, John. *John Keats: Selected Poetry and Letters*. Ed. Richard Harter Fogle. Rev. ed. San Francisco: Rinehart Press, 1969.

Kittay, Jeffrey, ed. *Towards a Theory of Description*. Yale French Studies, No. 61. New Haven: Yale Univ. Press, 1981.

Knechtges, David R. *The Han Rhapsody: A Study of the Fu of Yang Hsiung (53 B.C.—A.D. 18)*. Cambridge: Cambridge Univ. Press, 1976.

———. "A Journey to Morality: Chang Heng's *The Rhapsody on Pondering the Mystery*. In *Essays in Commemoration of the Golden Jubilee of the Fung Ping Shan Library (1932–1982)*. Ed. Chan Ping-leung, et al. Hong Kong: Fung Ping Shan Library, 1982, pp. 162–182.

———. Rev. of *The Lament of the South: Yü Hsin's "Ai chiang-nan fu,"* by William T. Graham, Jr. *Harvard Journal of Asiatic Studies*, 42, No. 2 (1982), 668–679.

———. *Two Studies on the Han Fu*. Seattle: Far Eastern and Russian Institute, Univ. of Washington, 1968.

———, trans. *Wen xuan, or Selections of Refined Literature, vols. 1: Rhapsodies on Metropolises & Capitals*. Compiled by Xiao Tong (501–531). Princeton: Princeton Univ. Press, 1982.

——— and Jerry Swanson. "Seven Stimuli for the Prince: The *Ch'i-Fa* of Mei Ch'eng." *Monumenta Serica*, 29 (1970–1971), 99–116.

Konishi Jin'ichi 小西甚一. "The Genesis of the *Kokinshū* Style." Trans. Helen

Selected Bibliography

C. McCullough. *Harvard Journal of Asiatic Studies*, 38, No. 1 (1978), 61–170.

———. *A History of Japanese Literature. Vol. I, The Archaic and Ancient Ages.* Trans. Aileen Gattan and Nicholas Teele. Ed. Earl Miner. Princeton: Princeton Univ. Press, 1984.

Kroll, Paul W. *Meng Hao-Jan*. Boston: Twayne Publishers, 1981.

———. "Portraits of Ts'ao Ts'ao: Literary Studies on the Man and the Myth." Diss. Univ. of Michigan 1976.

———. "Verses From on High: The Ascent of T'ai Shan." In *ESP*.

Kūkai 空海. *Bunkyō hifuron* 文鏡秘府論. Peking: Jen-min wen-hsüeh ch'u-pan-she, 1975.

Kuo Mao-ch'ien 郭茂倩, comp. *Yüeh-fu shih-chi* 樂府詩集. Ed. Editorial Board of Chung-hua shu-chü. 4 vols. Peking: Chung-hua shu-chü, 1979.

Kuo Shao-yü 郭紹虞, ed. *Chung-kuo li-tai wen-lun hsüan* 中國歷代文論選. Rev. ed. 4 vols. Shanghai: Ku-chi ch'u-pan-she, 1979–1980.

———. *Chung-kuo wen-hsüeh p'i-p'ing shih* 中國文學批評史, 1956; rpt. Hong Kong: Hung-chih shu-chü, 1970.

Lau, D. C., trans. *Lao Tzu: Tao Te Ching*, 1963; rpt. New York: Penguin Books, 1983.

Ledderose, Lothar. "The Earthly Paradise: Religious Elements in Chinese Landscape Art." In *Theories of the Arts in China*. Ed. Susan Bush and Christian Murck. Princeton: Princeton Univ. Press, 1983, pp. 165–183.

Lee Chik-Fong 李直方. *Hsieh T'iao shih yen-chiu* 謝朓詩研究. Printed with *Hsieh Hsüan-ch'eng shih chu* 謝宣城詩注. Hong Kong: Universal Book Co., 1968.

———. *Han Wei Liu-ch'ao shih lun-kao* 漢魏六朝詩論稿. Hong Kong: Lung Men Book Store, 1967.

Levy, Ian Hideo. *Hitomaro and the Birth of Japanese Lyricism*. Princeton: Princeton Univ. Press, 1984.

Li, Ch'i. "The Changing Concept of the Recluse in Chinese Literature." *Harvard Journal of Asiatic Studies*, 24 (1962–63), 234–247.

Li Po 李白. *Li T'ai-po ch'üan-chi* 李太白全集. Commentary by Wang Ch'i 王琦. 3 vols. Peking: Chung-hua shu-chü, 1977.

Li Tse-hou 李澤厚. *Mei te li-ch'eng* 美的歷程. Peking: Wen-wu ch'u-pan-she, 1981.

Li Yen-shou 李延壽. *Nan shih* 南史. Ed. Editorial Board of Chung-hua shu-chü. 6 vols. Peking: Chung-hua shu-chü, 1975.

———. *Pei shih* 北史. Ed. Editorial Board of Chung-hua shu-chü. 10 vols. Peking: Chung-hua shu-chü, 1974.

Liang Ch'i-ch'ao 梁啓超. *T'ao Yüan-ming* 陶淵明. 1923; rpt. Shanghai: Commercial Press, 1947.

Liao Wei-ch'ing 廖蔚卿. "Nan-ch'ao *yüeh-fu* yü tang-shih she-hui te kuan-

Selected Bibliography

hsi" 南朝樂府與當時社會的關係. In *CKWH*, pp. 569–589.

———. "Ts'ung wen-hsüeh hsien-hsiang yü wen-hsüeh ssu-hsiang te kuan-hsi t'an Liu-ch'ao ch'iao-kou hsing-ssu chih yen te *shih*" 從文學現象與文學思想的關係談六朝巧構形似之言的詩. In *Chung-kuo ku-tien wen-hsüeh lun-ts'ung* 中國古典文學論叢. Vol. I. Taipei: Chung-wai wen-hsüeh yüeh-k'an-she, 1976, pp. 39–70.

Lin, Shuen-fu. "The Nature of the Quatrain from the Late Han to the High T'ang." In *ESP*.

——— and Stephen Owen, eds. *The Evolution of Shih Poetry from the Han through the T'ang*. Princeton: Princeton Univ. Press. Forthcoming.

Lin Wen-yüeh 林文月. "The Decline and Revival of *Feng-ku* (Wind and Bone." in *ESP*.

———. "Nan-ch'ao kung-t'i shih yen-chiu" 南朝宮體詩研究. *Wen-shih-che hsüeh-pao* 文史哲學報. 15 (August 1966), 433–451.

———. *Shan-shui yü ku-tien* 山水與古典. Taipei: Ch'un wen-hsueh ch'u-pan-she, 1976.

———. "'Southern Mountain' and 'Spring Grass.'" Trans. Felicia Hecker. *Renditions*, 16 (Autumn 1981), 44–61.

Ling-hu Te-fen 令狐德棻, et al. *Chou shu* 周書. Ed. Editorial Board of Chung-hua shu-chü. 3 vols. Peking: Chung-hua shu-chü, 1971.

Liu Hsiang-fei 劉翔飛. "Lun chao-yin shih" 論招隱詩. *Chung-wai wen-hsüeh* 中外文學, 7, No. 12 (1979), 98–113.

Liu Hsieh 劉勰. *Wen-hsin tiao-lung* [*chu*] 文心雕龍[注]. Commentary by Fan Wen-lan 范文瀾. 1947; rpt. in 2 vols. Peking: Jen-min wen-hsüeh ch'u-pan-she, 1978.

———. *Wen-hsin tiao-lung* [*chu shih*] 文心雕龍[注釋]. Commentary by Chou Chen-fu 周振甫. Peking: Jen-min wen-hsüeh ch'u-pan-she, 1981.

Liu I-ch'ing 劉義慶. *Shih-shuo hsin-yü* [*chiao-chien*] 世說新語[校箋]. Ed. Yang Yung 楊勇. Hong Kong: Ta-chung shu-chü, 1969.

Liu, James J. Y. *The Chinese Knight-Errant*. London: Routledge & Kegan Paul, 1967.

———. *Chinese Theories of Literature*. Chicago: Univ. of Chicago Press, 1975.

———. *The Interlingual Critic: Interpreting Chinese Poetry*. Bloomington: Indiana Univ. Press, 1982.

———. "The Paradox of Poetics and Poetics of Paradox." In *ESP*.

Liu K'ai-yang 劉開揚. "Lun Yü Hsin chi ch'i *shih fu*" 論庾信及其詩賦. In his *T'ang shih lun-wen chi* 唐詩論文集. Shanghai: Chung-hua shu-chü, 1961, pp. 136–166.

Liu Lin-sheng 劉麟生. *Chung-kuo p'ien-wen shih* 中國駢文史. 1936; rpt. Taipei: Commercial Press, 1976.

Liu Ta-chieh 劉大杰. *Chung-kuo wen-hsüeh fa-chan shih* 中國文學發展史. Rev. ed. 3 vols. Shanghai: Ku-tien wen-hsüeh ch'u-pan-she, 1957–58.

Selected Bibliography

Lo Ch'ang-p'ei 羅常培. *Han-yü yin-yün hsüeh tao-lun* 漢語音韻學導論. Hong Kong: T'ai-p'ing shu-chü, 1970.

———— and Chou Tsu-mo 周祖謨. *Han Wei Chin Nan-pei ch'ao yün-pu yen-pien yen-chiu* 漢魏晉南北朝韻部演變研究. Peking: K'o-hsüeh ch'u-pan-she, 1958.

Lo Ken-tse 羅根澤. "Chüeh-chü san-yüan" 絕句三源. In his *Chung-kuo ku-tien wen-hsüeh lun-chi* 中國古典文學論集. Peking: Wu-shih-nien-tai ch'u-pan-she, 1955, pp. 28–53.

————. *Chung-kuo wen-hsüeh p'i-p'ing shih* 中國文學批評史. 1957; rpt. Hong Kong: Tien-wen ch'u-pan-she, 1961.

Lo Lien-t'ien 羅聯添, ed. *Chung-kuo wen-hsüeh shih lun-wen hsüan-chi* 中國文學史論文選集. Vol. II. Taipei: Student Book Co., 1978.

Lovejoy, Arthur. "The Chinese Origin of a Romanticism," in his *Essays in the History of Ideas*. Baltimore: The Johns Hopkins Univ. Press, 1948, pp. 99–135.

Lu Ch'in-li 逯欽立. "T'ao Yüan-ming shih-chi shih-wen hsi-nien" 陶淵明事迹詩文繫年. In *TYMC*, pp. 261–290.

Lu Hsün 魯迅 (Chou Shu-jen). "Wei Chin feng-tu chi wen-chang yü yao chi chiu chih kuan-hsi" 魏晉風度及文章與藥及酒之關係. In his *Erh-i chi* 而已集. Vol. 17 of *Lu Hsün san-shih nien-chi* 魯迅三十年集. Hong Kong: Hsin-i ch'u-pan-she, 1967.

Lu K'an-ju 陸侃如 and Feng Yüan-chün 馮沅君. *Chung-kuo shih-shih* 中國詩史. 3 vols. Peking: Tso-chia ch'u-pan-she, 1957.

Mao shih chu-shu 毛詩注疏. 6 vols. In *Shih-san ching chu-shu* 十三經注疏. Rpt. Hong Kong: Chung-hua shu-chü, 1964.

Marney, John. "Cities in Chinese Literature." *Michigan Academician*, 10 (1977), 225–238.

————. *Liang Chien-Wen Ti*. Boston: Twayne Publishers, 1976.

Mather, Richard B. "The Controversy over Conformity and Naturalness during the Six Dynasties." *History of Religion*, 9, No. 2 and 3 (1969/70), 160–180.

————. "The Landscape Buddhism of the Fifth Century Poet Hsieh Ling-yün." *Journal of Asian Studies*, 18, No. 1 (1958), 67–79.

————. "The Mystical Ascent of the T'ien-t'ai Mountains: Sun Ch'o's *Yu-t'ien-t'ai shan Fu*." *Monumenta Serica*, 20 (1961), 226–245.

————., trans. *Shih-shuo Hsin-yü: A New Account of Tales of the World*. By Liu I-ch'ing (403–444). Minneapolis: Univ. of Minnesota Press, 1976.

McCullough, Helen C., trans. "The Genesis of the *Kokinshū* Style." By Konishi Jin'ichi 小西甚一. *Harvard Journal of Asiatic Studies*, 38, No. 1 (1978), 61–170.

Miao, Ronald C. "Palace-Style Poetry: The Courtly Treatment of Glamor

Selected Bibliography

and Love." In *Studies in Chinese Poetry and Poetics*. Ed. Ronald C. Miao. Vol. I. San Francisco: Chinese Materials Center, 1978, pp. 1–42.

Miao Yüeh 繆鉞. *Shih tz'u san-lun* 詩詞散論. Rpt. Taipei: K'ai-ming shu-chü, 1953.

Miner, Earl. *Japanese Linked Poetry: An Account with Translations of Renga and Haikai Sequences*. Princeton: Princeton Univ. Press, 1979.

———. "The Social Mode." In his *The Cavalier Mode from Jonson to Cotton*. Princeton: Princeton Univ. Press, 1971, pp. 3–42.

Morino Shigeo 森野繁夫. "Ryō no bungaku shūdan—Taishi Kō no shūdan o chūshin to shite." 梁の文学集団—太子綱の集団を中心として. In *Nippon Chūgoku gakkai hō* 日本中国学会報, No. 20 (1968), 109–124.

———. "Ryōsho no bungaku shūdan" 梁初の文学集団. In *Chūgoku bungaku hō* 中国文学報, 21 (1966), 83–108.

Mote, F. W. "The Arts and the 'Theorizing Mode' of the Civilization." In *Arts and Traditions: Uses of the Past in Chinese Culture*. Ed. Christian Murck. Princeton: Princeton Univ. Press, 1976, pp. 3–8.

———. "Confucian Eremitism in the Yüan Period." In *The Confucian Persuasion*. Ed. Arthur F. Wright. Stanford: Stanford Univ. Press, 1960, pp. 202–240.

———. trans. *A History of Chinese Political Thought*. By Hsiao Kung-chuan. Vol. I. Princeton: Princeton Univ. Press, 1979.

———. *Intellectual Foundations of China*. New York: Knopf, 1971.

———. "The Transformation of Nanking: 1350–1400." In *The City in Late Imperial China*. Ed. G. William Skinner. Stanford: Stanford Univ. Press, 1977, pp. 101–153.

Mou Tsung-san 牟宗三. *Ts'ai-hsing yü hsüan-li* 才性與玄理. 1962; rpt. Taipei: Student Book Co., 1975.

Murck, Christian, ed. *Arts and Traditions: Uses of the Past in Chinese Culture*. Princeton: Princeton Univ. Press, 1976.

Obi, Kōichi 小尾郊一. *Chūgoku bungaku ni arawareta shizen to shizenkan—Chūsei bungaku o chūshin to shite* 中国文学に現われた自然と自然観—中世文学を中心として. Tokyo: Iwanami, 1962.

Ou-yang Hsün 歐陽詢, et al. Comp. *I-wen lei-chü* 藝文類聚. Ed. Wang Shao-ying 汪紹楹. Rev. ed. 4 vols. Shanghai: Ku-chi Ch'u-pan-she, 1982.

Owen, Stephen. "Deadwood: The Barren Tree from Yü Hsin to Han Yü." *Chinese Literature: Essays, Articles, Reviews*, 1 (1979), 157–179.

———. *The Great Age of Chinese Poetry: The High T'ang*. New Haven: Yale Univ. Press, 1981.

———. "A Monologue of the Senses." In *Toward a Theory of Description*. Ed. Jeffrey Kittay. No. 61 of *Yale French Studies* (1981), pp. 244–260.

———. *Traditional Chinese Poetry and Poetics: Omen of the World*. Madison:

Univ. of Wisconsin Press, 1985.

———. *The Poetry of Meng Chiao and Han Yü.* New Haven: Yale Univ. Press, 1975.

———. *The Poetry of the Early T'ang.* New Haven: Yale Univ. Press, 1977.

———. "The Self's Perfect Mirror: Poetry as Autobiography." In *ESP*.

Pao Chao 鮑照. *Pao Ts'an-chün shih [chu]* 鮑參軍詩[注]. Ed. Huang Chieh 黃節. Rpt. Hong Kong: Chung-hua shu-chü, 1972.

———. *Pao Ts'an-chün chi [chu]* 鮑參軍集[注]. Ed. Ch'ien Chung-lien 錢仲聯. Shanghai: Ku-chi ch'u-pan-she, 1980.

Pei Yüan-ch'en 貝遠辰 and Yeh Yu-ming 葉幼明, eds. *Li-tai yu-chi hsüan* 歷代遊記選. Hunan: Jen-min ch'u-pan-she, 1980.

Plaks, Andrew. "The Chinese Literary Garden." In his *Archetype and Allegory in the Dream of the Red Chamber.* Princeton: Princeton Univ. Press, 1976, pp. 146–177.

Po Chü-i 白居易. *Po Chü-i chi* 白居易集. Ed. Ku Hsüeh-chieh 顧學頡. 4 vols. Peking: Chung-hua shu-chü, 1979.

Pollack, David. "Linked-Verse Poetry in China: A Study of Associative Linking in *Lien-Chü* Poetry with Emphasis on the Poems of Han Yü and His Circles." Diss. Univ. of California, Berkeley, 1976.

Preminger, Alex, et al. *Princeton Encyclopedia of Poetry and Poetics.* Enlarged ed. Princeton: Princeton Univ. Press, 1974.

Rabinovitch, Judith. "The Poetic Code of Fujiwara no Hamanari (772)." Draft translation, 1984.

Rickett, Adele Austin, ed. *Chinese Approaches to Literature from Confucius to Liang Ch'i-ch'ao.* Princeton: Princeton Univ. Press, 1978.

Robertson, Maureen. "Periodization in the Arts and Patterns of Change in Traditional Chinese Literary History." In *Theories of the Arts in China.* Ed. Susan Bush and Christian Murck. Princeton: Princeton Univ. Press, 1983, pp. 3–26.

Russell, Bertrand. "Knowledge by Acquaintance and Knowledge by Description." In his *The Problems of Philosophy.* 1959; rpt. London: Oxford Univ. Press, 1975, pp. 46–59.

Schafer, Edward H. *The Divine Woman: Dragon Ladies and Rain Maidens in T'ang Literature.* Berkeley: Univ. of California Press, 1973.

Shen Ts'ung-wen 沈從文. *Chung-kuo ku-tai fu-shih yen-chiu* 中國古代服飾研究. Hong Kong: Commercial Press, 1981. Vol. I.

Shen yüeh 沈約. *Sung shu* 宋書. 8 vols. Ed. Editorial Board of Chung-hua shu-chü. Peking: Chung-hua shu-chü, 1974.

Shih, Vincent Yu-chung, trans. *The Literary Mind and the Carving of Dragons.* By Liu Hsieh. Rev. ed. Hong Kong: The Chinese Univ. Press, 1983.

Ssu-ma Ch'ien 司馬遷. *Shih-chi* 史記. Ed. Editorial Board of Chung-hua shu-chü. 10 vols. Peking: Chung-hua shu-chü, 1959.

Stankiewicz, Edward. "Centripetal and Centrifugal Structures in Poetry." *Semiotica*, 38, nos. 3–4, (1982). 217–242.

Stimson, Hugh M. *Fifty-five T'ang Poems*. New Haven: Far Eastern Publications, Yale University, 1976.

———., trans. "Preface to the *Orchid Pavilion Collection*." Unpublished trans., March, 1983.

Su Shih 蘇軾. *Su Shih shih-chi* 蘇軾詩集. Commentary by Wang Wen-kao 王文誥. 8 vols. Peking: Chung-hua shu-chü, 1982.

Sui Shu-sen 隋樹森. *Ku-shih shih-chiu shou chi-shih* 古詩十九首集釋. Hong Kong: Chung-hua shu-chü, 1958.

Sullivan, Michael. *Symbols of Eternity: The Art of Landscape Painting in China*. Stanford: Stanford Univ. Press, 1979.

Sung Ch'iu-lung 宋丘龍. *Su Tung-p'o ho T'ao Yüan-ming shih chih pi-chiao yen-chiu* 蘇東坡和陶淵明詩之比較研究. Taipei: Commercial Press, 1980.

Suzuki Torao 鈴木虎雄. *Fushi taiyō* 賦史大要. Tokyo: Fusanbō, 1936.

T'ai Ching-nung 臺靜農. "Wei Chin wen-hsüeh ssu-hsiang te shu-lun" 魏晉文學思想的述論. In *CKWH*, pp. 449–460.

T'ang Hai-t'ao 唐海濤. "T'an Pao Chao te 'Mei-hua lo'" 談鮑照的"梅花落", *Ming Pao Monthly*, 19, No. 10 (1984), 60–61.

T'ang Yung-t'ung 湯用彤. *Han Wei Liang-Chin Nan-pei ch'ao fo-chiao shih* 漢魏兩晉南北朝佛教史. Peking: Chung-hua shu-chü, 1963. Rpt. in one volume. Taipei: Ting-wen shu-chü, 1976.

———. *Wei Chin hsüan-hsüeh lun-kao* 魏晉玄學論稿. Peking: Jen-min wen-hsüeh ch'u-pan-she, 1957.

T'ao Ch'ien 陶潛. *Ching-chieh hsien-sheng chi* 靖節先生集. In *Ssu-pu pei-yao* 四部備要. Shanghai: Chung-hua shu-chü, 1936.

———. *Sou shen hou-chi* 搜神後記. 10 chüan. In *Ku chin shuo-pu ts'ung-shu* 古今說部叢書, chi 2. n.d.

———. *T'ao Yüan-ming chi* 陶淵明集. Ed. Lu Ch'in-li 逯欽立. Peking: Chung-hua shu-chü, 1979.

———. *T'ao Yüan-ming chi [chiao-chien]* 陶淵明集[校箋]. Ed. Yang Yung 楊勇. Hong Kong: Wu-hsing chi shu-chü, 1971.

———. *T'ao Yüan-ming shih-hsüan* 陶淵明詩選. Ed. with notes by Hsü Wei 徐巍. Hong Kong: Joint Publishing Co., 1982.

T'ao Yüan-ming shih-wen hui p'ing 陶淵明詩文彙評. Ed. Department of Chinese, Peking Univ. Peking: Chung-hua shu-chü, 1961.

T'ao Yüan-ming yen-chiu tzu-liao hui-pien 陶淵明研究資料彙編. Ed. Department of Chinese, Peking Univ. Peking: Chung-hua shu-chü, 1962.

Teng Shih-liang 鄧仕樑. *Liang Chin shih lun* 兩晉詩論. Hong Kong: Chinese

Selected Bibliography

Univ. of Hong Kong, 1972.

Teng, Ssu-yü, trans. *Family Instructions for the Clan*. By Yen Chih-t'ui. Leiden: Brill, 1968.

Ting Fu-lin 丁福林. "Pao Chao shih-wen hsi-nien k'ao-pien" 鮑照詩文系年考辨. *Chung-hua wen-shih lun-ts'ung* 中華文史論叢, 27, No. 3 (1983), pp. 277–287.

Ting Fu-pao 丁福保, ed. *Ch'üan Han San-kuo Chin Nan-pei-ch'ao shih* 全漢三國晉南北朝詩. Shanghai, 1916. Rpt. in 3 vols. Taipei: Shih-chieh shu-chü, 1969.

Tseng Chün-i 曾君一. "Pao Chao yen-chiu" 鮑照研究. In *Wei Chin Liu-ch'ao shih yen-chiu lun-wen chi* 魏晉六朝詩研究論文集. Ed. Chung-kuo yü-wen hsüeh-she 中國語文學社. Hong Kong: Chung-kuo yü-wen hsüeh-she, 1969, pp. 134–158.

Tu Fu 杜甫. *Tu shih* [*hsiang-chu*] 杜詩[詳注]. Commentary by Ch'iu Chao-ao 仇兆鰲. Peking: Chung-hua shu-chü, 1979.

Tu, Wei-ming. "Profound Learning, Personal Knowledge and Poetic Vision." In *ESP*.

T'ung Shu-yeh 童書業. "Chung-kuo shan-shui hua ch'i-yüan k'ao" 中國山水畫起源考. In *Shan-shui hua shih chih yen-chiu* 山水畫史之研究. Vol. I of *Chung-kuo hua lun-ts'ung* 中國畫論叢. Ed. Ts'un-ts'ui hsüeh-she 存萃學社. Hong kong: Ta-tung t'u-shu kung-ssu, 1978, pp. 27–35.

Twitchett, Denis, ed. *The Cambridge History of China, Vol. 3: Sui and T'ang China, 589–906, part 1.* Cambridge: Cambridge Univ. Press, 1979.

Uchida Michio 內田道夫. "Kōnan no shi to sakuhoku no shi" 江南の詩と朔北の詩. *Shūkan tōyōgaku* 集刊東洋学, no. 16 (1966), 1–8.

Wang, C. H. *The Bell and the Drum: Shih Ching as Formulaic Poetry in an Oral Tradition*. Berkeley: Univ. of Calafornia Press, 1974.

———. "Lu Chi *Wen-fu* chiao-shih" 陸機文賦校釋. *Wen-shih–che hsüeh-pao* 文史哲學報, 32 (December 1983), 159–256.

———. "The Nature of Narrative in T'ang Poetry." In *ESP*.

——— (Yeh Shan 葉珊). "Shih Ching kuo-feng te ts'ao-mu ho shih te piao-hsien chi-ch'iao" 詩經國風的草木和詩的表現技巧. In *Chung-kuo ku-tien wen-shüeh yen-chiu ts'ung-k'an—Shih-ko chih pu* 中國古典文學研究叢刊—詩歌之部. Vol. I. Ed. K'o Ch'ing-ming 柯慶明 and Lin Ming-te 林明德. Taipei: Chü-liu t'u-shu kung-ssu, 1977, pp. 11–45.

Wang Chung 汪中. "Lun Pei-ch'ao yüeh-fu" 論北朝樂府. In *CKWH*, pp. 591–598.

Wang Chung-lo 王仲犖. *Wei Chin Nan-Pei-ch'ao shih* 魏晉南北朝史. 2 vols. Shanghai: Jen-min ch'u-pan-she, 1979–1980.

Wang Fu-chih 王夫之. *Ku-shih p'ing hsüan* 古詩評選. In Vol. 15 of *Ch'uan-shan ch'üan chi* 船山全集. Facsim. reproduction. Taipei: Hua-kang ch'u-pan-she, 1965.

Selected Bibliography

Wang K'ai-yün 王闓運. *Pa-tai shih-hsüan* 八代詩選. Rpt. in 2 vols. Taipei: Kuang-wen shu-chü, 1970.

Wang Kuo-ying 王國瓔. "*Ch'u-tz'u* chung te shan-shui ching-wu" 楚辭中的山水景物. In *Chung-wai wen-hsüeh* 中外文學 8, No. 5 (1979), 80–97.

———. "Han fu chung te shan-shui ching-wu" 漢賦中的山水景物. In *Chung-wai wen-hsüeh* 中外文學, 9, No. 5 (1980), 4–34.

———. "*Shih-ching* chung te shan-shui ching-wu" 詩經中的山水景物. In *Chung-wai wen-hsüeh* 中外文學, 8, No. 1 (1979), 118–136.

Wang Li 王力. *Han-yü shih-lü hsüeh* 漢語詩律學. 1958; rpt. Hong Kong: Chung-hua shu-chü, 1973.

Wang Yao 王瑤. *Chung-ku wen-hsüeh feng-mao* 中古文學風貌. 1951, Shanghai; rpt. Hong Kong: Chung-liu ch'u-pan-she, 1973.

———. *Chung-ku wen-hsüeh ssu-hsiang* 中古文學思想. 1951, Shanghai; rpt. Hong Kong: Chung-liu ch'u-pan-she, 1973.

———. *Chung-ku wen-jen sheng-huo* 中古文人生活. 1951, Shanghai; rpt. Hong Kong: Chung-liu ch'u-pan-she, 1973.

Wang, Yi-t'ung, trans. *A Record of Buddhist Monasteries in Lo-yang.* By Yang Hsüan-chih. Princeton: Princeton Univ. Press., 1984.

———. *Wu ch'ao men-ti* 五朝門第. Rev. ed. 2 vols. Hong Kong: The Chinese Univ. Press, 1978.

Wang Yün-hsi 王運熙. *Han Wei Liu-ch'ao T'ang tai wen-hsüeh lun-ts'ung* 漢魏六朝唐代文學論叢. Shanghai: Ku-chi ch'u-pan-she, 1981.

———. *Yüeh-fu shih lun-ts'ung* 樂府詩論叢. Shanghai: Ku-tien wen-hsüeh ch'u-pan-she, 1958.

Watson, Burton, trans. *Chinese Rhyme-Prose: Poems in the Fu Form from the Han and the Six Dynasties Periods.* New York: Columbia Univ. Press, 1971.

———., trans. *Records of the Grand Historian of China.* By Ssu-ma Ch'ien. 2 vols. New York: Columbia Univ. Press, 1961.

———. *Ssu-ma Ch'ien, Grand Historian of China.* New York: Columbia Univ. Press, 1958.

———, trans. *The Complete Works of Chuang Tzu.* New York: Columbia Univ. Press, 1968.

Wei Chin Liu-ch'ao shih yen-chiu lun-wen chi 魏晉六朝詩研究論文集. Ed. Chung-kuo yü-wen hsüeh-she 中國語文學社. Hong Kong: Chung-kuo yü-wen hsüeh-she, 1969.

Wei Ch'ing-chih 魏慶之. *Shih-jen yü-hsieh* 詩人玉屑. Ed. Wang Yün-wu 王雲五, et al. Taipei: Commercial Press, 1972.

Weintraub, Karl Joachim. *The Value of the Individual: Self and Circumstance in Autobiography.* Chicago: Univ. of Chicago Press, 1978.

Welsh, Andrew. *Roots of Lyric.* Princeton: Princeton Univ. Press, 1978.

Westbrook, Francis A. "Landscape Description in the Lyric Poetry and '*Fu* on Dwelling in the Mountains' of Hsieh Ling-yün." Diss. Yale Univ. 1973.

Selected Bibliography

———. "Landscape Transformation in the Poetry of Hsieh Ling-yün." *Journal of the American Oriental Society*, 100 (1980), 237–254.
Wilhelm, Hellmut. "The Scholar's Frustration: Notes on a Type of 'Fu'." In *Chinese Thought and Institutions*. Ed. John K. Fairbank. Chicago: Univ. of Chicago Press, 1957, pp. 310–319.
Wilhelm, Richard, trans. *The I Ching, or Book of Changes*. Rendered into English by Cary F. Baynes. Princeton: Princeton Univ. Press, Bollingen Series 19, 1967.
Wixted, John Timothy. "The *Kokinshū* Prefaces: Another Perspective." *Harvard Journal of Asiatic Studies*, 43, No. 1 (1983), 215–238.
———. "The Nature of Evaluation in the *Shih-p'in* (Gradings of Poets) by Chung Hung (A.D. 459–518)." In *Theories of the Arts in China*. Ed. Susan Bush and Christian Murck. Princeton: Princeton Univ. Press, 1983, pp. 225–264.
———. *Poems on Poetry, Literary Criticism by Yuan Hao-wen (1190–1257)*. Wiesbaden: steiner, 1982.
Wong, Siu-kit, ed. and trans. *Early Chinese Literary Criticism*. Hong Kong: Joint Publishing Co., 1983.
Wright, Arthur. *Buddhism in Chinese History*. Stanford: Stanford Univ. Press, 1959.
———. *The Sui Dynasty: The Unification of China, A.D. 581–617*. New York: Knopf, 1978.
Wu Hung. "A Sanpan Shan Chariot Ornament and the Xiangrui Design in Western Han Art." *Archives of Asian Art*, 37 (1984), 38–59.
Wu Shu-t'ang 吳叔儻. "Hsieh T'iao nien-p'u" 謝朓年譜. In "Chung-kuo wen-hsüeh yen-chiu" 中國文學研究 of *Hsiao-shuo yüeh-pao* 小說月報. Vol. 17 (1926). Rpt. in *Chung-kuo wen-hsüeh yen-chiu* 中國文學研究. Ed. Chao Tsu-fan 趙滋蕃. Taipei: Ch'ing-liu ch'u-pan-she, 1976, I, 125–138.
Yang Hsüan-chih 楊衒之. *Lo-yang ch'ieh-lan chi* [*chiao-shih*] 洛陽伽藍記 [校釋]. Ed. Chou Tsu-mou 周祖謨. Hong Kong: Chung-hua shu-chü, 1976.
Yao Ssu-lien 姚思廉. *Liang shu* 梁書. Ed. Editorial Board of Chung-hua shu-chü. 3 vols. Peking: Chung-hua shu-chü, 1973.
Yeh Chia-ying 葉嘉瑩. *Chia-ling t'an-shih* 迦陵談詩. 2 vols. Taipei: San-min shu-chü, 1970.
———. "Ts'ung Yüan I-shan lun-shih *chüeh-chü* t'an Hsieh Ling-yün yü Liu Tsung-yüan te *shih* yü jen" 從元遺山論詩絕句談謝靈運與柳宗元的詩與人. In her *Chung-kuo ku-tien shih-ko p'ing-lun chi* 中國古典詩歌評論集. Hong Kong: Chung-hua shu-chü, 1977, pp. 31–71.
——— and Jan W. Walls. "Theory, Standards, and Practice of Criticizing Poetry in Chung Hung's *Shih-P'in*." In *Studies in Chinese Poetry and Poetics*. Vol. I. Ed. Ronald C. Miao. San Francisco: Chinese Materials

Center, 1978, pp. 43–80.
Yeh Hsiao-hsüeh 葉笑雪. "Hsieh Ling-yün chuan" 謝靈運傳. In *HLYS*, 143–220.
Yeh Jih-kuang 葉日光. *Tso Ssu sheng-p'ing chi ch'i shih chih hsi-lun* 左思生平及其詩之析論. Taipei: Wen-shih-che ch'u-pan-she, 1979.
Yen Chih-t'ui 顏之推. *Yen shih chia-hsün [chi-chieh]* 顏氏家訓[集解]. Commentary by Wang Li-ch'i 王利器. Shanghai: Ku chi ch'u-pan-she, 1980.
Yen K'o-chün 嚴可均. *Ch'üan Shang-ku San-tai Ch'in Han San-kuo Liu-ch'ao wen* 全上古三代秦漢三國六朝文. Peking: Chung-hua shu-chü, 1965. Rpt. in 5 vols. with index. Taipei: Hung-yeh shu-chü, 1975.
Yü Chien-hua 俞劍華, ed. *Chung-kuo hua-lun lei-pien* 中國畫論類編. Hong Kong: Chung-hua shu-chü, 1973.
Yü Hsin 庾信. *Yü Tzu-shan chi [chu]* 庾子山集[注]. Commentary by Ni Fan 倪璠. Peking: Chung-hua shu-chü, 1980.
———. *Yü Hsin shih fu hsüan* 庾信詩賦選. Ed. with notes by T'an Cheng-pi 譚正璧 and Chi Fu-hua 紀馥華. Shanghai: Ku-tien wen-hsüeh ch'u-pan-she, 1958.
Yu, Pauline. "Formal Distinctions in Literary Theory." In *Theories of the Arts in China*. Ed. Susan Bush and Christian Murck. Princeton: Princeton Univ. Press, 1983, pp. 27–53.
———. "Metaphor in Chinese Poetry." *Chinese Literature: Essays, Articles, Reviews*, 3 (1981), 205–224.
———. *The Poetry of Wang Wei: New Translations and Commentary*. Bloomington: Indiana Univ. Press, 1980.
Yü Ying-shih 余英時. *Chung-kuo chih-shih chieh-ts'eng shih-lun, Ku-tai p'ien* 中國知識階層史論, 古代篇. Taipei: Linking Publication Co., 1980.
———. "Individualism and the Neo-Taoist Movement in Wei-Chin China." Draft, 1982.
———. *Li-shih yü ssu-hsiang* 歷史與思想. Taipei: Linking Publishing Co., 1976.
———. *Shih hsüeh yü ch'uan-t'ung* 史學與傳統. Taipei: Shih-pao wen-hua ch'u-pan shih-yeh yu-hsien kung-ssu, 1982.
———. *Trade and Expansion in Han China: A Study in the Structure of Sino-Barbarian Relations*. Berkeley: Univ. of California Press, 1967.
Zürcher, E. *The Buddhist Conquest of China: The Spread and Adaptation of Buddhism in Early Medieval China*. 2 vols. Leiden: Brill, 1959.

INDEX

Ancient Style poetry, 138, 138n
artistic similitude. *See* verisimilitude

Birrell, Anne, 156n
Book of Changes, 66
Book of Songs. See *Shih ching*

Chang, H. C., 7n
Chang Hsieh, 54–57, 95
Chaves, Jonathan, 33n
Ch'en Yin-k'o, 17n, 23n, 117n, 118, 118n, 119n, 180n
Cheng, François, 121n
chih-yin (the one who knows the tone), 25, 102; in Hsieh Ling-yün, 75–76; in Pao Chao, 96–97; in T'ao Ch'ien, 25, 27, 30–31, 32–33
ch'ing-t'an (pure conversation), 5
Ch'ü Yüan, 36–37, 75, 125n
Chuang Tzu, 18n, 30, 39, 48, 58n, 129n
Chung Jung, 3, 9, 14, 41, 48, 54, 80n, 119, 119n; on Hsieh Ling-yün, 51, 54; on Hsieh T'iao, 117–118, 122; on Pao Chao, 81–82, 95; on T'ao Ch'ien, 13–14, 14n
Confucius, 18n, 60n, 129n

descriptive similitude. *See* verisimilitude

Eliot, T. S., 79
Emperor Wu of the Liang. *See* Hsiao Yen
Emperor Yüan of the Liang. *See* Hsiao I

Fan Yeh, 113, 116, 116n
Fang, Achilles, 43n
"four tones, eight prohibitions," 117–121
Frankel, Hans H., 59n, 68n, 101n, 180n
Frodsham, J. D., 27n, 97n
fu, 68n, 68–70; compared with *shih* poetry, 72–73; in *yung-wu* mode, 93, 152; versus *shih*, 161

Graham, William T., 166n, 168n, 178n, 182n, 183n, 184n

Hawkes, David, 37n, 73n, 75n, 125n
Hightower, James R., 11n, 17n, 18n, 25n, 30n, 41, 42n, 43n, 44n, 45n, 46n, 68n, 69n, 166n, 168n
Ho Hsün, 121
Holzman, Donald, 27n, 167n, 168n
Hou Ching rebellion, 165–166, 180n, 182, 183
Hsi K'ang, 103n, 178
Hsiang Hsiu, 178
Hsiao I, 154, 159; as a painter, 159; as author of "Chin'lou tzu," 154; as Emperor Yüan, 165, 166, 167, 168, 183
Hsiao Kang, 79, 153–154, 158, 160; and Palace Style poetry, 154–157; criticizing Hsieh Ling-yün, 122; death of, 165; "Ode on the Beauty Viewing a Painting," 155–156; praising Hsieh T'iao, 122
Hsiao T'ung, 26n, 41, 41n, 46n, 152, 183, 183n; death of, 154; different from Hsiao Kang, 153; editor of T'ao Ch'ien's works, 152–153; *Wen-hsüan* by, 152, 156
Hsiao Yen, 117n, 121; as a Buddhist, 151–152; as Emperor Wu, 146–147, 154, 156, 160, 163, 182, 183; as one of the "eight friends of Prince Ching-ling," 144; death of, 165; poems by, 148, 149–151
Hsieh An, 53, 54
Hsieh Ling-yün: as champion poet of "mountains and waters" poetry, 49; as first ranking poet, 51; as one of the "Three Literary Giants in the Yüan-chia Reign," 14; compared with Chang Hsieh, 56, 57; compared with T'ao Ch'ien, 63, 74, 75, 76, 77; "*Fu* on Dwelling in the Mountains," 70–72, 115; in Yung-chia, 62, 62n; influence of, 79–80; official career of, 77; "On My Way from South Mountain to North Mountain," 51, 66; "Return to the Old Garden," 60; "Travels to Famous Mountains," 49, 88. *See also* "mountains and waters" poetry
Hsieh T'iao, "A Prince Went Wandering," 144; and Prince Sui of Ching-chou, 128–131; and "semi-eremitism," 134–135,

Index

170; and Shen Yüeh, 120; *chüeh-chü* quatrain by, 142–144; "Climbing the Beacon Fire Tower," 127–128; compared with Hsieh Ling-yün, 115, 135, 138; compared with Pao Chao, 123–124; farewell poem by, 125–126; "*Fu* on Visiting a Private Garden," 113–115; influenced by Hsieh Ling-yün, 133–134; "Looking Out Leisurely from the Lofty Study in My Commandery," 136–137; "Making an Excursion to the Mountains," 134; "On Our Way to Ching-t'ing Road," 139–141; related to Hsieh Ling-yün, 113; "The Sorrow of Bronze Bird Tower," 142–143; "The Zither," 123. *See also* "mountains and waters" poetry

Hsü Ling, 147n, 156, 160, 177. See also *Yü-t'ai hsin-yung*

hsüan-yen poetry, 5, 7, 9, 12, 13, 54

Juan Chi, 27, 27n, 28, 103, 103n, 166, 167, 168, 169

Kao, Yu-kung, 144n
Karlgren, Bernhard, 164n
Keats, John, 158
Knechtges, David R., 13n, 14n, 68n, 110n, 118n, 119n, 152n
Konishi Jin'ichi, 67n, 122n
Kuo P'u, 103n

landscape painting, 159–160
landscape poetry. *See* "mountains and waters" poetry
Lao Tzu, 3, 48, 100n, 128n
Lee, Chik-fong, 103n
Li Po, 120n, 137
lien-chü (quatrain sequence), 139–141
Lin, Shuen-fu, 81n, 143n
Liu Hsieh, 3, 9, 47, 48, 65, 82
Liu, James J. Y., 12n, 30n, 116n, 158n
Liu Yü, 20, 22, 32, 61
Lu Chi, 14, 39n, 43, 69, 103, 103n, 182

Marney, John, 146n, 161n, 183n
Mather, Richard B., 49n, 70n, 74n, 78n, 117n, 170n
Mei Sheng, 71
Mei, Tsu-lin, 144n
Miner, Earl, 122n, 139n

Mote, F. W., 41n, 112n, 118n
"mountains and waters" poetry, 48; and *fu*, 70–72; by Hsieh Ling-yün, 51, 53, 59, 61, 63; by Hsieh T'iao, 133–134, 137–138; by Pao Chao, 83–87. *See also* parallelism

Neo-Taoism, 6
Neo-Taoist, Naturalism, 40
Neo-Taoist poetry. See *hsüan-yen* poetry

Orchid Pavilion gathering. *See* Wang Hsi-chih
Owen, Stephen, 46n, 72n, 139n, 170n

Palace Style poetry, 154–157, 163, 165, 172
Pao Chao, "A Letter to My Sister after Arriving at Ta-lei Riverbank," 87–92; "An Imitation of T'ao Ch'ien's Style," 103; as one of the "Three Literary Giants in the Yüan-chia Reign," 14, 82; as "the people's poet," 97; *chüeh-chü* quatrain by, 141; compared with Hsieh Ling-yün, 83, 86, 88; compared with T'ao Ch'ien, 86, 104–106; "*Fu* on the Desolate City," 108–111, 182; "I Met a Lonely *T'ung* Tree," 92–93, 124n; "Imitation of 'the Hardships of Travel,'" 99–101, 102, 105, 106–107; "Imitation of the Old Style," 94–95; influenced by Hsieh Ling-yün, 83, 103; influenced by T'ao Ch'ien, 103–105; on Hsieh Ling-yün, 83; praised by Tu Fu, 103; "The Songs of Chung-hsing," 150n; "To the Tune, 'National Revival,'" 150, *yüeh-fu* by, 80–82, 104. *See also* "mountains and waters" poetry
Pao Ling-hui, 87, 97n, 108
parallelism, 64–65; in *fu*, 69; in Hsieh Ling-yün, 64, 65–68; in Pao Chao, 86
Plaks, Andrew H., 45n, 71n
Po Chü-i, 53, 78
poetry of Wandering Immortals. *See* *yu-hsien* poetry
poetry on objects. See *yung-wu* poetry
Prince Chao-ming. *See* Hsiao T'ung
Prince Ching-ling, 112, 114, 115, 115n, 117, 118, 119, 125, 128, 133, 146, 148, 150; eight friends of, 112, 113
Prince Sui of Ching-chou, 112, 125, 128, 132, 133
prose on mountains and waters, 87
pure conversation. *See* *ch'ing-t'an*

214

Index

Recent Style poetry, 120. *See also* Regulated Verse
Regulated Verse, 117, 121, 126, 127, 128, 160, 160n, 161

shan-shui poetry. *See* "mountains and waters" poetry
Shen Te-ch'ien, 83
Shen Yüeh, 69, 117, 117n, 118, 118n, 119, 120, 122, 146, 151n, 160
Shih, Vincent Yu-chung, 69n, 82n, 116n
Shih ching, 12, 97, 164n
Shih-shuo hsin-yü, 49, 84
Stimson, Hugh M., 7n
Ssu-ma Ch'ien, 25, 30n, 180, 181
Ssu-ma Hsiang-ju, 69, 169n
Su Shih, 25n, 33, 46n
Sun Ch'o, 5, 9, 70
Sung Yü, 45, 184n

T'ao Ch'ien, "An Outing to Hsieh Brook," 9; as a recluse, 41–42; as middle-ranking poet, 13; attitude toward death, 39–40; autobiographical mode in, 16; "Begging for Food," 34–35; compared with Chang Hsieh, 57; compared with Hsieh Ling-yün, 63, 74, 75, 76, 77; "Complaint in the Ch'u Mode," 34; concept of *tzu-jan* (nature), 41, 46; criticism of, 13–14; "Dirge" series, 12–13, 38–39; "Elegy for Myself," 39–40; expressive mode in, 12; fiction and autobiography, 24–26; "Form, Shadow, and Spirit," 40; "*Fu* on Calming the Passions," 43–46, 69, 96n; historical odes, 27; "Imitations of the Ancient Style," 24–25, 27, 28–30, 43n; individuality of, 12, 16; influenced by Wang Hsi-chih, 9, 11; "Kuei-ch'ü-lai-hsi *tz'u*," 21; loyalism in, 31–32; "Miscellaneous Poems," 28; name changed to Yüan-ming, 32; "Ode to Ching K'o," 27, 30–31; "Ode to the Three Good Men," 27; "Ode to the Two Shus," 27; "Odes to the Impoverished Gentlemen," 27; official career of, 20–21; opposed to verbal embellishment, 15; "Poems on Drinking Wine," 36–37; "Returning to My Farm to Dwell," 22–23; "The Biography of Mr. Five Willow Trees," 25–26; "The Peach Blossom Spring," 16–19, 17n, 18n, 22, 23
Ts'ai Yung, 150n

Ts'ao Chih, 45, 87, 103
Ts'ao P'i, 80n
Ts'ao Ts'ao, 142–143, 168
Tso Ssu, 27, 103n, 107n, 107–108, 110
Tu Fu, 3, 41, 103, 120n, 179–180
Tu, Wei-ming, 65n

Verisimilitude, 48, 48n, 51, 53, 54, 65, 69, 82, 92, 103, 115, 158, 161; and parallelism, 68

Wang Hsi-chih, 6, 6n, 9, 20, 49, 49n, 54; and Orchid Pavilion gathering, 6, 7–9, 11, 51, 60
Wang Jung, 118, 146
Wang Ts'an, 69
Watson, Burton, 18n, 25n, 34n, 39n, 68n, 69n, 109n, 110n, 171n
Westbrook, Francis A., 70n
White Lotus Society, 42
Wilhelm, Richard, 66n
Wright, Arthur F., 163n

Yeh, Chia-ying, 14n
Yen Yen-chih, 14, 14n, 35, 57, 61, 62, 82; "Eulogy on T'ao Ch'ien," 14, 35, 48
Yü, Ying-shih, 5n, 40, 40n, 45n, 65n, 87n
Yü Hsin: and Regulated Verse, 160; as diplomatic envoy to the north, 163–165, 166; at court, 157; *chüeh-chü* quatrain by, 176–178; compared with Hsieh T'iao, 178; compared with Pao Chao, 182; comparing himself to T'ao Ch'ien, 170–171; contrast between north and south in, 171–172; *fu* by, 163; "*Fu* on a Small Garden," 171; "*Fu* on the Barren Tree," 170; "*Fu* on the Spring," 161–163; influenced by Hsiao Kang, 157; influenced by T'ao Ch'ien, 160, 165; "Lament for the South," 178–184; "Looking at the Moon from My Boat," 160n; "Odes on Paintings on a Screen," 158, 175–176; Palace Style poetry by, 157–159, 173; "The Imitation of *Yung-huai*," 166–169; "To Hsü Ling," 177; "To Wang Lin," 177; "Written While I Was a Hydraulic Grandee," 174–176
yu-chi (travel literature), 49, 88
yüeh-fu, 97, 101, 102–103, 104, 146, 147, 148
yu-hsien poetry, 41, 56
Yung-ming poetry, 121n

Index

Yung-ming poets, 115, 116, 117, 119, 120, 121, 126
yung-wu poetry, 139, 152, 156, 163; by Hsieh T'iao, 123; by Pao Chao, 93, 94; by Yung-ming poets, 122–125
Yü-t'ai hsin-yung, 156

**Library of Congress
Cataloging-in-Publication Data**

Chang, Kang-i Sun, 1944–
Six dynasties poetry.

Bibliography: p.
Includes index.
1. Chinese poetry—Northern and Southern
dynasties, 386–589—History and criticism.
I. Title.

PL2319.C46 1986   895.1′12′09   85-43274
ISBN 0-691-06669-8